T0034697

BETWEEN WORLDS

BETWEEN WORLDS

A QUEER BOY FROM THE VALLEYS

JEFFREY WEEKS

PARTHIAN

Parthian, Cardigan SA43 1ED
www.parthianbooks.com
First published in 2021
© Jeffrey Weeks 2021
All Rights Reserved
ISBN 9781914595097
eISBN 978-1-912681-92-1
Cover design by www.theundercard.co.uk
Typeset by Syncopated Pandemonium
Printed and bound by 4Edge
Published with the financial support of the Welsh Books Council.
British Library Cataloguing in Publication Data
A cataloguing record for this book is available from the British Library.

In memory of my mother and father
Eiddwen Weeks, 1921–2014
Raymond Hugh Weeks, 1924–1976

CONTENTS

ACKNOWLEDGEMENTS

A memoir requires a lifetime of gratitude. I'll limit myself here to acknowledgement and warm thanks to those who have given immediate and direct help and support for me in writing this book. My first thanks are to those friends and colleagues who over the years, against my doubts, have encouraged me to write this book. I am particularly grateful to Richard Allen, Matt Cook, Richard Dyer, Mary Evans, David Horbury, Karin Lützen and Pat Macpherson for their support. They are not, of course, responsible for the end result.

I owe a special thanks to Daryl Leeworthy, who was very keen to see the book in print, and introduced me to Parthian, for which I am eternally grateful. Dai Smith, editor of the Modern Wales series, was a superb editor and encourager, reading drafts carefully and creatively, coming up with always sympathetic and empathetic proposals for improvement. My warmest thanks. Richard Davies of Parthian has been a very supportive publisher, and my thanks to him and his colleagues, especially Robert Harries, for making the production a pleasurable experience.

I am deeply grateful to all the photographers whose work

is reproduced in this book. Unfortunately, passing time makes it impossible to record all their names, but I am particularly grateful to Micky Burbidge, Angus Suttie, Philip King, Philippe Rougier and Mark McNestry.

Mark lived through every stage of my writing this memoir, with patience, support and care. He read my drafts with a keen eye for typos and meanings, and the warmest understanding of what I was trying to do. He helped me to carve a coherent story from a mass of memories. I hope the final book gives some insight into what I owe to him.

Jeffrey Weeks
2 March 2020

PREFACE

I was born on 1 November 1945 in the Rhondda, the most famous of the South Wales mining valleys. It was a birthplace that has marked and shaped me in ways that for a long time I did not really understand or fully accept. Because of my sexuality I felt I had to escape its all-embracing intensity as soon as I could, but what my life became has always remained entwined with how my life began – as a queer boy from the Valleys.

The mythology of the Rhondda remains strong to this day, even in the marketing of Wales. A little while ago I happened to come across a copy of *The Rough Guide to Wales*, one of a series of well-known tourist handbooks. It opened with a list of 'thirty-one things not to miss' in the country. Among various tourist delights, from male voice choirs to railways, bridges to beaches, cathedrals to bog snorkelling, the number one choice is the Valleys: 'Colourful terraces of housing, hunkered down under the hills, are the hallmark of Wales' world-famous Valleys, the old mining areas in the south'.[1] It is an image from the Rhondda that illustrates the piece.

The almost bucolic photo is of three rows of terraced houses precariously set against a vibrantly green hillside. It is a picture of the last straggling streets in Llwyncelyn, a ribbon extension of Porth, the small town at the gateway of the twin valleys. The terraces overlook at the valley bottom the old colliery complex of Lewis Merthyr, once one of the largest coal mines in the world. Its existence gave these houses meaning and justification; it is now the site of a mining museum.

The first of these three terraces is Nyth Bran, eighty or so small near-identical houses, though now nicely distinguished by different coloured doors and roofs. The uniform grey slate roof tiles of my childhood have long been replaced by red or green or duller imitation slate, markers of a new individuality that has grown hand in hand with the passing of the coal industry. Just out of sight in the picture is number 38. This was long my family home: the house where my mother's father and mother lived and died, where my mother grew up with her sisters, got married and nurtured her husband and three children, where my father spent all his adult life and died, and finally where my mother herself passed away after living in the house for ninety-odd years. This is the house where I was born, just after the end of the Second World War.

The Rhondda then was about halfway along a trajectory that took it from the feverish growth of the mining industry before the First World War to the romanticised tourist fantasy of the twenty-first century. In 1945 it was still world renowned for its coal, carrying the greatest burden of history of all the South Wales Valleys. The string of terraced houses, small villages and townships that clung precariously to the hillsides made up a homogeneous and, although only fifteen or so miles from Cardiff, geographically self-contained culture. Despite this, it had never been totally isolated from the outside world. From before the First World War it had been at the heart of a militant socialist culture, and it had exported thousands of its young to the rest of Britain and wider, to mine, work in factories and offices, and to teach, preach, nurse, act, sing, box, play rugby or write. The mobility forced by economic depression and the Second World War had given younger people a glimpse of other ways of life, but in many ways it had strengthened the ties of home. My father's family had left the Rhondda *en masse* in the 1930s for Bristol in pursuit of employment and better prospects, but my grandmother had been acutely homesick, and Dad's immediate family had returned to Tonypandy. My mother, like two of her sisters, had also left South Wales in search of work. Two became nurses, and settled in Oxford and Croydon, while my mother ended up in Slough, working for a while in the kitchens at Eton College. This was a period of high adventure for my still-teenage mother-to-be, who looks fashionable and glamorous in the surviving photographs. However, she was called back when war broke out to be with her mother, and to work in the munitions factory in Bridgend, where she spent the rest of the war.

Many of the young men, including my father, fought all over the world in the war; others stayed put to work in the pits, which had zoomed back into full production to power the war effort after nearly twenty years of disastrous under-use in the great strikes and lockout of the 1920s, and the Great Slump, which sucked the lifeblood out of the Valleys in the 1930s. War mobilisation provided new work opportunities for women in the factories and service industries, but as normal conditions resumed after the war a more traditional division of labour reasserted itself. After demobilisation my father moved into number 38 with my mother; her mother, who was the presiding mam of the family; my mother's sister, Aunty Lily, and later her husband, Uncle Frank; my brother Dennis, born in 1947; and me. My other brother Robert came along much later, in 1963. This overcrowded little house at the edge of

Porth was home, the focus of intense domestic life until I left for university in 1964, and the heart of family life until my mother died in 2014.

That longevity in itself tells a story and marks a critical element in my own life history. I grew up deeply rooted in a particular social world and way of life. Although there were frequent rows and we often lived at the top of our voices, it was a loving and caring household. I grew up as a bright and imaginative child but was also sulky and grizzly, hypersensitive and acutely shy, blushing at everything, with a host of what my family called my habits, nervous tics and jibs, and was terrified by loud noises, especially fireworks: I managed to dodge going out every Bonfire Night, thanks to the reluctant connivance of my parents. I must have been a bit of a trial for everyone, but I can see now, and sort of took for granted then with the ruthlessness of the young, that I was deeply loved, even doted on, especially by the three forceful women at the heart of my life: my mother, Aunty Lily and their mother, Rosie – Nanny Evans (always just Nanny to me; my other grandmother was invariably 'Nanny Weeks') – who lived with us until she died in 1961. My relations with my father, to whom everyone said I was so similar, both physically and in personality, were more fraught and tense, with constant rows. Yet I never really doubted he was proud of me and wanted me to succeed; and I eventually recognised – too late – his own vulnerabilities, an acutely sensitive man trapped in an overwhelmingly macho identity and culture.

But there was a problem that soon became obvious to everyone, especially my father, I suspect, although it was never fully vocalised, and one that was to shape my life. In a world where boys were boys and girl were girls, by the standards of the time and place I was not quite either. I was bookish, not sporty. I preferred playing with girls rather than boys, and dolls rather than guns. When I was no longer allowed to play with dolls, I adopted a glove puppet with a sweet face and cwtched it in secret. I used my Meccano set to construct simple little houses and palaces rather than trains or pieces of machinery. I fantasised about imaginary kingdoms rather than model motor cars or football or rugby teams. I was horribly bullied by other boys and cried easily. I was slight, ginger-haired, couldn't roll my Rs, couldn't whistle to save my life and had a lisp. I never wanted to be a girl, but I felt a peculiar sort of little man. I was a classic sissy boy.

When my school class broke into separate teams for football or cricket the team captains used to toss a coin not to pick me. I was endlessly teased and made fun of, and on several occasions in school I was piled on between lessons by some of the class heavies and left in impotent tears and shame as the teacher came in. I didn't come to any serious physical harm, and certainly till my mid-teens I had no sense that my increasing social and gender difference was related to being sexually different. Yet being simply a queer child, in the broadest sense, was difficult enough, and the source of constant guilt and misery. When I read much later the African-American (and gay) novelist James Baldwin's dismissal of his childhood and schooling as 'the usual grim nightmare', the words stuck. I instantly identified: with his sense of exile and his minority status, his Otherness, and the deep unhappiness and isolation those produced. I know now, of course, that many thousands of little Jeffreys, as well as Jennifers, were going through similar experiences to me in hundreds of towns and villages at the same time and ever since, but the sense of being an outsider, of not fully belonging, shaped me fundamentally.

The Rhondda I grew up in was a byword for community, for neighbourliness, for warmth and mutual support. All this was true. The downside was that it was also a conservative, defensive, inward-looking culture. It bred intense local trust and strong social bonds, but also a prickly distrust of the wider world, and an acute sensitivity to criticism, especially from insiders. I vividly remember the bitterness caused by the darkly sardonic witticisms of the novelist Gwyn Thomas, a Cymmer boy who had gone to my old school thirty-odd years before and loved the Rhondda deeply, but never uncritically, and who never seemed off the television in the 1960s. It was ironic that the Rhondda proudly presented itself to the world as a politically radical society, with a strong allegiance to trade unionism and socialism, and to social transformation, yet rarely questioned the patterns of traditional everyday life. And it did not take easily to outsiders or those who were radically different. It was, as T. Alban Davies, a long-time Nonconformist minister in the Rhondda, commented, 'a community in which it was a heresy to think differently' – or be out of the ordinary in any way.[2] As I write this I suddenly realise that my own continuing self-consciousness, diffidence and habit of walking backwards into the limelight have deeper social and cultural roots than I consciously realised.

Anyone growing up in the 1940s and 50s in the Rhondda will remember the subtle distinctions made about people that policed nonconformity and difference, even in a culture that was overwhelmingly manual working class: the comments about rough families who lived in disreputable areas ('What do you expect? They come from . . . '); about loose girls, who went to the pub unaccompanied, or went wild at Christmas parties in local factories; about dandified young married men who 'fancied themselves' a bit too much, and were rumoured to betray their wives – whether with men or women was never clear. Newcomers to the street, even after thirty years or more, could be treated as outsiders. 'Blacklegs' in local strikes would be sent to Coventry forever, with no redemption. None of this was peculiar to the Rhondda; years later I grew to know the former mining village of Chopwell in the Durham coalfield, the home of my partner Mark's parents, and I could instantly recognise the many commonalities: the warmth, the deep local loyalties, the conformism, the curiosity about strangers and the suspiciousness about change. But the Rhondda also had its own distinctive ethos, part of a South Wales mining history where the Valleys shared a common experience of labour and struggle with other parts of the UK, yet managed to produce significantly different ways of being.

The Valleys not only had an iconic social, economic, cultural and political history, which came to define what Daryl Leeworthy calls 'Labour country', the heartland of radical social democracy that was not just about politics but demarcated a way of life.[3] They also had a distinctive sexual and family history, which was to shape me and my generation indelibly, even as we were swept up in wider historical shifts and moved into a wider world. The dust of that past is ingrained in my body and mind like the coal residues that veined my grandfathers' hands.

I left the Rhondda just before my nineteenth birthday, and despite regular visits in the fifty-odd years since never lived there again. I moved into different worlds, became a different person, not despite but in large part because of the love and support provided by my parents, and through the opportunities that as a bright grammar school boy in the post-1944 Education Act world the social democracy of the Rhondda offered me. Yet as a queer boy from the Rhondda I had to flee its intense embrace in order to become myself. What that self was or could be I have spent a lifetime exploring. However much it felt like it at the time, it has not been a unique or singular journey. This book is a record – inevitably partial and fragmentary – of a personal journey but also of a social and cultural transformation that has remade the world I was born into and propelled me into different worlds.

When my close friend and former partner, Angus Suttie, died in 1993 of AIDS-related illnesses a friend wrote a note of condolence containing the thought that we are 'caught between worlds and ways of being . . . '. It resonated with me then and continues to echo now, because it put into words a sense of living in multiple worlds that coexisted side by side but could rarely find the words to talk easily to one another. The AIDS crisis was one of a number of critical moments in my life that have dramatised both the resilience and impossibilities of traditions that were crumbling, and the potentiality but fragility of new forms of living and loving that had yet to find full validation. This book is an attempt to make sense of the different worlds, ostensibly irreconcilable but actually deeply imbricated, that I have lived in and between, and which have made me what I am today.

But let me begin at the beginning.

CHAPTER 1

A QUEER BOY FROM THE VALLEYS

BEGİNNİNGS

I was the product of a wartime marriage, hastily arranged by my nineteen-year-old father over Easter in early April 1944, on his last weekend of leave before D-Day, the beginning of what my mother into extreme old age still called the 'second front'. Ray (always Raymond to his parents, Ray to my mother and his new family) was a stoker and petty officer on a minesweeper in the home seas, and present at the Normandy landings. He had joined up as soon as he could, apparently falsifying his age, so was already a young veteran when he got married. My mother Eiddwen, nearly three years older, lived with her mother and worked in the munitions factory in Bridgend. Both Mam and Dad were children of mining families, deeply rooted in the Rhondda.

The Rhondda of the 1940s was still recognisably a product of its formative experiences at the end of the nineteenth century and the early twentieth century as the twin valleys (Rhondda Fach and Rhondda Fawr, the little valley and the big valley) became for a while the most important coal-mining area in the world, a vast 'black Klondyke', the vibrant heart of a South

Wales that had become a 'metropolitan hub' of Empire, with the Atlantic as its lake.[4] It had seen explosive growth with the population increasing by over a third between 1901 and 1911, three times the UK average, and had some of the ethos and spirit of a frontier town, with a vibrant and raucous cultural and political life, and pubs vying for space with chapels. By 1913, the high peak of the Rhondda's glory days, there were 53 large collieries in the two winding valleys. Coal poured down the Rhondda and Taff valleys to the ports of Cardiff and Barry, making a few people immensely wealthy, and for a while drawing thousands of men and women from all over the British Isles and beyond who were never destined to be rich but could build here a viable life. Rapid growth of population and of the higgledy-piggledy terraces, overcrowding and the unpredictable rhythms of the trade-cycle fuelled acute political and social tensions, most famously epitomised by the Tonypandy riots of 1910–11, when the Home Secretary, Winston Churchill, notoriously 'sent in the troops' to quell the disturbances among the miners and was never forgiven. As a young boy in the early 1950s I vividly remember cinemas audiences still erupting in loud boos whenever Churchill, by then in his second term as prime minister, appeared in a newsreel. The period before the First World War was a period of passionate political radicalisation in the Rhondda. *The Miners' Next Step*, a pamphlet that grew out of the strike that had led to the riots, explored the possibilities of syndicalism and workers' control as a direct challenge to the long history of Lib-Labism, the deeply embedded collaboration between the Liberal Party and the forces of Labour that the long-standing local MP William Abraham – 'Mabon' – personified. The Tonypandy riots, a 'carnival of disorder' in Dai Smith's words, had crystallised a sense of identity and community that was to shape Rhondda life for the next half-century.

By 1913, on the eve of war, the community was stabilising, and with it its values and family patterns. The real story of the Rhondda, wrote E. D. Lewis, is 'how large masses of people from all parts of Wales and England were adventitiously thrown together to achieve, in spite of all kinds of difficulties, a quality of personal living which was probably unsurpassed among the ordinary folk of that time'.[5]

The journeys of my mother and father's families to this vibrant if precarious world had been varied, each in their own way illuminating a bigger social drama. By 1911, when the Rhondda bubbled with industrial and political energy and conflict, my mother's mother, my future nanny, Rosie, born in 1885, was living in Glyn Street, Cymmer, overlooking Porth. In the 1911 census she is named as housekeeper to her parents, David Rees, then just 60, and Elizabeth Mary Rees, ten years younger. The house, with seven rooms, was a step up from the modest terraced houses recently built all around, a mark of David's status as a colliery foreman and later undermanager. Family history has not recorded his role in the strikes and riots of 1910–11, but it is unlikely to have been a militant one. Certainly, unlike my contemporary Dai Smith, I have no memory of heroic stories binding me to the militant past. David and Elizabeth Rees were respectable, middling people, more chapel than pub or miners' lodge. Both had farming backgrounds: David came from a small farm of 14 acres between nearby Pontypridd and Llantrisant, and was proudly a 'freeman of Llantrisant Common' – an honour to which I am apparently now entitled by descent but have never had any inclination to claim – while Elizabeth's parents had a farm in Glynfach, just above where David and she now lived. There was no absolute divide, however, between farming and mining. Family members had worked in the pits in the Rhondda as early as the 1840s, and the men of the family are variously

3

listed as quarrymen, hauliers and labourers. The farms were too small, the families too large and the market too fragile to make farming on its own a viable career. Coal mining, a highly dangerous industry beset by pit explosions and disasters, was nevertheless a lifeline to a better existence.

The outward respectability of the Rees household hid a family secret with long-term consequences for Rosie. Also living in the house in 1911 was a two-year-old child, Olwen, listed as the daughter of David and Elizabeth. In reality she was the illegitimate daughter of Rosie – the offspring, according to my mother, of a relationship with a local married policeman. Illegitimacy at that time, and for long afterwards, could hardly have been more shameful for the woman who bore the child, and scarcely less shaming for the child. A rigid moral code particularly framed women's sexual lives, in large part a community response to the accusations of female immorality that had marked the publication of the infamous Blue Book on education in Wales in the 1840s. Guarding the reputation of women was a prime collective commitment. This did not prevent a lively premarital sex life among young men and women, at least as suggested by the high incidence of prenuptial pregnancies, but community pressures usually enforced marriage. When that failed other subterfuges were necessary. Rosie's parents informally adopted their granddaughter and brought her up as their own, though in these early years her actual birth mother was at hand as 'the housekeeper' to care for her. Like so many family secrets this was one that everyone in the neighbourhood probably knew about, but no-one spoke about. However, while growing up I developed an acute ear for these sexual misdemeanours and complexities. As an inquisitive teenager, I found out about Nanny when the minister at Rosie's funeral spoke of her four daughters – I only knew of three. Looking around the room it dawned on me

4

that Aunty Olwen was the fourth, which Dad later confirmed. Olwen's own daughter remained officially ignorant of this even in her eighties. No-one, least of all her mother, had ever spoken of it to her.

This family embarrassment and shame inevitably pushed my grandmother down the minutely calibrated social ladder, only partially redeemed when she married my grandfather William in 1916, already pregnant by him with her second daughter. She had known William, eldest son of a farmer from Llanfair Clydogau, just outside Lampeter in west Wales, for some time: in 1911 he was a lodger in Rosie's grandparents' farm in Glynfach, employed as a shepherd. Like many of his generation, William had moved east to escape the agricultural slump but continued to utilise his rural skills: he subsequently worked as an ostler, looking after the pit ponies, in what became Lewis Merthyr colliery. My mother, born in 1921, was the youngest daughter of Rosie and William, and her father's favourite. By all accounts he was a gentle, bookish, self-educated man, deeply religious and a lay preacher. On my mother's death I uncovered a mass of his books, many of which I had read as a child, in an upstairs cupboard: the classic anti-slavery novel, *Uncle Tom's Cabin* jumbled with Milton's *Paradise Lost* and Bunyan's *Pilgrim's Progress*, an illustrated book on Venice, Bible commentaries, and copies of the Bible itself in English and Welsh. He died of 'dust' – pneumoconiosis – in 1930, when my mother was 9. In her last years she would still mourn his loss.

My father's parents had a more hazardous pathway to the Rhondda. The family of my grandfather, Uriah Weeks (always known as Hughie), came from the Monmouthshire valleys, near Pontypool in the old Abergavenny Hundred. There were strong earlier links into England via both Gloucestershire and Somerset. Hughie's paternal grandfather, also Uriah, and his wife Mary lived on the edge of the law, a long way from respectability: in 1861 they were charged with others for forging half-crown coins, and sentenced to prison for three years and nine months respectively. He was further cautioned in 1867 for selling rotten herrings in Pontypool market, and a year later was imprisoned for another year's custody. He seems to have had severe mental health problems, and by the 1881 census was a patient in the local lunatic asylum, where he died. The messiness of his and his wife's lives had a direct impact on their nine children. My great-grandfather John Weeks, Hughie's father, was listed as a two-year-old pauper in the 1861 census, when his parents were in gaol, and seems to have been in and out of the Pontypool workhouse for the rest of his youth. He was obviously a survivor, however, and eventually became a miner in the Rhondda. John and his wife Rebecca had thirteen children, eight of whom died very young. Their third child, my grandfather Hughie, was born in 1891 in Talywain, a rural coal-mining village just north of Pontypool, and by 1911 was living in Llwynypia in the Rhondda with his family, listed as a coal trimmer, and close to the epicentre of the disturbances.

The journey of my father's mother, Meg, born in 1898, to the Rhondda is less clear-cut than either her husband's erratic path or the upper working-class respectability of my mother's side. She gives three different surnames in various documents, and this is explained by the complexity of the immediate circumstances of her upbringing. She was informally adopted, but her birth mother, Gwen, returned intermittently into her life and still lived locally. Her birth father also lived nearby, at one time on the same street as her mother, but seems to have played no part in Meg's life. Meg's mother outlived her, living a mile or so from Meg's last home. Despite this constant proximity, I have absolutely no memory of having met Gwen. Meg married Hughie in 1921. Raymond, born in 1924, was the second of three sons, with a daughter following on much later.

A striking feature of these family journeys is that while they were epic in many ways, none of them were long distance. They represent a shaking up and ingathering of the population of South Wales and the English borders. My father's side was the more 'English' one, with little Welsh-speaking tradition, and a surname most common in various forms (Wicks, Weakes, Weekes) in the English borders of Wales. All sides of my mother's family, on the other hand, were solidly rooted in south or west Wales, and were Welsh speaking or bilingual. My DNA profile indicates overwhelmingly 'British Isles' origins, though there was a small admixture of north European ancestry, a very common pattern, suggesting a deeply mixed original make-up stabilised by centuries of relative population continuity. The only hint of more ancient exotica is a suggestion in my mother's mitochondrial DNA of ancient Middle Eastern and Romany ancestry.

At my first formal dinner when I went to university, I sat next to Professor Joel Hurstfield, the leading expert of Queen Elizabeth I at the time. Hearing my still-thick Welsh accent and peering at my ginger hair and pale skin, he said, 'second wave of Celts, just like Elizabeth'. Historians and geneticists are now more sceptical of whether the Celts really existed, let alone two waves of them, but there was undoubtedly striking evidence on all sides of long association with Wales and its peripheries, and with the fair-headed part of its ancestry. From every quarter, there was reddish/gingery hair, which I inherited.

By the eve of the First World War, in the boom years, all the elements in my family had reached the Rhondda: my mother's side settled in Porth, my father's in the Tonypandy/Llwynypia area. But by the early 1920s, when both my parents were born, the short-lived boom that followed the war was collapsing, and the hectic bonanza years that had created the Rhondda, with its passion and militancy, ended. The 1920s saw acute industrial strife, the prolonged miners' strike, culminating in the general strike of 1926, and the succeeding lockout that brought poverty and despair to the community.[6] The Rhondda, like other primary producing areas, suffered further in the interwar depression. William's death in 1930 left Rosie and her children in dire poverty, refused compensation ('compo') by the pit, and dependent on haphazard income. Rosie took in washing, and she was helped out by William's family farm in 'the country', as the Lampeter area was always known. Even in the 1950s they would send us a chicken or goose through the post every Christmas, an echo of that earlier support. Rosie's father David and his second wife Sarah, however, clearly did not approve of her and gave little material support, though they brought up Olwen as their own daughter. Further up the valley, Dad's family, after their migration to Bristol, returned to long-term unemployment, accentuated by Hughie's chronic chest and heart problems. Dad won a scholarship to Tonypandy Grammar School (where George Thomas, later Speaker of the House of Commons, was one of his teachers), but left early to work in a local men's clothing shop to support the family income – and then enlisted in the navy, whose glory years of supremacy had been fuelled in large part by Rhondda's steam coal.

Despite the renewed wartime demand for coal from 1939 and the reconstruction that followed, by 1947 the number of mines was reduced to twelve, and the story of the Rhondda for the next half-century, despite the post-war move towards 'affluence', was the struggle to survive as a viable community while freeing itself from the glories and burden of coal. But coal, for good or ill, made the Rhondda, and shaped its everyday life. Coal gave the place its identity, especially its sense of itself as a community and a good place to live despite its hardships. The idea of 'community' as a dense network of kin, neighbours, friends and local organisations had a long resonance in the Rhondda and was an essential part of its political and moral imaginary. It was fundamentally rooted in family and place, in the dusty soil of the Valleys, but it was also diasporic, uniting those who had left across distance. 'When are you coming home?' was a question echoing in the ears of many an exile from the Valleys down the years, especially in the 1930s as thousands left in search of work and opportunities, but also throughout my lifetime.

It was, during all the fluctuations of the economic cycle and the fantastic rise and painfully prolonged fall of an industry, a warm, vibrant, rugged, close-knit place. Community was sustained in the hard labour and mutual dependencies of the pit, the union, the club, the chapel, the neighbourhood and the home. It was an all-encompassing ideal, yet it was also intensely local. In many ways, said Ken Hopkins, a prominent South Wales educationalist and, as it happens, my former English teacher, 'we are of a village society. The school, the club, the chapel never more than just around the next corner'.[7]

My parents' marriage in 1944 epitomises for me the culture and values of the Rhondda at that time. The urgency of the marriage was shaped by the imminence of the invasion of Europe, and the very likely possibility that my father would not survive. My father arrived in Nyth Bran without warning flourishing a special marriage licence. Nothing had been planned, nothing prepared. The neighbourhood community immediately took charge. Thomas', the general store a few doors up the street, provided the food for the wedding. Mr Thomas' daughters helped my mother get together her trousseau. The close families on both sides, who had never properly met before the wedding (though my mother had gone out for a while with my father's elder brother) rallied round, and the wedding picture, which I am looking at now, fading round the edges, looks serious rather than joyous, solidly respectable rather than wildly romantic – yet to my mind now that's what it was, a commitment until death in the midst of war: at the centre, my father youthful, slight and strikingly handsome in navy uniform, standing; my mother, pretty and fashionable, seated in her pink two-piece suit.

EVERYDAY LİFE

The Rhondda world they married in, and I was soon born into, had a gender and sexual order that was quite distinctive from the overall British pattern. In many ways it was, according to demographic historian Simon Szreter, closer to a surprisingly different culture. The Welsh, he argues, 'appear to have behaved more like the French, the antithesis of the English model'.[8] Couples married younger than elsewhere, and had larger families, like my great-grandparents' generation, characteristically up to eight to ten children, though with a high infant mortality rate. Miners as a group across Britain were among the last to limit family sizes, though their fertility began to decline markedly from the 1920s, and by the time I was born both South Wales and, by extension, my parents were reverting to the British norm during the twentieth century of two or three children. As family size declined marriage became ever more normative, a pattern that survived into the 1980s in the Rhondda, as marriage rates declined elsewhere but remained high there. Marriage was the gateway to adulthood, to legitimate sex and mutual support, to respectability and a solid family life. That is not to say that marriages did not break up, but 'the family' in all its complexity was the glue that held everyday life together.

At the heart of family life was a sharp division of labour

that seemed like a law of nature: men were the breadwinners, while women looked after the home and offspring. The origins of these patterns lay in the dependence on work in the mines, seen overwhelmingly as a man's job, and the lack of work outside the home for women. Being able to maintain your family properly was a matter of male pride. Failure to do so was deeply shameful, in effect an emasculation. In 1935 the Rhondda MP, W. H. Mainwaring, one of the militants of 1910–11, put the position in the context of protests against unemployment and the hated means' test with stark clarity: 'They wanted security for their homes, sustenance for their wives. If they were not prepared to strike a blow for these things then they were not fit to be called men'.[9]

The family wage was an ideal that shaped values and beliefs well into the post-war world, with at first few opportunities for women's employment outside the home. My mother worked part time in Thomas' grocery when we were young, and then for a local catering firm. Later she cleaned for the Asian family doctor who lived in the bungalow at the bottom of the street, and eventually until her retirement worked as a school dinner lady. Dad invariably and inevitably called the little she earned her 'pin money', though it was more important than that for family prosperity, and by the late 1960s after Dad's breakdown her's became the prime household income. Though she slogged away at these jobs on top of her domestic work, my mother seemed to enjoy them, as they took her out of the house and gave her new friends. They also produced the occasional treats, especially from the catering firm: delicious cream cakes or tasty pies left over from the functions she worked on. Male culture remained distinctly patriarchal and separate. Even into the 1960s it was thought a bit shocking to see a woman in a pub on her own (a 'slag') – my mother certainly would never have dreamt of doing so, or even of smoking in the street – and women were excluded from working men's clubs except on special occasions when their husbands could sign them in.

These segregated patterns were common throughout the mining communities of Britain. A well-known study of the 1950s (based in Yorkshire), *Coal Is Our Life*, described sharply gender-divided and embittered mining communities, with men and wives leading essentially 'secret lives' from one another, reflecting, perhaps, a hardening of gender divisions and an embattled sense of male pride in the difficult conditions of the 1950s.[10] In the cramped and gossipy ambience of the Rhondda there was little prospect of secrets being kept for too long. There is no doubt, however, that casual violence by men against each other, and especially against their womenfolk often belied the sense of mutuality and community that was supposed to be the hallmark of the local culture. The refuge movement for women was one of the first manifestations of second-wave feminism in South Wales in the 1970s, suggesting an enduring problem of domestic violence. I have a distinct memory that the portrait of a coal-mining community in *Coal Is Our Life*, serialised in a Sunday paper, was heavily criticised as unfair and inaccurate even at the time in South Wales, and Philip Dodd, brought up in Grimethorpe, the area of Yorkshire described in the book, has rightly argued that it turned 'into a collective singular what were "varying forms of life"'.[11] The Rhondda and other mining areas were complex societies where the relations between men and women, though highly gendered and often fractious, and frequently violent, were not always or straightforwardly power struggles. Confrontational male dominance is not the only story. Most men and women tried to please each other and work together, and love and generosity were as common as disputes. Despite my father's quicksilver temper and sharp, defensive and often unforgiving tongue, this was certainly true in my family. Dad, short and wiry, was proud of his toughness and would tell me and my brother about the brawls he would get involved in as a young man, but he was not physically violent towards my mother or, apart from quick slaps, us boys.

Dad never questioned the dominant forms of masculinity, which he was proud to embody, though in later life I often wondered about the degree to which he really felt comfortable with his predestined role. He was in many ways a devoted family man and took seriously his responsibilities as the main source of household income. After demobilisation, and a restless spell in the immediate post-war period in which he tried various jobs, he eventually began working in a tool-making factory in Taff's Well near Cardiff, staying there for the next twenty years, proud that he rarely missed a day from ill health (when of course he lost pay). He was heavily involved for a while in trade union activities as a shop steward but never at the expense of his family, which was central to his existence. He always gave my mother his pay on Friday night, minus his own pocket money that he would use for travel, his Player's cigarettes, his small bets on the horses and his Friday night out at the club with the boys. Every Sunday he would take Dennis and me to visit his parents in Tonypandy and would slip his out-of-work father a few bob. Whenever there was a family crisis around his parents or their other offspring, Ray was the son they turned to for help. He was also the go-to scholar in our immediate neighbourhood, filling in forms for neighbours terrified by petty bureaucracy. He was a kind and generous man, and I loved him deeply, but we never really got on. I found his quick temper and sharp tongue difficult to accept, especially as he always seemed so critical of my peculiarities. He was much closer to Dennis than to me, especially as my brother was more practical than I was – then as always since clumsy and totally unable to do the simplest household task without a struggle and moan.

I got on much better with the women in my life, promiscuously close to Nanny and Aunty Lily as well as my mother. She was a proud parent, always keeping us well dressed and well spoken, and was indulgent to our eating foibles – perhaps too indulgent, but she also had a husband who could be very picky. For Mam, food was the music of love. She was not a particularly versatile cook but some of her specialities – corned-beef pasties and Welsh cakes baked on a griddle – have remained treats for me all my life. Mam's routines inevitably revolved much more than Dad's around domestic rituals, but she also strove to carve out something of an autonomous life. She would go out regularly on a Wednesday night, sometimes with an old friend from the munitions factory days, more often on her own, to one of the local cinemas, the Central or Empire in Porth. Dad would then prepare our supper, especially potato scallops, which Dennis and I loved and looked forward to, while we watched a cowboy series on television. But by ten o'clock Dad was on edge waiting for Mam to come home, having an outburst if she was a bit late, even though she had usually rushed out before the national anthem to get home quickly. For my mother cinema was the world of escape, thrills and romance, echoed in the mysteries and Mills & Boon novels she loved to read. By the early 1960s, with greater affluence, and before my youngest brother Robert was unexpectedly born in 1963, Mam and Dad would regularly go out together on a Saturday night. What they never did together was go dancing, which my mother loved (she still had a little bop on her ninetieth birthday) but Dad loathed. They had met at a local dance hall, the Rink, but once they had hooked up Dad rarely went again. *Come Dancing* on television on a Monday night was my mother's surrogate during the rest of their marriage.

My parents were in many ways well matched. Their rows could be fierce and noisy, but they usually made up quickly. When I was growing up with them, I used to think my father was the dominant character, and I usually sided with my mother when they clashed. Mam had the more emollient style, and although she had a sharp temper herself, especially in defence of her clan, her instinct was always to smooth things down. She was more diffident than my father, and it must have been difficult for my mother to assert herself fully as the dominant woman in the household when my forceful grandmother was still around. Yet by the late 1960s it was my mother who proved the more resilient of my parents, growing into her predestined role as the stoic guardian of the family as my father's health frayed.

Like every other woman of her generation in the Rhondda, my mother had to live up to the mythologised role of 'Mam' in the culture: 'The quiet, strong woman selflessly working for the good of the family, holding the purse strings, holding the family together and keeping a meticulously clean and tidy home'.[12] For earlier generations of women living up to that myth was a herculean task, with large families, poor domestic conditions, overcrowding and a constant battle against grime and coal dust. Things were changing for my mother's generation, and growing affluence and new gadgets eased domestic labour, and provided greater leisure opportunities. Sexual repression and hypocrisy, which had so shaped Rosie's life, was also easing, and there was a certain sexual frankness, even bawdiness, at home, especially at family celebrations or Christmas, as drink weakened inhibitions – though I was too shy or prissy to enjoy or participate in such exchanges.

Yet inherited traditions of what constituted a respectable home, forged in the early days of the community, lingered on. This is nicely captured by Dai Smith: 'Dress suits for male-voice choirs, Sunday-best outfits, China-dogs on the mantle-piece over a fire-grate blackleaded daily, the front room and tea service kept, like museum pieces, for special occasions or visitors . . . This desire for respectability, for things in the local parlance, "tidy", could exert an almost immoveable hegemony over individual behaviour and family ambition' – especially for women.[13] Change was certainly in the air by the mid-1950s, but Nanny and my mother still blackleaded the fireplace and scoured the front doorstep, and while many other things changed in the decades that followed my mother still kept a glass-fronted cabinet full of the best china, and had Nanny's china dogs on the mantlepiece when she died in 2014.

Like in many working-class and minority communities elsewhere, blood and neighbourliness overlapped, so that neighbours and friends were known as honorary kin, elder members called Aunty and Uncle, so that for a child it was often confusing who was blood and who was not. I was shocked as a young boy to learn at the death of our neighbour two doors down, who I knew as Aunty Crease, that she was not a blood relative, and that her sons were not my cousins. Front doors, still secured with a heavy key like the one I saw exhibited many years later for Oscar Wilde's Reading gaol cell, were rarely locked, and neighbours were constantly popping in for a gossip or to 'borrow' a cup of sugar or milk.

Our house was, if warm and all-embracing, small, often uncomfortable and overcrowded, certainly in my early years, with my parents, Nanny and us boys taking up the three small (and unheated) bedrooms upstairs, and Aunty Lily and Uncle Frank lodging in the front room before they moved to a house of their own. Until the early 1950s we were still lit by gaslight, and we would struggle out to the back yard for the outside loo with a candle or a torch (that Dennis and I would get every year as one of our Christmas stocking fillers, as Dad had done in his childhood). The tin tub would be dragged into the kitchen for our weekly bath, usually on a Friday, in front of the fire. We only had a bathroom fitted, with an indoor toilet, as I went to university, built by my father – the National Coal Board that by then owned the house were not devoted to modernising their housing estate, and eventually sold them off. In my first job as a teacher in the late 1960s, I was able to take out a bank loan to help my parents, Dad by then being unable to work, to buy the house.

For most of my childhood we lived in the back kitchen. Here was the wash basin and one cold tap, the table, a couple of easy chairs huddling the open coal range, where the cooking was done, often by Nanny. An abiding memory is of Nanny cooking the Sunday dinner, the smell of roasting beef pervading the house, her face red from bending over the fire, singing a Welsh hymn as she listened to the wireless broadcast of the morning service on the Welsh programme of the BBC, with tears pouring down her cheeks from deep unspoken memories. When I hear some of this music today, wherever I am, I weep too, an unconscious homage, perhaps, to a world long gone.

From August 1953, after the Coronation, we had a small 12-inch Bush television, which was on a trolley kept in the middle room and wheeled into the kitchen once the TV service began at 7 PM. Over time, as we became more affluent, a glass-roofed extension – the 'glass house' – opened up the kitchen, and housed the new wash basin (with hot water), gas cooker, which took over from the range, and the fridge. Gas fires replaced the coal fires throughout the house by the mid-1960s, and we gradually colonised the middle room as the living room, while I took over the back-bedroom after Nanny's death (and it remained 'Jeffrey's room', despite my living away, till my mother's death). The front parlour, however, remained more or less sacrosanct except at Christmas or special occasions, till my mother out of necessity made it her bedroom in the last years of her life so that she wouldn't have to climb the stairs.

The increasing emphasis on the comforts of home into the 1960s was paralleled by a decline in what had once been the glue of family and community life. My mother and her sisters, like their friends, had been regular chapel goers in the 1930s, yet by the time Dennis and I were growing up religion played very little part in our lives. Nanny's commitment was nostalgic and personal rather than institutionalised, and she now rarely went to the Welsh chapel in Porth. Dad's parents, on the other hand, were for a while in my childhood deeply committed, regular attendees at Trinity chapel in Tonypandy, which had a succession of charismatic preachers. I vividly remember listening to passionate discussions about freewill and predestination over Sunday tea at their house. At various times Dennis and I were persuaded to go to Sunday school at St Luke's church at the bottom of Nyth Bran, or the English Cong (English Congregational Church), where Mam and Dad had married, in Porth itself, but there was no real enthusiasm on either my parents' or our part. When I got religion in my late teens it was a private and personal faith that didn't last long.

We were much more enthusiastic about other things to do on Sundays, especially going on day trips. We typically had three or four Sunday bus trips every summer, usually to Barry Island or Porthcawl, which were organised by Dad's club, a local chapel or an enthusiast in the street. We always had annual summer holidays, usually by the seaside or with my aunt and uncle in London. We also had annual trips to the National Museum in Cardiff, followed by fish and chips in one of the old cafés near the General station that Dad remembered from his sailor days. Once we had a car in the early 1960s we would have a trip together every weekend, but I grew to dread these as Dad would regularly get testy as I fumbled over my route directions, and there would often be a temper explosion with my father tense and white behind the wheel and me in tears. My parents were always very protective of me and my brother going off any distance on our own, but by my mid-teens my closest friend Alun and I would do bus and train trips together, with regular trips to Cardiff. When I was growing up in the Rhondda in the 1940s and 50s Cardiff felt like a foreign country with a different language, not really Welsh at all, and going there as a schoolboy from Porth by a slow bus on winding roads or on one of the new diesel trains on a creaky line was like crossing the Channel. It was an invitation to a different world where lunch in the old Kardomah on Queen Street seemed like the height of sophistication, a visit to Lear's bookshop an opening to a new life, and a quick read of the graffiti in the public lavatories brought intimations of inexplicable delights yet to be fully imagined.

The intensity, warmth and all-encompassing grip of family life as I was growing up still lingers in tastes, smells and sounds. I've spent a lifetime running away from it, but it still shapes my ways of life. I enjoy the busyness of domestic life – the sound of music playing in another room, the dog barking at outside noises, my partner chatting while making us coffee as I sit at the table writing. I could never work in a padded room. Yet as I was growing up in that intense family atmosphere, I needed also to develop a life of my own. Withdrawal into myself was a form of self-protection and has lingered with me all my life. It was a way of developing a life of the mind where other lives became possible, re-imagined from the books I read, the dreams I was beginning to have. This fed into the everyday battles I was having with my parents about needing more space for myself. Privacy was a distant ideal, and something I had to struggle for in the early 1960s as I worked for my O- and A-level school exams, and I would retreat to the (freezing) bedroom to do my homework or revision, my parents not quite understanding my anger or my need. There was of course an even more imperative reason for my fury and frustration. As my vague feelings began to crystallise into fantasies and clearer hopes and wishes, and desire and ambition shaped a guilty aspiration to escape, my sexuality became an increasingly dominant part of my secret life.

BEİNG QUEER

I can't remember exactly when my amorphous feelings about being different firmed into a realisation that I had strong sexual attraction and desires for other males. From my mid-teens, however, I increasingly became aware that whatever the explanation of my peculiarity was, it separated me off from other boys and needed to be kept a deadly secret. I could scarcely give it a name, though others tried. I remember being asked loudly as I got onto a school bus – I must have been about 14 – if I was a queer. Though I'd never heard the word in this context, I guessed what it must mean and muttered something self-mockingly – but I felt marked for ever, in front of the whole bus and, it seemed, the whole world. The irony of this was that years later, I met by chance in London the guy – his name, I remember, was Terry – who had asked me the question, and of course he turned out to be gay too, though tortured into middle age about coming out to his mother who still lived in Porth.

Words can be weapons, but they also help to give meaning to barely formed feelings, and I gradually learned through words my desires had a name, many names, which said something about me, what I was and could be. I picked up hints about what that might be from occasional insults or teasing questions, as from Terry, from snatches of information in newspapers, reports of court cases in the *Rhondda Leader* and *Porth Gazette*, oblique pieces in the columns of agony aunts in my mother's women's weeklies, even accounts of 'inversion' and 'homosexuality' in decrepit medical texts I found among the books of my long-dead grandfather. Much of what I learned was still confined to my private thoughts and fantasies. I never experienced any sexual advances from adults. Perhaps I was too naïve to notice them, perhaps I was too unsporty, and too poor a mixer to have regular extracurricular encounters with teachers, coaches or scout masters. But I did learn to masturbate (I can't remember how – a school friend must have shown me), and my fantasies were increasingly of men, though I remained naïve about what I was supposed to do with them for a long time. Eventually I had brief and mainly unsatisfactory encounters with school friends, often starting with playing forfeits, and for several years I had sexual fumblings with my friend Gavin who lived up the street. We regularly met in his house on Friday evenings when his parents went to the club. They were not very fulfilling encounters – Gavin refused to kiss or undress – but they inflamed my imagination. Soon after I went to university I came across James Baldwin's *Another Country* and thought it wonderful, life-changing. I copied out a few paragraphs in a letter to Gavin hoping he would think them equally inspiring. A couple of days later I got his reply. As I opened the envelope the charred remains of my own letter fell out: that, the cover note said, was what he thought of my disgusting message. Next time I went home I saw Gavin as usual and we went for a drive, as if nothing had happened. As we stopped in a quiet road up the mountain, he grabbed me, and the usual messy groping followed. I was still desperate for physical contact, any contact, however unsatisfactory. So, apparently, was he. He later moved to Swansea, got married, had children and cut any further contact with me. I've no idea what happened to him after that, but I suspect his was probably a more typical queer life at the time than mine was to become.

As all this suggests, homosexuality existed in the Rhondda as everywhere else, though rarely as a distinctive way of life, but I only began to learn about the covert friendship and sexual networks that existed as I was about to leave for university. Same-sex activity was subtly crafted into the heterosexual dynamic. Leo Abse, the Labour MP for Pontypool and one of the authors of the Sexual Offences Act, which partially decriminalised male homosexuality in 1967, saw in the gender order one of the likely 'causes' of what he described as endemic homosexuality in the Valleys. The dominance of 'Mam' in the family, he once told me (over a boozy lunch at *The Spectator* with the novelist-to-be Peter Ackroyd), produced a large number of 'mammy's boys' in the Valleys. As he wrote elsewhere, in his rather crude pseudo-Freudian language, 'excessive attachment to the mother can be evoked and encouraged by too much tenderness on the part of the mother herself and can be significantly reinforced by the small part played by the father during the boy's childhood'.[14] Superficially, at least, here was an explanation for my personal history. But it was, of course, complete psychobabble. Luckily, by then, in the early 1980s, I was way past such intellectual contortions.

Sadly, I had had no sense of other mammy's boys like me when I was growing up, and no identification with possible others. As I discovered much later, the obvious candidates for suspect homosexuality in the 1950s and early 1960s conformed to a pattern common in highly gender-segregated societies like the Rhondda of effeminate men and butch women. The effeminate man would in all likelihood be called a 'proper bopa' (aunty) and tolerated as a harmless freak, as long as he respected the gender order. The dapper, dandified or camp men I knew from the neighbourhood were usually married men, and there was no public hint of sexual aberrance. Two women living together down the street might be acceptable as close friends, with a wink or two. I used to occasionally see in the next street a local woman, who was a headteacher, work in her front garden with a cigarette hanging from her lips while her female companion watched languidly, but I had no definite knowledge at the time about what this might mean. In any cases neither mincing men nor butch women provided role models for me. I just felt a bit of a freak. As I engaged half-heartedly with the bracing and scary macho atmosphere of a boys' school with its overwhelming zeal for sport, I could only assume that a shameful and mocked effeminacy was my lonely destiny.

My overriding problem as an adolescent was that I had a visceral knowledge that my feelings were deep but painfully wrong, and that my being was somehow a betrayal of what the Rhondda and my family stood for. My existence was invalidated by my closest bonds and the values I had imbibed. I had no sense of what an alternative narrative could be. What I lacked above all, without really knowing it at the time, were stories of others like me who I could recognise myself in, identify with and feel a sense of belonging through. Stories, says Ken Plummer, who has written richly and passionately about sexual narratives over many years, 'help us to imagine, animate and value human life'. We live and desire through stories, they place us in relation to a past, a present and a future. But they are never neutral, for they embody sedimented meanings, and have power to welcome or reject, affirm or shame.[15] The stories of love, sex and relationships I had learnt at home as a child excluded me, made me invisible or derisory. One of my inspirations for becoming a historian of gay life in the 1970s was to uncover and animate collective stories that made sense of my life and thousands like mine. This was to be a much more complicated commitment than I ever imagined, but one of its happy by-products was that through this I learned much more about same-sex attraction and its hazards in South Wales long after I left than when I was growing up there. Three stories of men of my grandfathers' generation showed the painful effects of lacking strong stories of belonging.

I met Fred, who lived in Barry with his daughter, in the mid-1970s at a Campaign for Homosexual Equality (CHE) meeting in Cardiff, and during several interviews over the next few years he told me about his life. He was born in Cadoxton in 1894, just round the corner from where he was living when I met him, one of eleven children. The family was desperately poor and broke up when he was 13 upon his mother's death and his father's subsequent descent into drunkenness. He recalled that 'homosexual inclinations started when I was a boy of about 14. I didn't understand it then, you see ... And I've been reaching out all my life to put my arms round another man'. He fell in love and had sex with another conscript for the first time during the First World War, 'the first time I felt the love and affection of a man ... And oh, it was lovely. I'll never forget it. Never forget it'. But after this he returned home to Barry, got married, had a child, bred pigs and largely suppressed his feelings for men for the next fifty years. On the verge of 80, and after his wife's death, he learnt about gay meetings in Cardiff from an advertisement in the local paper, phoned up, and for the first time in his life became part of a company of other gay men. 'And of course I've become one of the old contemptibles, one of the regulars, aye'.[16] It was at one of these meetings that I met Fred, sitting with a group of much younger friends, his flat cap on his head, a traditional South Wales working-class man whose life had begun again in his eighties. After I later interviewed him about his life, I kept in touch, visiting him on my trips back to Wales. When he died, I was deeply touched that he left me a small bequest.

Trevor was more flamboyant and outgoing and became an icon of the gay liberation movement in London during the 1970s, but his earlier life had seen glittering promise destroyed by his homosexuality. Born in the Gwent valleys in 1907, not far from where my dad's father was born, he too came from a mining family. He went to University College Wales, Aberystwyth and then had a rapid advancement in the museum world, culminating in a leadership role in Leicester's museum and art gallery. On the verge of a further promotion, he was caught up in a cottaging case and was forced to resign, his career destroyed. He too then got married, had children and suppressed his homosexual feelings. It was nearly thirty years later, with his wife estranged and his children grown up, that he again felt able to explore the new gay world opening up from the early 1970s. For a while he was a constant presence at CHE events. His epiphany occurred at a gay conference in Sheffield in 1974 when, as the oldest person there, he embraced the youngest who had said he felt lonely in such a crowd, and made an impassioned speech about everyone working together and loving each other. The room erupted in applause. As Trevor later put it, 'I was now "out" and couldn't have been more out, if ever'.[17]

It was not to prove so easy. As he got older and frailer, Trevor retreated once more from the gay scene, and established a new relationship with a man who didn't want any involvement in gay politics. Trevor himself had been badly scarred by a threatening writ from Olwyn Hughes, sister of poet laureate Ted Hughes. Trevor had lived in a flat underneath that of the poet Sylvia Plath, and it was he who had smelt the gas that she used for her suicide. He wrote a private memoir of the incident, critical of Ted Hughes, and when the Hughes family heard of this they sought – successfully – to suppress it. The whole incident deeply depressed Trevor. I visited Trevor and his partner in the last year of his life, and still have the painting I bought from him on that occasion.

Much later I came across the story of Rhys Davies, the Rhondda-born short-story writer and novelist. Born in 1901 in Clydach Vale in the Rhondda, he was of lower middle-class (a shopkeeper's son) rather than mining stock, and that probably distanced him a little from the local community, but it is clear now that it was predominantly his developing homosexuality that pushed him into a lifelong exile, mainly in London, though his younger brother was also homosexual and seems to have been less inhibited. He published his first novel in 1927 and was later befriended by D. H. and Freda Lawrence. His work had echoes of Lawrence's preoccupations with a puritanically repressed sexuality, and his stories often evoke a utopian Welsh past where sexuality was more protean and liberating. But in his own life the contradictory pressures of a narrow Nonconformity and cloying warmth undoubtedly constricted his sense of growing difference. He had to leave to be. Yet like many an exile, he never escaped fully the Rhondda, writing about it throughout his career, and returning frequently to write. He never explicitly writes about homosexuality, and you need to be a subtle reader of the codes to see any reference to it in his autobiography, *Print of a Hare's Foot*, but same-sex desire suffuses his writing as it did his life. Posthumously he was rediscovered by a new generation, including queer theorists who saw in his writing a precocious destabilisation of gender and a fascination with masks and masquerade.[18] He died in 1978, long before such concerns entered mainstream discourse, but just as much younger people from the Rhondda like myself were beginning to feel freer to talk about our gayness and the arbitrariness of sexuality and gender categories more widely. He lived in his later years near Russell Square, in central London, just yards from where I had been a student – I like to feel we may have crossed paths, strangers in the night – but he died unheralded by the new gay movement by then highly active all around him. For Rhys Davies, as for the vast majority of his generation, reticence remained the necessary condition of his sexuality.

These personal stories have become important to me because they are so varied, linked only but always by the pervasive shame of sexual unorthodoxy. Their lives were lived in another time from mine. My journey was distinct. Yet through them I have a sense of what can unite us in difference: the threads of history that make possible identification across the chasms of time and memory.

In the years since I grappled with my sexuality as a teenager in South Wales a vast literature has developed, and most of it now readily available online. Life chances have been transformed. Strangely, it is only very recently that a specifically Welsh history of same-sex love has emerged that is helping people like I once was to make sense of their past.[19] Writers like Daryl Leeworthy have pointed out that South Wales was not especially homophobic during this period in comparison with, say, London or other parts of the country. A fascination with cross-dressing had a long resonance in the Rhondda and suggests deep tensions around binary divides between men and women. I have strong memories of my uncle regularly in drag at local carnivals. There are also suggestions that prosecutions for homosexual offences were rare in the Glamorgan constabulary area during this period, and as I have suggested there were forms of accommodation with same-sex partnerships, a sort of live-and-let-live attitude as long as you did not bring shame on the family. That was the great taboo. It wasn't so much the weight of the law that I experienced as a teenager but the weight of prejudice and the fear of rejection – by family and community. When I came out to my father in the early 1970s, he said he would accept it because he loved me, but he wanted me not to do anything at home that would embarrass the family. For years after, though I had by then become internationally well known as a gay historian, I still found myself bound by that promise and kept my gay life quite separate from my birth family's. In the usual way they sort of knew but never had to confront it, and I found it difficult to confront them with it. The bonds of love had become bonds of duty, discretion and necessary silence.

By my late teens I guiltily knew I had to leave the Rhondda and my family to become whatever I could be. Luckily, education proved a route out. Despite, or perhaps because of, my growing sexual misery, I was determined to succeed at school in order to escape. My school, Porth County, was renowned at the time as the top school in the Rhondda. As my English teacher, Ken Hopkins, put it, 'To be top of the Rhondda in the "scholarship" was to bring honour to the family, the street and the village. To wear the Porth County green blazer was to become one of the chosen few'.[20] Porth County was the school attended by the novelists Rhys Davies and Gwyn Thomas, numerous worthy public servants, actors, singers and sportsmen, who went to seek their fortunes and make their names in the wider world. But in the 1950s and 1960s, as a consequence of the 1944 Education Act, it was part of a highly selective system – a two-tier grammar school system in the Rhondda – that risked breaking the ties that bonded you to family and friends. For reasons I can now barely comprehend, my going to County irrevocably split me from my two closest friends in junior school, who failed to get in and I rarely spoke to again. It also created a long-lasting tension with my brother who went to the local secondary modern. Porth County was hardly a blissful escape. It had a strong sporting ethos and tradition that I felt no identity with. With one or two friends I found a niche by becoming militantly unsporty, dodging games and gym periods, and becoming the class nerd, especially in history, where my hand would be permanently floating up to answer questions. None of this enamoured me to classmates, and further isolated me from my peers. At the same time, the school gave me a strong intellectual grounding, a growing self-confidence and belief in myself, and a broadening horizon. My history teacher, David Thomas ('Dai Chips'), encouraged my passion for history, while Ken Hopkins ('Hoppy') in particular used to encourage a wider grounding through his enthusiasm for the moral importance of literature – he was a bit of a Leavisite – and his encouragement to read the weekly journals to follow what was going on in the wider political and cultural world. Every week he would bring in his copies of *The Spectator*, *New Statesman* and *The Listener*. I would grab them and devour them. I also started reading the serious papers, having orders of the *Sunday Times* and *Observer* home-delivered from the age of 15, thanks to the indulgence of Mam and Dad. Buying my first copy of *The Times* itself, still with small ads on the front page, gave me an electric, almost sexual, charge as I looked into other worlds.

My school experiences inevitably did something else: they began to unravel my ties to the Rhondda itself. As Hopkins suggested, a school like Porth County risked losing the virtues of community for another world: 'It was a bitter irony that economic necessity should have forced a socialist community to such an elitist system, but it was inevitable. Survival had a higher priority than equality'.[21] But it wasn't just economic necessity that propelled me. Personal survival for me meant finding ways of exploring my deepest desires, and increasingly I saw going to university in London as the essential next step.

In many ways I have never fully left the Rhondda. Many of my growing preoccupations as a queer boy in the Valleys – about who or what I was, about belonging, about finding a valid way in the world – became translated into my later intellectual and writing concerns: about identities, community, social activism, personal liberation and collective involvements. And my personal ties with the Valleys have remained strong to this day. I still visit regularly, my brothers and their families still live close by where I was born, and it's only a few years since my mother died there, very much by then a matriarch who kept us all together. But the journey that took me from Trehafod station to Paddington in late September 1964 did more than transmit me to university and new career possibilities. It opened the way to my becoming a fully sexual being, and to all the joys and pleasures, pains and delights that that would involve.

CHAPTER 2
LONDON CALLING

FORGING AN IDENTITY

The London I came to in 1964 was on the cusp of change. It still bore the scars of a war that had ended nearly twenty years before. Many buildings had remained derelict, and bomb sites in prominent places like Leicester Square were fenced off as long-lasting temporary car parks. Most of the famous buildings, from St Paul's Cathedral to the Houses of Parliament, Westminster Abbey to Buckingham Palace, were still saturated in inches of soot. The prevailing colour was grey. Modernity was popping through, however, in a vibrant cultural, musical (the Beatles' sound was everywhere), social and street life, and in gradual changes to the cityscape. Out of the windows of University College London's (UCL) seminar rooms in Gordon Square you could see the glistening new Post Office Tower, with its revolving restaurant near the top promising a new London, and indeed a 'new Britain'.

Within days of my arriving in London a Labour government was elected guaranteeing just that, though its wafer-thin majority indicated that the country was a bit hesitant in committing to that vision. The rest of the decade was to bring deepening distrust and disillusionment as the nation zig-zagged from crisis to crisis as it attempted to ride the rapids of 'modernisation', economic uncertainty and a threatening international climate, and as a cultural revolution began to intrude, unevenly, on every aspect of life, including mine. My immediate political hopes and dreams were yet to be tested as I watched the election results on 15 October and into the early hours of the next morning in the students' union. The news broke during the coverage that a coup had ousted Khrushchev from leadership of the Soviet Union. I remember someone shouting, 'Forget our election. This is the change that counts'. Later we heard that China had tested its first nuclear weapon. These events changed the global balance. I was for the time being happy that we would have a Labour government at last, after thirteen 'wasted years' as the party slogans stated. I wandered down to Trafalgar Square to watch the celebrations there, and then caught the first tube back to my digs in East Finchley, still feeling a bit lost and lonely.

That was the thing about those first days at college in London. I had spent a hectic couple of weeks careering from freshers' meetings (I joined the Labour Club) to cheese-and-wine receptions to a weekend History Department induction at Cumberland Lodge near Windsor (where I appalled Professor Cobban sitting next to me at breakfast by using the butter knife for my jam). Lectures had started, where I quickly realised I could no longer dazzle or irritate by striking my hand up to answer questions. No-one asked questions, and anyway most lecturers did not give space for anyone to try. Unlike American undergraduates, I discovered, British university students were usually passive in class, if not outside. I had had friendly conversations with numerous people, including for the first time in my life with middle-class public school-educated fellow students, who seemed so much more self-confident than me. Years later at a reunion I learnt that they were just as ill at ease as I was in those early days, they were just better at hiding it. Coming from an all-boys school it was also the first time I had mingled easily with many young women. It was all very warm and chummy, but as yet I had no intimate friends. At half-term at the end of October I fled back to Porth for my birthday. The warmth of home was still an effective antidote to my sense of isolation.

Things improved after that, and I did make close friends, as at school in a small tight-knit group rather than an extensive network. I settled into study routines and was boosted by generous comments on my essays. As usual my success as a student allowed me to sublimate my anxieties and sense of inadequacy. I was still intensely shy, and the inability of some of my fellow students to understand my Welsh accent was a burden. I have to confess that I also had difficulty understanding other people's accents and speech rhythms, especially Scottish and Geordie – ironic, given that I was eventually to spend most of my adult life living with men from Scotland and the north-east of England. We all instinctively softened our speech patterns just to be understood. My real problem, however, was the question of my homosexuality, especially as I now had the opportunity to experience it fully for the first time. How was I going to fit it into my student and London life?

During my confused, fearful and anguished mid-teens, I used to pray every night that I wasn't really homosexual. I certainly was that, but I eventually realised what I *wasn't* was at all religious – my prayers were more a just-in-case Pascalian wager. When I stopped praying at 18, on the eve of leaving for university, I also stopped fretting endlessly about my sexual desires and fantasies, my emotional needs and physical longings: I was what I was – a realisation confirmed by my reading of James Baldwin's *Giovanni's Room* when I was 18, which had convinced me of the validity of my feelings. Of course, I was still fearful of rejection by my family and friends, I had a background terror of having to live an illegal life, and I was all too aware of the threat of physical violence and verbal abuse that policed the boundaries between normal and queer. But by now I knew that my sexuality was fundamental to me, central to what I was and wanted to become. I could not believe I was sick or mentally deranged, evil or morally corrupt, despite the best efforts of some of the books about homosexuality I was now able to get hold of to persuade me otherwise. My sexuality felt perfectly normal to me, even if it was extraordinary to the world I knew. The only troubling question – and it was a huge one – was how I could, should or would live my life well in a world that seemed to invalidate by its very structures and values my deepest feelings.

I always found it difficult to be concerned about the question that seemed to obsess the experts and other people like myself: why we were queer. For generations, as I was to discover, thinking about same-sex desire has been bedevilled by questions around the causes of homosexuality, and I have spent a professional lifetime having to engage with them. Is it inborn or socially induced, a sign of degeneracy or a hormonal imbalance, a chromosomal mismatch or a quirk of nature, a genetic variation or a male soul in a female body and vice versa? Should we blame a distant father and overindulgent mother (Leo Abse's view), or perhaps too weak a father and a cold mother? Maybe a general lack of moral fibre, the effect of a malign seduction, the result of the decline of the family, or a symptom of the collapse of civilisation? To state the arguments like that to my mind displays the absurdity of the whole pointless debate, but that has not stopped the argument continuing to revolve. For one brand of contemporary gay activists, especially in the USA, such questions are existential: if we were not born this way then how can we justify our claim to minority status, what would be our purchase on the pursuit of social justice? My own view has long been that such arguments are almost entirely irrelevant to the fundamental issue: not what causes homosexuality, but, as my future friend and colleague Mary McIntosh put it, why do so many societies in so many different histories think it a relevant question, and have so much difficulty in accepting different sexual practices and ways of life?[22] I couldn't have put it in such words when I was 18, but once I encountered these insights I knew instantly they were right. They have proved a lifelong inspiration for my work as a historian and sociologist.

So, the first problem for me as a young man discovering the pleasures and perils of London lay not in 'discovering' or 'coming to terms with' my homosexuality as if it was a fixed essence, a pregiven destiny that had to be revealed or endured. As my experience with my friend Gavin confirmed, there was no necessary link at all between sexual desires and self-identification, what you did and who you were, subjectivity and sense of being in the world. Rather, the challenge facing me was how to forge an identity and find a way of life that made sense of my feelings, aspirations and desires, and allowed me to survive with and, where necessary, against others. This became a prolonged process during my first years in London, whereby the queer boy from the Valleys reinvented himself and became gay.

THE LURE OF THE CITY

An early gay liberationist, Carl Wittman, called San Francisco a refugee camp for homosexuals.[23] London, I soon discovered, was Britain's oldest and best refuge. Although I didn't fully know that when I chose to go to university in London – Oxford having turned me down – I was at least familiar with the city from regular summer holidays staying with my mother's older sister, Aunty Betty, and her husband, Uncle Bill, who lived in Earls Court in the early 1960s as housekeepers to an artist's widow in Redcliffe Square. The area, with its prevailing air of genteel decay (now, of course, it's a millionaires' paradise), nevertheless breathed a raffish, cosmopolitan liveliness and sense of openness and excitement, sustained by an ever-changing population of young Australians, compared with the Valleys. Even before moving to London as a student I had a strong sense of the possibilities available in its size, secret byways and the anonymity of the night, and unknowingly encountered the symbiosis in some parts of the capital between ordinary and queer life before I went to live there. My aunt lived round the corner from what I later learnt were two famous queer pubs, the Coleherne, later a famous leather bar which I went to regularly for many years, and the Boltons, which my father unwittingly or not used to go to for a lunchtime drink. Two worlds only a blink or drink apart, and that was to become a vital aspect of the excitement and lure of London.

My immediate milieu in University College was not particularly promising for a new sexual life. It was less stuffy and more classless than I had imagined. 1964 was the first year when it had deliberately attempted to broaden the student intake, with the majority, like me, coming from grammar schools, and half of our year were women. Despite, or because of, its aspirational ethos, UCL's broad liberalism went side by side with a bracing heterosexual assumption that I couldn't identify with at all. Rather than integrating into the relaxed, if sporty, prevailing ambience, I gradually tried to become the all-round intellectual I fantasised about being. I went regularly to the film programmes put on by the Slade, part of UCL, and tried to enjoy the films of Jean-Luc Godard and the 'nouvelle vague' (and did actually enjoy the films of François Truffaut). I went to the theatre with my friend Peter, and discovered a vast range of plays, including early on *The Prime of Miss Jean Brodie* and *Who's Afraid of Virginia Woolf*, plays by Harold Pinter and musicals like *Funny Girl*. I found I liked musicals and loved the film of *The Sound of Music*. I also grew into opera and started going to Covent Garden, and to concerts at the Royal Albert Hall and the Royal Festival Hall. I secretly and passionately fell in love with a fellow (male) student in my first year – my unknowing, unacknowledged first love – but he rapidly distanced himself when he began to suspect my attraction, and in my secret anguish I buried myself further in work – and won the first year history prize, the Dolley Prize. When I told my old school headmaster this, he said he would mention it in assembly, but would not refer to the title: it would make the pupils laugh. He had me, and them, taped. I came out to another student friend who I suspected might be queer on an evening walk through the sex sites of Soho, but he vehemently denied that he was. It took another ten years for him to come out as gay himself, though since then he has been a stalwart of local gay politics, and a lifelong friend. But that didn't help me at that moment.

Some years later I discovered that our senior tutor who was very supportive of me came out as gay in middle age, and left his wife and children, but none of us had any suspicions at the time. His end-of-year parties at his large comfortable home in north London were models, so I thought, of upper middle-class (heterosexual) domestic bliss, with deep settees and *The Spectator* casually resting on the coffee table. By the time I had graduated I had 'confessed' my homosexuality to a small group of my fellow students, including a woman with whom I had a brief and not particularly satisfying affair, but essentially my queer sexual life developed in a discrete and discreet world quite apart from student life.

From my first weeks in London I had an urgent desire to find the queer world. What I lacked at first was a map. I was not helped by my diffidence about approaching people and uncertainty about my attractiveness and what I actually wanted to do sexually. Gradually through casual encounters I began to explore tentatively some of the more accessible pathways into what I found at first to be a baffling and sometimes intimidating world, but also a space for desire and disappointment, anguish and passion, and of companionship and humanity. It turned out we were everywhere, if you knew how to see.

Many differing styles and types of queer men and women co-resided in the vast anonymity of the city. The queer world then, as now, was made up of a multitude of different social worlds, many of them overlapping, but some quite distinct and segregated from others, often with a long history then largely unknown. Mary McIntosh had referenced some of the evidence in her 1968 article, 'The Homosexual Role', though I did not read this till the early 1970s. Later, colleagues, friends and scholars such as Randolph Trumbach and Alan Bray brilliantly traced the emergence of distinctive London queer cultures from the seventeenth century, which provided the nexus where heterosexuality and homosexuality began to emerge as binary concepts and ways of being, though the divisions were always blurred in practice.[24] By the later nineteenth century male homosexuality was deeply woven into the city culture, making an immediately recognisable world of pleasures and dangers. It was a world where male homosexuality, if you sought it, could be encountered anywhere and everywhere, though totally illegal in public and private since 1885, fenced in by the possibility of shame, disgrace and prison: in trains, tube stations, theatres, streets, music halls, public houses, squares, Turkish baths, urinals, parks, cafés, gentlemen's clubs, settlement houses, churches, hotels, shops, barracks. It was a world of friendship networks and of casual sexual encounters, of high-minded philosophising about the nature of love, and of lowlife trade. This was very much still there in the early 1960s, on the eve of my arrival in the city, a world of diverse life patterns rather than settled identities, where 'queens' and 'queers', 'homosexuals' and 'trade' lived and engaged side by side, often unknowingly.[25] But times were a-changing. By the 1960s, a new breed of largely middle-class queers was emerging, who set out to reinvent themselves as respectable homosexuals, and who began to speak for themselves in print and on the occasional television programme, though usually filmed discreetly in the shadows. Homosexual people were beginning to be defined and define themselves as full human beings, part of a vibrant if hidden minority as opposed to the bearers of the shame and guilt, albeit now with an 'unfortunate condition' rather than being specimens of various types of sick or corrupt monsters.[26] The television journalist and later MP, Bryan Magee, famous for his kindly moral earnestness, did two TV programmes on male and female homosexuals in 1964 and 1965, which I saw (nervously and silently with the family!) at the time, and he later published a sympathetic book based on the programmes, which nevertheless confirmed the difficulty of balancing recognition and othering: 'Homosexuals are not just people who indulge in certain sexual practices ... their sexual practices are the expressions of a whole way of feeling, of responding to other people, and this they cannot help'.[27] The electric shock came in that final phrase, as if we were in the grip of some painful compulsion. Many in the queer world did indeed feel this way and would anguish to me about their/our awful fate, usually after vigorous sex. Others were more robust, but angry and frustrated at British hypocrisy. London offered opportunities for all of us.

Even in sober, suburban East Finchley, where I had my first student digs, I could have casual sexual encounters walking back from the tube, or in dimly lit conveniences, or walking in the woods by the North Circular Road. Later, when I moved to Notting Hill Gate, I shared a bedsitter (with a very straight fellow Welsh student) just round the corner from a famous queer pub, The Champion, which I visited occasionally, at first unknowingly. I learnt the skills of trolling, not then the name for online harassment but the traditional name for cruising and picking up. I got to know the best stations of the Circle Line to meet other men. I went regularly to a few pubs, such as the Salisbury in St Martin's Lane, where you could find Sir John Gielgud and other familiar actorly faces having a quiet drink, and the William IV in Hampstead, usually full of queer men discreetly eying one another and occasionally copping off.

I was deeply attracted to the style and ethos of the counterculture as it was emerging in the 1960s in London, but it did not seem particularly welcoming to someone like me. Along with most of the pub-goers I remained quite straight in my appearance at this stage. I let my hair grow a bit, but it always felt unruly, and eventually I kept it fairly short – and shorter and shorter as the years went by. My beard came later, in the early 1970s, with my political radicalisation and settling into my first long-term relationship, and in various styles it has remained part of my facial furniture ever since. Most of the men I got to know, usually a little older than myself, were drawn from the new type of homosexuals, generally largely unashamed about their sexuality but discreet in their public behaviour: teachers, an actor or two, artists, a well-known theatre director, businessmen, a shoe salesman, a nurse, a policeman (who scared me to the core when he admitted his career), a would-be vicar, shop assistants, occasional political activists (sometimes Tory, even . . .), a Professor of Economics.

Many were one-night stands (or less), few lasted long. I was learning through such fleeting encounters the complexities and multiple varieties of queer lives. My economics professor boyfriend in his forties had a straight son just a couple of years younger than me, and we would be left together in the William IV while he completed some errand. Through these encounters I learnt the rules of the game and the languages of the sexual world. More critically, I realised that in having sex I could find a sort of validation, a confirmation of being, a sense of my selfhood.

I never got to know anyone quite as outrageous as Quentin Crisp (I would have been terrified) and the only thing I knew of Polari, the legendary secret argot of queers, was via the camp chit chat of Sandy and Julian on BBC Radio's *Round the Horne* and *Beyond Our Ken*, which made no sense to me until I took an academic interest in it in the 1970s. We universally called ourselves queer, less often poofs and almost never gay, which was the term used for the more piss-elegant clubs in the West End, which I never frequented. Despite the frequent rapid-fire banter, playful campiness and gender inversion that seemed compulsory to many on the scene, I personally never used female pronouns to describe either myself or other queers, not so much because I disapproved but because I was too self-conscious and diffident to perform in that way. I had a strong self-knowledge, however, that I was certainly not and never wanted to be a woman. I no longer felt I was especially effeminate, though my masculinity was muted.

London was like a great big laboratory of sexual life. Through my own little experiments and these many encounters – usually brief and casual but some becoming long-term friendships – I built up a small circle of queer friends. It was at this time, in 1966, that I met my lifelong friend Micky, ten years older than me, but that rare figure in the 1960s: a 'mature student'.

Characteristically, though casual lovers might become friends, there usually developed an implicit incest taboo preventing you having sex with a friend, or friends of a friend. Love and sex were sharply separated. In the meantime, I was finding out what I liked doing or having done to me sexually and what I desired, developing confidence and sexual experience. I found out that I was attractive to other men and was also getting to know about the wider world of queerness.

I remember keeping one very early bedmate awake all night through a feverish mix of erotic play and excitedly asking him who else was queer. W. H. Auden and Christopher Isherwood, of course. Noel Coward, Ben Britten and Peter Pears, Dirk Bogarde, Lenny Bernstein, Rudolph Nureyev, Lord Mountbatten? Who else? Another told me about the political world, and the queer MPs, one of whom was his lover. I was piecing together a sense of belonging and identity from these bits of information, fragments of knowledge. And I was reading avidly.

I would explore the public library at East Finchley as well as the university's Senate House Library for authors and novels that would tell me more about homosexuality: Mary Renault, André Gide, Jean Genet, Angus Wilson, Gore Vidal, Gillian Freeman, and later as a postgraduate research student I devoted enormous time to reading Marcel Proust rather than burying myself in dusty manuscripts and old newspapers. My favourites were E. M. Forster (long before *Maurice* was published), the Berlin stories and the more obscure novels of Christopher Isherwood, like the then little-regarded *Down There on a Visit*, the poems of W. H. Auden and, above all, the essays and novels of James Baldwin. Baldwin was the most momentous.

I first encountered Baldwin in my final year at school, on a trip to Oxford to be interviewed for a college place. I was humiliated at the interview itself by my inarticulacy, and by being told by the first upper-class academic I had ever met (who was also a baronet) that the handwriting of my entrance examinations papers was 'ghastly, ghastly, ghastly, ghastly'. He asked me to rewrite a paper, obviously seeing some promise in me, but it did nothing to bolster my fragile self-confidence. I found solace – and indeed, as it turned out, life-changing inspiration – in a novel I had bought in Blackwell's bookshop, Baldwin's *Giovanni's Room*. Like many queer novels of the time, this ended in death and apotheosis, but I found hope and inspiration in the descriptions of same-sex love and the evocation of sexual passion, even if the exalted prose did not quite tell me what was actually going on when the central characters were having sex. I wept as I finished reading the book on the train back from Oxford, sure at last of my sexuality, if not of my university place.

Baldwin's experience was obviously honed in very different places from mine, a long way from the mining valleys of South Wales – in the Black churches and streets of Harlem, in exile in France and the queer bars of Paris, in the civil rights movement, and in the turmoil of 1960s America, with its riots and assassinations apparently fulfilling his awful Biblical prophecies: 'God gave Noah the rainbow sign. No more water, the fire next time'. The dialectic of exile and home was bisected less by the class antagonisms of old Britain than by the embedded experience of racism in the United States. And yet I could identify with Baldwin in a way I found difficult with many other contemporary white writers, because his sexual honesty and exploration of enforced Otherness resonated forcefully in my mind. *Giovanni's Room* was the first novel dealing explicitly with homosexuality and same-sex love I had read. The epigraph, from Walt Whitman, exploded in my mind then, and remains with me all these years later: 'I am the man; I suffered, I was there'.[28]

This, before gay liberation, was to my mind like Martin Luther's 'Here I stand, I can do no other'. It was an assertion of subjectivity and selfhood, if not yet of a clear-cut gay identity, of which Baldwin was in any case a lifelong sceptic (nobody's perfect). It offered the possibility of belonging, of community across the chasms of difference, of those endless connections across class, race, nationality, place and time that bred our mutual involvements and responsibilities.

I read Baldwin's *Another Country* soon after I went to university, in early 1965, not long after the book came out. I madly identified with one of the central characters, Eric, a southern white man who loved Rufus, the Black man at the core of the book. Like me, Eric was homosexual, and as an added bonus, like me at the time he had reddish hair. But that character lived with me because he taught me an important lesson. 'The trouble with a secret life,' says Eric, 'is that it is very frequently a secret from the person who lives it and not at all a secret for the people he encounters.'[29] My friend Gavin's visceral reaction to my letter about the book at the time told me a lot about the lies and denials that secrecy bred, but it took me a while longer to find my own key to escape that prison-house. In the meantime Angus Wilson's clinical dissection of the muddle and hypocrisies of middle-class morality, Forster's subversive celebration of human connections and unexpected transgressions, Genet's eroticisation of abjection, Isherwood's cheerful amorality and Baldwin's angry passion provided the threads from which I could weave my own web of meaning, and forge a language to express it.

ON THE MARGINS

As I was discovering, it was very possible to have a full queer life in the London of the mid-1960s as long as you accepted its rules. But these rules were increasingly constraining for many of my generation. The city, the country, were in a strange, liminal place. The public rhetoric echoed with paeans to London's cutting-edge fashions, pop music, theatre and art, at the forefront of a country that was pushing towards a modern, hip Britain. Yet the roads there seemed desperately narrow and tortuous if you were queer. Britain remained deeply entwined in coils of traditional attitudes and structures. Nostalgic memories of the 1960s often celebrate the rise of soon-to-be-famous queer artists and writers like David Hockney and the poet Thom Gunn, but I still find it difficult to forget that they preferred the sunshine and sexual freedom of sunny California to the restrictions of a grey London, whether swinging or not. The black humour and transgressive spirit of the young playwright Joe Orton was shaped in part by his encounters with the hypocrisies of old London, especially his imprisonment alongside his lover Kenneth Halliwell for wittily and erotically defacing Islington Library's books. But his Wildean eruption on the London scene was soon cut short by his murder by Halliwell. Like the heroes of many of the gay novels I was reading, his glittering life also ended in tragedy

Years later I used to give an annual lecture to sociology undergraduates on the roots of the social and sexual revolutions since the 1960s. My students (the majority of whom were female, Black and often single mothers) would gasp with disbelief when I described what Britain was like in the 1950s and early 1960s. Suicide, I would say, was a criminal offence until 1962, so if you survived an attempt you could be prosecuted and imprisoned. Even if you died, the families had to live with a sense of shame and guilt. I vividly remember my father inveighing bitterly against a poor neighbour who had gassed herself, for her selfishness. Unmarried mothers, I would remind my students, were still regularly forced into mother and baby homes, and compelled to give up their children for adoption. An unwanted pregnancy was still a desperate fear of my women friends in college. Despite the advent of the pill, access to it was restricted for single women until the late 1960s, and friends would go through contortions to get access. Abortion was illegal until 1967 and backstreet abortionists were a regular folk devil in the press, and a reality in all too many women's lives. Meanwhile, male homosexuality was totally illegal, whether in public or private, as I knew only too personally. The fact that my students were so surprised at any of these examples is a marker of how rapidly attitudes were to change in the next few decades. But while many of us hoped that the iceberg was at last beginning to crack by the mid-1960s, its pace appeared truly glacial.

1967 was the year I graduated. It was the year of *Sgt. Pepper's Lonely Hearts Club Band*, which provided the soundtrack for that first 'summer of love'. It was also the year when male homosexuality was partially decriminalised through the hard-won Sexual Offences Act. Like many of my generation I was intoxicated by the music, the vibrancy and new energy, though not at this stage by the drugs. But I was all too aware that I was still on the margins of all this excitement, and the 1967 Act did little to alleviate this.

As an obsessive devourer of newspapers I had followed the tortuous progress of the parliamentary debates, and respected from afar the work of the Homosexual Law Reform Society (HLRS), not knowing at this stage that its work was being carried out overwhelmingly by homosexual volunteers. It appeared as the acme of establishment respectability, fronted by liberal intellectuals, bishops, peers and expert psychologists. I greatly admired the reforming endeavours of the great liberal Home Secretary Roy Jenkins in giving parliamentary time and support for the passing of what was officially a private members' bill. But I also felt curiously detached from it all.

I was working that summer after graduating as an unlikely labourer on a building site back in the Rhondda when the Sexual Offences Act actually passed in late July. None of my workmates mentioned it, nor of course did I, but I had a strong fear that their warm, teasing friendship for such a hopeless nine-stone weakling would rapidly disappear if I told them I was queer, whether now legal or not. The Act removed the immediate fear of imprisonment for me, as I was now over 21, lived in England and Wales, and was not in the armed forces or the merchant navy. But I was aware of what a compromise the Act was, and how restrictive the law remained. It did not legalise homosexuality, nor did it remove the specifically homosexual offence of 'gross indecency'. It merely decriminalised consensual activities 'in private', which was very restrictively defined. Nowhere did it validate my sexuality.

The major parliamentary proponents of reform had made clear how limited the aims of the Act were. Lord Arran, who pushed the law through the House of Lords, famously declared, 'I ask those who have, as it were, been in bondage, and for whom the prison doors are now open to show their thanks by comporting themselves quietly and with dignity'.[30] And the immediate effects were contradictory: years later, at a lunch to celebrate the fiftieth anniversary of the 1967 Act, I heard Dick Taverne, who had been a parliamentary under-secretary to Jenkins at the Home Office at the time, express surprise on being told that the initial result of the Act had been a tripling of prosecutions for homosexual offences by men. He had never noticed. But that was indeed the case and was the inevitable result of the logic of the proposals of the 1957 Wolfenden Report, which were largely enacted in 1967. The proposals were built on a clear and highly utilitarian principle: the law's role was to safeguard and police public behaviour; it should not interfere in private behaviour unless there was a danger of harm. However, applied to homosexual behaviour this had unanticipated consequences. Once you define more closely the gap between public morality and private actions, strengthening the safeguards of the first while liberalising actions in a narrowly defined private as 1967 did, there was a logic to a tighter policing of public displays of indecency, and this is precisely what happened. So, despite the accretion of myths around the 1967 Act, especially marked in the fiftieth anniversary celebrations of 2017, it wasn't the end or even the beginning of the end of legal discrimination against homosexual people, more like the end of the beginning. Modest efforts to critique and reform the Labouchère Amendment of the Criminal Law Amendment Act had begun in the 1890s, as I later documented. It took seventy years before the limited gains of 1967 were won. It was to take a further thirty-seven years before any further relaxation of the law passed parliament.

It had required a herculean effort to get this far. A few years later, when I began writing the history of homosexual activism, and with the arrogance of youth rejecting father figures, I was highly critical of the caution, timidity and half-baked nature of the changes, and those who had fought for them. Michael Schofield, who had written the pioneering book *Society and the Homosexual* under the pseudonym Gordon Westwood in the darkest moments of post-war anti-homosexual hysteria in the early 1950s, was bitterly upset at my critique, threatened to sue for alleged errors and never quite forgave me, despite the efforts of a number of mutual friends to reconcile us. Later, frank memoirs by two other crucial pioneers, who I got to know, D. J. West and Antony Grey, movingly describe the sheer courage and resilience it took to go against the grain in the

1950s and early 1960s, when Britain was still one of the most morally conservative of major countries, on this issue at least.

Donald West's *Homosexuality*, first published in 1955, and then in regular Pelican editions thereafter, was an attempt, as he put it, to deal with the 'problem' of homosexuality in a dispassionate and popular manner. It was the first serious non-fiction book on the subject that I had encountered in the mid-1960s, and it was a book that was to appear over and over again on the bookshelves of my friends as well as my own. It was very influential. What it was not was a call to arms. It concluded in a traditionally downbeat way by suggesting that no doctor should advise a young person to be content with his (sic) sexual orientation without a 'grave warning' – 'about the frustration and tragedy that so often attend this mode of life'.[31] It was the apologetic tone that many of my generation, including myself, objected to, and West compounded his error to the new activists by not really coming out as gay at the time. He had many difficult encounters with early gay liberationists who heckled his lectures. Not surprisingly, perhaps, caution was ingrained in his bones. Yet West's intention, as he makes clear in his frank memoir, *Gay Life, Straight Work*, was to help the cause, and he risked his career to do so, but he felt obliged to follow the conventions of the time in writing the book. He went about as far as he felt he could go. 'For a young, unmarried professional to have stuck his neck out so recklessly seems, in retrospect, quite crazy ... I was protected by the hypocritical medical label.'[32] By which he meant that the scientific and medical claims of the book gave it a necessary cover, just as his own professional credentials allowed him to write it. Even so, it was seized by Australian customs and appeared only with a bowdlerised title in the USA. Yet far from being 'reckless' to a young reader like myself, it seemed the very definition of a sell-out.

The campaigners for homosexual law reform in the 1960s had made a strategic, fateful but perhaps unavoidable decision to argue for law reform on the grounds that homosexuality was an unfortunate condition that the poor victims of should not be punished for. 'Would you lock an alcoholic up in a brewery?', as the maverick Tory peer Lord Boothby, bisexual lover of Prime Minister Harold Macmillan's wife, famously put it. The obvious alternative to prison at the time seemed to be 'treatment', and there were many well-meaning advocates of ever more refined forms of 'cure', leading in the 1960s to the horrors of electroconvulsive treatment and aversion therapy. I mercifully avoided these, though many of my generation did not. Antony Grey, pseudonym of A. E. G. (Edgar) Wright, and tireless organiser of the HLRS, has sharply described in his memoir, *Personal Tapestry*, that he personally believed in none of this but felt compelled as the public face of legal reform to bow to received opinion to get the 1967 Act passed.[33] Even so, it was a painful process, with the HLRS effectively bypassed as the parliamentary arguments dragged on. After the royal assent, support for the society rapidly ebbed away, and Grey found himself caught between his trustees, content the job was done, and some activist supporters of the HLRS, led by Allan Horsfall, working especially in the Manchester area, who wanted to go much further – the beginnings of what was to become CHE. They wanted to set up a chain of 'Esquire clubs' to provide social facilities for newly legalised homosexuals, but Lord Arran and Leo Abse bitterly protested that this was not what had been intended by them when they pushed law reform through. Grey felt obliged to strongly advise his overenthusiastic members to temper their activities.

When I later published a critical comment on this, based on the correspondence in the archives of the HLRS I had trawled through, Grey was very upset. I now feel guilty at my moralising tone, and I am pleased that before his death we were able to find closure over this. Grey, like his contemporaries in the 1950s and early 1960s, had risked his career and the ever-present threat of prosecution for homosexual offences, and like Schofield and West, remained faithful to the cause: he was to get involved in the early gay liberation meetings in London, and indeed proposed the subject for the first gay demonstration in November 1970 in Highbury Fields, north London. But sadly, ardent gay liberationists did not take to this serious, cautious, dedicated but slightly lugubrious man, and he got caught in a very early 1970s bout of paranoia: I was told with all earnestness at the time that he was an agent of the CIA. This was nonsense, but to many in my generation he represented the timidity of the past. He was effectively marginalised in gay liberation, and sidelined in later campaigning for homosexuality equality. For him, all was anticlimactic after 1967. But there is something deeply symbolic in this trajectory. Grey represented a moment that was passing. When asked in an interview in the late 1960s if there was any possibility of a group like the moderate American homophile group the Mattachine Society emerging soon in Britain, he thought it 'inconceivable' in the next few years. He was to prove dramatically wrong.

GETTING POLITICAL

Despite the efforts of people like Grey and his colleagues to change public opinion, what had made the 1967 reform possible in the end had been the return of a majority Labour government in 1966, which opened the way to a bill to pass through the Houses of Parliament. There had to be a political moment to make everything else possible. What began to change in the late 1960s was a growing belief that there were other forms of politics and other possible dynamics for transformational change rather than remaining trapped within the slowness of parliamentary compromises.

My own political formation, inevitably, was shaped by the radical but pragmatic social democratic culture of the Rhondda that Daryl Leeworthy has described so powerfully.[34] I came from a tribal Labour voting family, though Dad had flirted with a local Ratepayers' Association in the early 1960s, disillusioned by the perceived corruption of the local Labour Party. By the 1960s, with an overwhelming majority of members of the council and vast majorities in parliamentary elections, much of the local party had degenerated into a closed clique, with networks of patronage and rampant clientelism. When I tried to join the local branch in 1965, I was told after a long delay that membership was full. Everyone knew that if you wanted something – a job with the council, a quick house repair – you had to nobble a councillor first. I got my summer labouring job with the council after graduating because my Aunty Lily spoke to a local councillor; I couldn't bring myself to ask if any money changed hands. I continued to support the Labour Party nationally because of their support for sexual reform, especially when Roy Jenkins was Home Secretary. I was, however, increasingly influenced by new strands of more radical politics. The foremost influence on me at this time was Raymond Williams, the cultural critic and novelist. (His biographer, Dai Smith, makes clear that for Williams himself the novels were his most important contribution.) Like Jenkins, his exact contemporary (both born, like my mother, in 1921), he came from a working-class family in the Monmouthshire valleys, went to a prestigious Oxbridge college, and became an influential writer – though it is difficult to imagine more different kinds of Welshmen or more different career successes.

My Penguin copy of Raymond Williams' *Culture and Society*

is dated 17 May 1968. I bought it just as the excitement of the would-be revolutionary May events in Paris were beginning to pass. The revolution had largely passed me by, watched on television. I spent most of that May in bed, not with anyone else, sadly, but with glandular fever, the 'kissing disease' as I was told by my doctor, though I hadn't yet done as much kissing as I would have liked. So, I missed, for the time being at least, the music of the streets that many of my contemporaries heard. But Williams' book resonated powerfully with my growing political radicalisation.[35]

I had read a library copy of *Culture and Society* earlier in the 1960s, but now there were many reasons for taking it seriously. By 1968 I was trying, without great success, to do postgraduate research on pre-First World War socialist thought. Williams' dissection of cultural critics of capitalism provided a framework for understanding what was going on in that period, and in the present. At about the same time, I bought the *May Day Manifesto*, edited by Williams and consisting of contributions from luminaries of the new, non-communist left, including Stuart Hall, Bob Rowthorne, Edward Thompson, Michael Rustin and Terry Eagleton. The *Manifesto*, the blurb says, 'brands this Labour government as the conscious agent of the new capitalism and closely studies the feasibility of a new left.'[36] What is striking today is that on the eve of the eruption of a movement that was to transform the left, the women's liberation movement, there is no mention of feminist politics at all, and no indication that there was such a thing as sexual politics.

Nevertheless, *Culture and Society*, with its analysis of a long anti-capitalist, anti-utilitarian critical tradition, offered a route map for my own developing intellectual and political commitments. Around this time I also read Williams' *The Long Revolution*, not so much a paean to gradualism as a perspective about the prolonged and convoluted process of the 'democratic revolution', and I found myself coming back to that metaphor frequently in my own later writing as I tried to analyse what I called the 'long, unfinished revolution' in sexual and intimate life that we are still in the midst of today.[37]

In retrospect, for me, Williams represented more than the contingent and conjunctural political moment. He epitomised a personal and political journey that I could in large part identify with. Like me he was from the border country, one as much in the mind as on the map. I was from the old coal-mining area of the Rhondda Valleys, he, like my father's line, from the Abergavenny area near the borderland of Wales, but both of us had made the journey away into a different life, from the Welsh margins to the margins of the centre. Recently graduated in 1968, I was still struggling to decide whether I should go back home to Wales, whether I had any prospects of a fulfilling career in London, whether I could ever get my act together to do my albatross of a thesis (which I was sure, rather than kissing, had pushed me into glandular fever), whether in fact I would ever do any real kissing and find a partner. He was by now a Cambridge professor, an omnipresent cultural commentator in the intellectual press and a guru of the left. But he too had made a journey from the working class and had not, it seemed, betrayed it in pursuing a different way of life.

The struggle that involved is fictionalised powerfully in Williams' first novel, *Border Country*. His biographer Dai Smith has written that '[t]he book for me was the instantly recognisable emotional and intellectual journey of a working-class boy who goes away from a shaping community', a journey that was increasingly common in the 1960s but no less powerful for being experienced individually.[38] Like Dai I found myself weeping with recognition when I read it on a train journey from Cornwall to London in early autumn

1970, after an emotionally fraught holiday. Unlike the sort of novel that sought 'room at the top' for its antiheroes, Williams was seeking a different sort of resolution, which respected and honoured the community and the people he had come from. At the end of the novel, its central character, Matthew Price, reflects on his journey and comes to a sort of reconciliation with where he came from and what he was: '[I]t seems like the end of exile. Not going back, but the feeling of exile ending. For the distance is measured, and that is what matters. By measuring the distance, we come home.'[39]

Exile and home: these are powerful terms and echoed then as they echo now in my mind. But there was a problem with Williams' reconciliation, also indicated by the omissions in the *May Day Manifesto*. For Williams it was a reconciliation of community, family, class and political commitment to socialism. But as has often been pointed out he was little interested in women in his fiction, and there was no place for me as a queer man, at least in his published fiction.[40] And that sense of community he celebrated, and which I sorely missed, that embraced you totally and warmly, was also the community that offered no space for difference. My exile and search for home and community had to go on.

My physical feebleness in the face of dramatic events of May 1968 now seemed to me a confirmation of my abjection and marginalisation. I was seeking something that integrated the various parts of my life – political, intellectual, emotional, sexual – and the existing left, old and new, had nothing to say. In the preface to his memoir, *Personal Tapestry*, Antony Grey spoke at the end of his life of his desire 'to draw together the personal and public sides of my life'. That was precisely the divide that increasingly preoccupied me in the late 1960s. I was beginning to have a comfortable life, with a school teaching job in London, a tight group of queer friends and a warm if not particularly open and honest relationship with my family in Wales. But I felt increasingly trapped by the constraints of what I would soon learn to call the closet. My life felt fundamentally compartmentalised and dishonest. The ending of a difficult emotional entanglement confirmed my sense that there was something deeply wrong with the way I lived. And my school teaching experiment was turning out to be a major personal mistake. By the eve of my twenty-fifth birthday in the autumn of 1970 I was ready for something new, though not yet sure what that would or could be.

CHAPTER 3
DREAMS OF LİBERATİON

'THE TURNİNG POİNT OF OUR LİVES'

In the early morning of 28 June 1969 a routine police raid on a gay bar in Greenwich Village, New York, sparked a fightback that became known as the 'Stonewall riots'. Shortly after, the Gay Liberation Front (GLF) was set up in New York City as a focus for a new militant activism. These events, soon heavily mythologised, have become the international symbol of the birth of a new liberation movement, ultimately one of the most successful of the radical social movements that emerged in the 1960s, and were widely celebrated across the globe in their fiftieth anniversary year of 2019.

Resistance to police raids was not unknown in the queer communities in the United States, going back to at least the 1950s. But the impact of the Stonewall uprising went much further than anything seen before. Stonewall, in the words of the central character in the American writer Edmund White's gay coming-of-age novel, *The Beautiful Room is Empty*, was 'the turning point of our lives'.[41] My encounter with the London GLF a year or so later was certainly the turning point of mine.

For many of us outside the United States, gay liberation was a slow burn in that first year, 1969–70. I heard rumours of a new excitement and militancy in New York, San Francisco and Los Angeles in the summer of 1969, but there was little coverage in the British Press. I had no American friends at the time, and little access to the masses of leaflets and pamphlets that were beginning to flood. A year later, on the first anniversary of Stonewall I heard a slightly sardonic report of the first Christopher Street Day parade by thousands of militant gay liberationists in New York on the BBC's *The World at One,* its premier radio news programme, and remember thinking that nothing so exciting and explosive could happen here in Britain anytime soon. I was wrong. Though I was completely unaware of it at the time, London was already buzzing that summer of 1970, with several local gay groups springing up under the umbrella of the embryonic Committee (soon to be Campaign) for Homosexual Equality, with the aim of creating a 'good image' and a growth of personal confidence, and providing a social space for gay people to meet and talk.[42] And within a few months London's own Gay Liberation Front, with much more ambitious aims, burst into life, and for me and many thousands of other queer people, nothing could be the same ever again.

I had started a new job as a research assistant at the London School of Economics (LSE) at the beginning of October 1970, having fled my school teaching job as soon as I could. The school was a highly conservative boys' grammar school in deeply suburban London, where senior staff still wore gowns, and I was told by my head of department that becoming a member of the National Union of Teachers, which I did, was like joining a cell of the Communist Party. This did nothing to make me feel more confident or resilient as an inexperienced teacher faced by classes of unruly boys. I felt trapped and frustrated and started looking for a new job within a month of appointment. It took me a year to find something I wanted to do, and that wanted me to do it. The job at LSE was a lifeline, but I had no idea when I started quite how significant my being there at that particular time would be.

By contrast to Chislehurst and Sidcup Grammar, LSE was then notorious for being radical and ungovernable, with regular student sit-ins and an intense bubbling among students and some staff of would-be revolutionary ideas, though the management remained deeply conservative, especially in the library where I was based. The tables in the canteen were always deep in leaflets about various left societies, revolutionary meetings and demos. A few weeks after I started I picked up a notice about a meeting, on 13 October 1970, to set up a London version of GLF at LSE. I was working there on a very sober research project in the library tracing the archives of prominent twentieth-century MPs, civil servants, military leaders and public intellectuals, the quintessential political and social elite, and I knew pretty certainly that gay militancy might be a step too far for my bosses (even though it eventually became clear that three out of four of our small research unit were gay, as of course were many of our research subjects, and I was later able to use my new skills and contacts to trace first-generation homosexual activists). So, I was a little wary – but at the same time excited and desperate to find out more. I couldn't go to the first couple of GLF meetings, but by early November I was geared up, and went to a meeting in one of LSE's lecture theatres. It was intoxicating.

For the first time in my life I was in a room filled with scores of openly gay men and women of all ages, hippy and conventional, flamboyant and sober, femme and butch, white and (some) Black, cis and trans (as we didn't then say), all apparently completely upfront and proud about their sexualities and gender diversities, and freely linking the fight for homosexual liberation to other radical political struggles, especially women's liberation and Black liberation. And I felt immediately that I had found a space that would be a political and sexual home.

Within weeks I had reinvented my entire way of being, with a new sexual identity, a new openness about my gayness, new friends, new ideas, new radical political commitments, a new lifestyle, a new home and a new, long-term lover, Angus Suttie. Between November 1970 and March 1971 when Angus and I moved into a new home with my old friend Micky, my life was transformed. A fellow early GLF-er, Alan Wakeman, in his memoir, *Fragments of Joy and Sorrow*, describes how he felt his 'soul come alive' when he first heard of GLF.[43] For me, less poetically, it was as if my whole being had exploded into a thousand pieces, and been refigured into a new form. And I finally came out, publicly and irrevocably, as gay.

The London GLF was set up by two young gay men, Aubrey Walter and Bob Mellors, who had met in the USA and had been enthused by the new gay militancy and revolutionary politics they had encountered there, and thought there should be something similar in London. In many ways they were unlikely revolutionaries. Bob was earnest but diffident, a slightly awkward public speaker, and by nature a backroom organiser, while the fey looking Aubrey had the air of an aspirant artist, a dreamer rather than an organiser, but with an ideological fervour for the new liberatory politics and a sharp tongue, especially for those who deviated from the line. They were able to draw on some support at LSE, including the young lesbian student Bev Jackson, who was the only woman among the small group who called the first meeting. Aubrey's lifelong partner David Fernbach was another key influence, the theoretical heavyweight among the founders. He had been a member of the *New Left Review* (*NLR*) editorial board, in which he had published a pioneering article on radical sexual politics. This was no mean feat, then as now: *NLR* never showed much interest in the topic.[44] This small disparate group lit the fire. The tens then hundreds who came to the early meetings, from all parts of the queer world, made it burn. The London grouping that emerged was a conscious echo of the New York GLF that was channelling the new energies unleashed by the Stonewall riots.

The new movement had rapidly taken fire across the USA, and quickly emerged in other countries over the next few years, from Canada to France, the Netherlands to Australasia, adapting to particular local histories but with common features. The London GLF saw itself from the start as part of an international movement, expressing and making a new spirit and consciousness among self-identified gay people. It was also an unlikely but heady mixture of sexual radicalism, countercultural lifestyle, political anarchism, reforming zeal, student passion, and social and community hopes and dreams, heaped on top of London's queer subcultural experience, which, despite initial mutual hostility, eventually provided the fertile ground in which it grew. It was held together by euphoria, energy and political enthusiasm that generated a distinctive perspective on the queer past and the gay future.

I have lamented the absence of stories about people like myself as I was becoming aware of my sexuality in South Wales. Gay liberation provided the inspiration for the growth of passionate new collective sexual stories that enabled us to tell our own individual stories in new ways.[45] For the first time I felt part of a narrative that made sense of my experiences, a new way of seeing ourselves in history and the present. It pointed the way to a different future: a story of sexual oppression marked by internalised shame and guilt counterposed to a new hope of collective struggle for liberation. Personal identity, a sense of who and what I was, and social identity, speaking of a common history, my relationship with others, and a sense of belonging, for the first time seemed to be seamlessly linked. In the past, as a well-known activist later put it, efforts at reform and social change, like 1967, had been largely done for us by a well-meaning straight elite, with the gay men and lesbians who did the grassroots work forced to stay in what we now began to call 'the closet'. This time real change would be brought about by we gays ourselves, acting for ourselves. The self-emancipation of homosexuals, an aspiration of the earlier homophile movements in Germany in the 1900s and America from the 1950s, now seemed a real possibility for the first time in our history. Gayness was not a personal peculiarity or just a private desire; it was a highly political issue with ramifications for every aspect of social and cultural life.

Gay liberation for me was primarily an assertion of this new collective consciousness, focused on a radical new sense of subjectivity and identity. To be a homosexual in our society, the Australian political scientist and gay activist Dennis Altman argued, in the first major exploration of gay liberation, *Homosexual: Oppression and Liberation* (which I read eagerly as soon as I got hold of it in 1971), is 'to be constantly aware that one bears a stigma'.[46] Gay liberation represented for my generation of queer men a quest for a new way of being that rejected the prejudices, stereotypes, insults, discriminations, guilt and shame that had up to then shaped our lives. The rapid abandonment of the old self-hating self-descriptions of 'queer', 'faggot', 'poofter' or worse in favour of our new universal self-description as 'gay' was itself an act of profound personal liberation. 'Gay is good', 'gay pride', 'gay power' – these were slogans that marked a new self-confidence I proudly proclaimed in the badges I wore on my chest. At first, gay was used as an all-embracing collective term, uniting men and women, young and old, Black and white, transvestites and transsexuals, as they described themselves at the time. That soon changed as other self-descriptions emerged, and more particular identities were affirmed. But adopting the word gay symbolised for me a break with an unforgiving past, and a new sense of belonging and self-esteem in the present. When twenty years or so later 'queer' came back into vogue among a new generation of militants in the wake of AIDS and the cultural backlash, especially in the USA, as a deliberately transgressive rejection of the limitations of the gay revolution so far, I was at first deeply reluctant to use the term again: it smacked too much of the world we had rejected in the early 1970s.

A key idea for me that signalled a dismal past was 'the closet', a concept that instantly evoked an image of being confined, trapped, locked away, hidden from and by history. Gay liberation offered a new visibility – 'out of the closets and into the streets' – with coming out, publicly affirming and celebrating our sexuality, a central strategy. Coming out was a mark of pride and self-confidence. The movement provided a supportive context in which being open about our gayness was now possible: it empowered us to act in the world. It signalled a new militancy and willingness to confront the oppression of our sexuality and gender nonconformity. The idea that gay sexuality had been oppressed by society over a long period was central to the new ethos and militancy. Oppression was structural not personal, it was a result of institutional discrimination rather than individual prejudice, and was a product of historically entrenched systems.

From second-wave feminism we borrowed the concept of sexism, a marker of male oppression of women. We highlighted the power of the Judaeo-Christian tradition, which embedded the idea of same-sex love as a sin and instilled guilt and shame. We challenged the dominance of the bourgeois heterosexual family, which by its very nature marginalised and excluded us. We saw in the intricate linking of capitalism, imperialism and patriarchy a common foundation of the oppression of women, Black people and gays. We had internalised all these structures and systems in our growing up. To combat them we needed a variety of responses, and these were rapidly invented in the early days, some adapted from the American movement, others growing out of British experience. The demonstrations, zaps, workshops, talk-ins, sit-ins, kiss-ins, gay days, dances, picnics, street theatre, occupations, cross-dressing, carnivalesque parades and marches that soon exploded were symbolic challenges to the status quo, practical demonstrations of what activism could do, and the means by which we could explore and build new ways of living, belonging and community. By coming out we could begin to show the world that we existed, that we challenged the system, and just as important it would show other lesbians and gay men that they were not alone, that through coming out all could come together, show solidarity in the struggle and tell our own stories about who and what we were. This was the basis for the new forms of activism that gay liberation embodied. And it inspired and transformed the most unlikely people.

Reading through Alan Wakeman's memoir I came across a story about my friend Micky that I had forgotten, but which is a good illustration of this. Micky by 1970 was a well-respected civil servant, specialising in housing research. A careful, cautious man, he was always soberly dressed, and whatever his efforts indelibly straight-looking. I persuaded him to come to an early GLF meeting, though I feared that it was not quite his thing. I was wrong. Here's Alan's note of an early encounter with Micky in June 1971.

I'm at a Gay Liberation Front meeting at All Saints Church in Notting Hill listening to Micky Burbidge of the counter-psychiatry group describe 'aversion therapy' to several hundred outraged gay people. 'In this so-called "treatment",' he says, 'gay victims are restrained and stimulated with erotic photos while electric shocks are administered to their genitals.' After the cries of anger have died down, he asks for volunteers to march down Harley Street and paint black crosses on the doors of the guilty psychiatrists. I am one of the many who raises their hands.[47]

A demo duly took place on 25 July 1971, with GLF activists distributing leaflets and doing street theatre. The crosses had been painted on doors the night before. Micky was to play a key role in many subsequent GLF and post-GLF campaigns, all while climbing the civil service hierarchy. At the height of the Thatcher government of the 1980s he would be advising senior ministers by day and staffing a helpline for isolated gays by night.

DOING IT

The first few meetings of GLF were life-transforming experiences for people like Micky and me.[48] For the first time I felt I was a foot soldier in a struggle that I could fully identify with, an activist in a movement that was about my life and lives like mine. My diffidence and reluctance to perform in public – I was terrified of public speaking at that stage, and my first interventions at meetings were awkward and ineffective – did not disappear, but the energy of the meetings gave me a new self-confidence, especially in doing new things and meeting new people. At my first couple of meetings I met numerous people with whom I established firm friendships that in many cases lasted a lifetime. Among them were Ken Plummer, then a research student, later Britain's foremost sociologist of sexuality; Mary McIntosh, already a well-established sociologist and theorist, and later a leading socialist feminist, who became a colleague and formative influence on my thinking about gay history; Elizabeth Wilson, Mary's then partner and a psychiatric social worker, and later an important cultural historian and novelist; Barry Davis, a fellow would-be historian and later an expert on Yiddish language and culture, who became my closest friend; and many others I worked with on various projects in the years ahead. And above all I met Angus, my first long-term lover and partner.

I had seen and felt attracted to Angus at the first GLF meeting I attended, but we got together properly after our first demo on 27 November 1970. This was a largely manufactured event, whose ostensible purpose was to defend the leader of the Young Liberals, Louis Eakes, who had been arrested for importuning on Highbury Fields in north London, a charge he vehemently denied. It was an obvious paradox that our first public event was in support of someone who claimed to be heterosexual and innocent of any homosexual activity. We decided to focus on police harassment, which so many of us had experienced. Later, reluctantly, after being arrested for a second time, Eakes came out himself as gay. But the real reason for the demo was to give ourselves a public presence, and *The Times* duly carried a piece about us the next day, which was important in telling the world we existed. We were on our way! As important as this was, the real success of the evening lay in what it did for the few dozen of us who were there. I had been on a few demos before as a student, notably in support of the anti-apartheid movement, but this was the first event that I could wholeheartedly identify with from personal experience. The candlelit parade around Highbury Fields in north London by a few dozen of us had a serious purpose, but above all it gave us a sense of exhilaration, solidarity and momentum. On the tube home afterwards, emboldened by our mass presence, a mixed bunch of us waved balloons and banners, kissed and embraced and took over the tube carriage. The other passengers would never have seen anything like this before. Neither had we. It seemed like a new dawn. And it certainly was for Angus and me.

We were both working-class young men from the Celtic fringe, eager to change our lives. Angus was from Forfar in Scotland, son of a milkman, and when we met he was slightly adrift, and very shy and withdrawn. He had been forced to leave drama school in Glasgow a few years before, having been told that his stammer was likely to prevent a successful acting career. He had taken a series of casual jobs, never lasting long in any of them. He was currently working on the Menzies newspaper stall on Paddington station, and was about to be made homeless. After an unexpected drama when he had to be rushed into hospital for an emergency operation for gallstones, which had the effect of solidifying our relationship, Angus moved into my chilly bedsitter in Blackheath at the beginning of 1971, and we became inseparable, building a life together while spending much of our time taking part in various GLF activities.

The dynamic and chaotic Wednesday meetings remained the beating heart of the movement, an intoxicating blend of passion, rhetoric, personal testimony, mutual learning and political education, first at LSE, then, when the meetings became too large, at the Middle Earth club space in Covent Garden in April 1971, and then from July 1971 at All Saints' Church Hall in Notting Hill Gate. It was a mass celebration as much as a decision-making meeting. It was anarchic in spirit, with a deliberate rejection of leadership, nominally coordinated by an elected steering committee, but with moods and actions swayed back and fore by whomsoever spoke last. Some naturally charismatic characters, like the Canadian Warren Haig, emerged for brief moments of leadership, but there was a strong aversion to those who offered themselves as leaders. The general meetings provided a good example of what the American feminist Jo Freeman described about this time as 'the tyranny of structurelessness', where hidden power hierarchies shaped direction until another hierarchy emerged.[49] It was most effective as a mass consciousness-raising group, and vital for generating a new popular movement, but it soon became clear that action would need to come from elsewhere, and there was an explosion of other activities. Like most of us in the early days, Angus and I joined a small consciousness-raising or awareness group, sharing our experiences, telling our buried truths, attempting to break down our internalised guilt, confronting our oppressions, challenging our hang-ups, especially around sex, and gaining confidence in being out and proud about our gayness. They were exciting and life-enhancing but sometimes scary meetings. I was once challenged by an immensely attractive and charismatic American member of our group for wearing an ordinary white shirt. Wasn't it a sign of my basic straightness? I couldn't wear white shirts for years afterwards. But more positively consciousness-raising meetings at their best were empowering forums for free and honest discussions, for personal growth and for changing lives.

Angus and I threw ourselves into other groups and actions. We went once to a meeting of the Media Workshop group that put together the GLF paper, *Come Together*, but it wasn't particularly welcoming – we were both terrified by the right-onness and ideological purity of the core members such as Aubrey and David, until they changed their minds and moved onto another pure position, and we looked elsewhere. We joined the Counter Psychiatry group, convened at first by Mary

McIntosh and Elizabeth Wilson, and explored the iniquities of the caring and psychological professions in relation to homosexuality, and the critiques offered by R. D. Laing and David Cooper and the like on the radical fringes of psychiatry. Activism flowed out of this. Mary and Elizabeth were angry at the hostility shown to GLF members like themselves by the Gateways club, which they had frequented in the 1960s. The Gateways was the most famous lesbian club in London, by now internationally famous as a location for the film *The Killing of Sister George*. Mary and Elizabeth proposed leafletting the club about GLF, and a group of us went along to support the women. After they were ejected by the management, the police intervened and in the resulting fracas with them an American guy named Marshall Weekes was arrested and eventually deported. We discovered pretty quickly that action was not risk free; we felt we were testing our limits. Another initiative of the Counter Psychiatry group that we were involved in was a challenge to the paperback publication of David Reuben's anti-gay book *Everything You Always Wanted to Know About Sex (But Were Afraid to Ask)*. We zapped bookshops in Charing Cross Road, putting GLF stickers inside the books warning about its contents.

There seemed to be endless things to do. We picketed pubs that refused to allow us to distribute leaflets and had tried to kick out GLF activists. We went to huge GLF discos in Camden Town Hall and Kensington Town Hall, which we saw as political statements in themselves, given the limitations of the 1967 Act, and in any case why shouldn't the revolution be enjoyable? We went to a new smaller disco in the Sols Arms near Euston, where the landlord seemed very welcoming, especially on a quiet night. But the police raided and searched us for drugs, and closed the disco. Angus and I walked home arm in arm rehearsing obscene comments about the 'pigs', the event confirming our sense that we could expect no favours from the powers that be. We went to picnics and gay days, and to parties in each other's houses, including our own. Lisa Power laconically records in her chronology of events for 14 May 1971, 'GLF Party at Ivor Street, Jeffrey Weeks and Michael Burbidge's place, happily remembered by some as their first orgy'.[50] My main memory of that event is a bit more muted, of an ostensibly straight friend parading around with a feather boa draped around him. Liberation should be fun. Fun could be a revolutionary act.

Then there were the more obviously earnest political actions. We proudly showed our solidarity with others in struggle. We joined the GLF contingent tagged at the end of the vast million-strong protest against the Heath government's Industrial Relations Act in January 1971, much to the discomfort of the organisers and trade union, communist and ultra-left militants around us. A couple of months later, in March 1971, we supported the International Women's Day parade, about four thousand of us walking in miserable weather through central London, the last occasion when men were unequivocally welcome at the event. Later that year, in August, a few hundred of us marched through the West End in the first effort at a major gay march, protesting at the discriminatory age of consent, beginning with a gay day in Hyde Park (a year before what some have claimed as the first official Gay Pride celebration in June 1972). A few of us later trudged around Earls Court, to my later embarrassment, urging the poor benighted souls in the queer pubs there to come out of the closets and onto the streets; few listened at that stage. At the beginning of the movement even the 'gay ghetto' seemed part of the enemy camp.

The most famous or infamous GLF action was the zap of the launch of the evangelical Festival of Light in early

September 1971, when the release of white mice and men dressed as nuns, carefully coordinated by GLF activists, caused mayhem. Angus and I were not involved in what became known as 'Operation Rupert'. I don't think we heard of it in advance – but we were involved in a footnote to it. At the suggestion of the artist David Hutter the awareness group we were involved in invited the most liberal of the leaders of the festival, Bishop Trevor Huddleston, to come and meet us to discuss our objections to it. The aim was to separate him from his more strident colleagues, like Mary Whitehouse, Lord Longford and Malcolm Muggeridge. Huddleston was famous as an outspoken opponent of apartheid and was rumoured to be gay himself. We never found out about that, but we had a courteous discussion, and he assured us that he was not anti-gay, but mainly concerned about pornography. Who knows if we had any effect, but he noticeably cut down his involvement in the Festival of Light thereafter. This was a different order of action from the more spectacular zaps and demos, and I was sceptical of it at the time, but it was part of a growing repertoire of interventions, big and small, public and private.

Like the gay liberation movement in the USA, we saw ourselves as part of a wider revolutionary upsurge – 'the movement'. The gay liberation movement's immediate inspiration lay less in predecessor homophile movements than in the counterculture, the opposition to American imperialism in Vietnam, the Black struggle, the anti-colonial movement and women's liberation. Much of its early rhetoric and style came from those movements: 'Gay power' echoed 'Black Power', gay liberation echoed women's liberation, and the use of 'Front' in GLF's name suggested affiliation with the anti-imperialist struggle in Africa and Asia. At first we were the newcomers on the block, eager to learn and borrow ideas and analyses. In retrospect, however, we can see that gay liberation proved to be one of the most important and innovative of the new social movements in shaping change. Its preoccupation with relating the personal to the political and vice versa was closely attuned to the types of grassroots movements that were emerging. As Alberto Melucci[51] has suggested, social movements are usually invisible networks of small groups submerged in everyday life. They tend to be concerned with individual needs and collective identities, but through the energies released in new forms of social action they constitute laboratories in which new experiences are invented and tested, in which reality is re-described and individuals can develop alternative experiences of time, space and personal relationships. Characteristically they offer symbolic challenges to the status quo, as our demos and zaps and kiss-ins were doing, but ultimately they are more concerned to reshape the grammar of everyday life than in developing political programmes.

Early gay liberation was certainly a laboratory for new ways of thinking and being. But laboratories can sometimes explode. GLF was dynamic and innovative but also increasingly unstable, held together by common slogans and aspirations that concealed different political, cultural and lifestyle commitments. We did have a list of demands on which we could all agree, including legal equality, the end of police harassment, and the right to kiss and hold hands in public together. We called each other brother or sister and took to greeting each other with a kiss whenever we met, in public or private. Angus and I would proudly, despite nerves, self-consciously link arms as we walked the streets, still a contested right in so many places fifty years later. There was also more earnest work to provide a clear basis for our activities. A small group of GLF leading lights, including Mary McIntosh and David Fernbach, produced an influential *Manifesto* towards the end of 1971 that attempted to link gay oppression with a wider analysis of the Judaeo-Christian tradition, capitalism, sexism and the heterosexual family. Although the language and argument now sounds dated it made a bold claim that, in various forms, has been a mainstay of radical analyses to this day: that the root of gay oppression was the 'gender role system', and the prime role of gay liberation was to challenge this.

It was the first statement of the theoretical basis of gay liberation in Britain, and it gave me a sense of the coherence and radical nature of what we were trying to do. Although drawing on feminist debates and locating itself within a broad Marxist framework it offered a distinctive framework for a radical gay liberation. For the leading activist Peter Tatchell, who came into the movement around this time, it was a 'revolution in consciousness'. I couldn't go that far, and I found its claim to offer a 'scientific analysis' a bit difficult to accept. Even in my wildest excesses of leftism I never succumbed to the fantasy that Marxism was a science, but in the years ahead I found myself continuously engaging with the *Manifesto*, and ultimately revising its analysis in my own writing.

The most challenging feature of it for many people, as it turned out, was its critical approach to the family, identified as the fundamental site of sexism and homosexual oppression. I had no difficulty with this at the time, but others, especially those coming from the traditional and communist left, did. Ironically, fifteen years later a selective quoting of key passages on the family was to be a major element in the attack on the gay community in the Thatcher government's Section 28. When a revised version of the *Manifesto* was republished in 1978, by a small group partly drawn from the traditional left, the only major change was the excision of the key sections on the family, ostensibly on the grounds that this would alienate a conservative working class.[52] The *Manifesto* offered a particular perspective that superficially we could all accept but actually glossed over fundamental divisions. It soon became clear that the publication of the *Manifesto* was the high point of GLF coherence, and by 1972 the various tendencies that made up GLF were beginning to whirl out of control.

I was outside the loop of the group that wrote the *Manifesto*, but I immediately took it to heart, and joined in post-*Manifesto* discussions. A small group of us, including Mary McIntosh, Nettie Pollard, Paul Bunting and me, produced a paper that was critical of developments in GLF, especially the increasing dominance of the 'radical feminist' men, an amorphous group that stretched at first from the theoretical anti-sexism of David Fernbach and Aubrey Walter to a group of men who described themselves as radical queens, including Stuart Feather and Bette, formerly Peter, Bourne who argued that the way forward was for men to focus on challenging the patriarchy through radical effeminacy, especially by getting into radical drag. I was not against countercultural politics, but I felt strongly that to impose a particular lifestyle politics on the movement was wrong in principle.[53] In the summer of 1972 I took my own first tentative steps to producing an alternative anatomy of the movement by writing an article, based on the paper I had written with Mary, for the new publication *Gay News*.

'Ideas of Gay Liberation' was my first attempt at gay journalism. In this I described three distinct flavours of gay politics, all of which had validity: gay activism, essentially reformist, pressing for practical interventions and legal reform; gay radical feminism, giving primacy to challenging sexism by lifestyle politics; and gay radicalism, with which I identified, based on the belief that gay liberation could not be achieved within capitalist society, and which sought to link the gay struggle with wider social struggles. The actual divisions were much more complex, but as I was trying to express, gay liberation was already too diverse to have a single programme except the most anodyne. As I modestly concluded, we needed to recognise that GLF was not an organisation but a movement, with as many different ideas as groups. There was no point in trying to impose a single ideology.[54]

HIGH TIDE

Whether by chance or prescience, by the time the article came out it echoed a growing feeling in GLF that something was going wrong. That summer of 1972 brought many of the tensions in the London gay liberation movement to a head. Ironically, they coincided with the largest gay parade so far, on 1 July. This has been claimed by many since, especially those involved in organising it, as the first official Gay Pride march in London, which ignores the earlier marches in 1971 that I and many others were enthusiastically involved in. It is certainly true, however, that the July parade was the biggest and best organised so far. About seven hundred of us – gay men, lesbians, bi and trans people, and straight friends and allies paraded from Trafalgar Square to Hyde Park in glorious confusion. Chanting Gay Pride slogans – 'Gay is good', 'Lesbians ignite', 'Avenge Oscar Wilde', 'Out of the closets into the streets' – popping balloons, handing out leaflets, holding hands and blowing kisses, it was a joyous and exhilarating celebration of our sexualities and our new sense of identity and belonging. We held an informal party in Hyde Park and danced later to the sexually ambivalent songs of David Bowie's *The Rise and Fall of Ziggy Stardust and the Spiders from Mars*, the soundtrack of that summer. We felt we were part of a new zeitgeist, on the crest of a wave that would finally sweep away the guilt, shame, hypocrisy, prejudices and oppression that had long shadowed our lives – or so we hoped.

Personal liberation, we believed, could only be fully realised through wider social liberation, and this marked us off from other more cautious gay organisations. In 1971 the general secretary of CHE had assured the respectable public that GLF's unruly behaviour was unrepresentative, but we despised such caution. Although by now CHE was growing rapidly and spreading outside both its Manchester base and London, I felt little identity with it, and especially its obsession with procedures, constitutions and social activity. As the poet Laurence Collinson, despite being a pioneer organiser of CHE in London, memorably put it, the Campaign was an organisation, the Front is a way of life.[55]

In retrospect it is clear that gay liberation was one of the last major eruptions of the cultural and social turmoil of the long 1960s. Both GLF and its sister movement, women's liberation, expressed some of that decade's famed iconoclasm and challenge, but were given a special energy by their reaction against the sexism and heterosexism of the dominant culture, including the male leadership of the radical left and the heavy masculinism of much of the counterculture. The new movements sought to change the terms of the debate about sexuality and gender, love and relationships. But history has a way of kicking back against those who want to escape its necessities. By 1972 the remaining optimism of the 1960s was beginning to shiver, and that July brought many of the tensions threateningly together. They symbolised the real end of the 1960s.

The brisk modernisation plans of Prime Minister Edward Heath were facing continuing turbulence. Industrial strife in particular was becoming uncontrollable. January saw the first national miners' strike since the 1920s, and the government had in effect surrendered to its demands. July saw the gaoling of the Pentonville Five, shop stewards arrested for mass picketing of an east London container depot, which led to the threat of a general strike, until the magical intervention of a government law official to release them.

If industry seemed chaotic, Northern Ireland was on the brink of civil war. The end of January 1972 saw Bloody Sunday, when the British Army shot twenty-eight unarmed civilians in Derry/Londonderry, fourteen of whom died; the ramifications are still with us today. July witnessed Bloody Friday, when a number of bombs exploded in Belfast, followed a few days later by Operation Motorman, where security forces invaded republican no-go areas. Many of the more radical elements in GLF were involved in the nascent Troops Out movement, which brought increasing security surveillance of gay liberation.

There was an increasing fear of complete political and social breakdown, feeding into conspiracy theories on both the left and right, and outright paranoia in the movement. Early in 1972 I had a phone call at work from a neighbour telling me that our house had been raided by the police. I dashed home expecting that this was a political fishing expedition looking for our links with leftist militancy. At the end of 1971 alleged members of the anarchist Angry Brigade had been arrested, accused of bombings and conspiracy. A GLF activist, Angela Weir, whom I knew, had been drawn in, though she was eventually acquitted at the end of 1972. Was the police bust on us part of the same witch hunt? In our case at least the reason for the raid was apparently more mundane: we were told by the police that someone had reported an attempted break-in on our house and they had investigated, found no signs of anything illegal and apologised for any inconvenience. We did, however, know for certain that an undercover policeman had come to meetings at our house about the same time. Like many others in the movement we were convinced that our phones were tapped. It was hard to think that anything Micky,

Angus or I were doing in gay liberation deserved police or MI5 attention, but in the fevered atmosphere of the time anything seemed possible.

Gay liberation was certainly seen in some official quarters as very much part of the general disruption. It fired our sense of history being on our side. Lesbians and gays were no longer hidden from history. They – we – were at the heart of a dynamic, rapidly changing world, where the old could not continue and the new could not yet be born.

But beneath the euphoria that fed into the Pride parade that July 1972, there were real problems. GLF was proving an unstable framework for the new energies it had unleashed. A sign of this had come a few months before in February with the departure of many women from GLF, alienated by the sexism of the men. The other tensions that I explored in my *Gay News* article were making meetings and campaigns increasingly fractious. Gay liberation was increasingly meaning different things to different people.

The recently established *Gay News* itself symbolised the ways in which the gay world was changing. Some militants in GLF, led by the radical queens, had been extremely hostile to the idea of a popular and commercial publication that would extend beyond an activist core and could be available in paper shops, and had physically tried to stop it. *Gay News* had started as a community-funded paper, with key input from activists, such as Andrew Lumsden, a journalist for *The Times*, and Denis Lemon, later the paper's long-lasting editor. Within a year it was attracting a wide readership and, crucially, advertising. Its regular publication, purchased at gay venues, and eventually in WHSmith, or delivered in a plain brown envelope to your home or preferred address, proved a lifeline for many gay people, and was a major factor in creating a wider sense of identity and community, as well as a considerable new market, in the years ahead.

The 'carnival parade' in July 1972 was a celebration of what had been achieved by GLF but also signalled its end as a dynamic single movement. Within months it had fragmented into a myriad of new groupings across London and Britain as a whole. Angus and I started going to the local Camden group rather than the all-London general meetings that continued in Notting Hill Gate. Gradually, there was a coming together of the gay movement born in 1970, and the subcultures around sexual and gender difference that had grown up over many years largely in the closet. 1972 was the year when the closet as a whole began to come out, and the gay world began a rapid expansion. Gay liberation lived on but GLF soon became a nostalgic memory. The London GLF was finally wound up in 1974, but in essence as a coherent movement it had died within a year of the first Pride.

It is difficult not to see the rise and fall of GLF as reflecting wider social developments. Just as the birth of GLF was the final flower of 1960s optimism, its demise was a harbinger of a much darker climate. The utopian hopes that had nourished GLF increasingly clashed with the harsher realities of 1970s Britain.

REMAKING PERSONAL LIFE

In the midst of this whirligig of activities that became our life, Angus and I were trying to make a relationship that would work for us. We were drawn together by strong sexual and emotional attraction and by a wish to remake our everyday lives together. There were competing pushes and pulls. Angus and I were immediately caught in an all-too-representative dilemma. We were both attracted by various aspects of the counterculture, which was the dominant style and strongest dynamic of GLF. The drive to personal liberation as part of a wider social transformation was immensely appealing, especially as it carried with it a vague but powerful commitment to breaking with conventional sexual norms. Yet neither of us felt that dropping out completely was an option we wanted to pursue. Given our class backgrounds, a commitment to paid work was a bare necessity. We had no alternative sources of income. Living on the dole was not appealing. Once or twice I was with friends from GLF who happily ripped off bookshops or stole food from supermarkets. These were bourgeois institutions and our needs were greater than theirs, was the general position. This wasn't just a gay thing but part of a general young radical ethos. A very keen liberator of books became later a very prominent and respected criminologist, and an advisor to the Labour Party. I may have been a bit uncertain of the ethics of all this, but I was also pretty certain I didn't want to take the risk. I had no desire to end up with a criminal record for a few books or a frozen chicken. I also had a commitment to get my struggling career off the ground, and Angus was tentatively taking the first steps towards what became a brilliant future in ceramics. Yes, involvement in the movement was crucial to us – it was a way of life, as Laurie Collinson said – but we wanted to achieve other things as well and build a good life together.

We fervently rejected the ideology of the monogamous couple, but found ourselves in a more or less monogamous relationship, with its usual crop of passion, anxiety and jealousies. The whole culture encouraged us to have open relationships, but the occasions when we tried invariably ended in tears and recriminations. We bought into the critique of the tyrannies of family life, which by its very nature excluded us – Angus later wrote a very moving essay on his background, 'From Latent to

Blatant', which dissected the pain of growing up gay in small-town Scotland – but we remained attached to our individual families of origin, despite the difficulties. We sought to create alternatives to the traditional family, and ended up in effect creating an alternative type of family. We were, of course, living many contradictions, and our families did not help. Soon after Angus and I got together we visited his brother Alan, who also lived in London, and came out to him. He got very angry, and we left with his words to Angus echoing behind us: that if he told their mother Alan would kill us. When I came out to my father in early 1972, he said he had suspected one of three things: I had got a girl into trouble, I wanted to marry a Black woman, or I was homosexual. It wasn't clear which he feared most, and I never asked, largely because he had made it so clear he did not want to talk about it. Each of the options carried stigma and social embarrassment that he did not want to face. The large-scale battle that GLF confronted might be about abstracts such as capitalism, sexism and patriarchy, but the real struggle against insult, rejection and shame still had to be fought at the level of daily life, and how we lived was as important as what we did.

In the heyday of GLF living in communes was the favoured option. Various GLF activists attempted to change their everyday lives by building communes, and Angus and I used to visit friends who lived in them, in Brixton, Stoke Newington and Notting Hill Gate. For a short while from 1973 Bethnal Rouge, a radical bookshop and commune in east London, became a magnet for activists and people passing through. But neither Angus nor I were keen on going the whole hog to collective living, not only sharing beds but clothes and lovers. Instead, with Micky and another friend Roger we moved in early 1971 into a rented house in Ivor Street, Camden Town. We tried to live as egalitarian a life as possible, sharing the cooking, shopping and cleaning, and paying the rent in proportion to our income. We did our best to ensure that Angus and I were not too coupley or exclusive, and to find ways of living together that provided mutual support without trapping us in an emotional pressure cooker. After Roger left, Micky, Angus and I lived together in this small house for several years.

From September 1976 we lived in an Edwardian house in Archway we bought together, again contributing what we could to the costs in proportion to our income. Micky, the most securely employed, put in the larger share, Angus the least, while I cashed in my pension contributions to pay my share, convinced that 'come the revolution' all would sort itself out. In fact it was the capitalist boom in housing values and the vast inflation in the value of the house rather than a socialist utopia that was to protect my old age. These two successive houses were fixed homes for us, whatever the ups and downs of our lives and relationships, the focus of our chosen family. They also became meeting places for various gay liberation activities: consciousness-raising groups, reading groups, meetings of various action groups one or other of us were involved in, planning meetings, and social gatherings. Here Micky regularly hosted Sunday afternoon tea parties of the Icebreakers befriending and support group he was involved with. I recently met a couple who had been together for forty-five years who had met at an Icebreakers meeting in our front room. Home and activism, the personal and the political, were inextricably intertwined.

Sex was of course at the heart of gay liberation and our personal lives. It was the main focus of the identities we were building, the consciousness raising we were struggling with, the relationships we were making, the politics we were developing, the campaigns we were waging. And sex was where we could find pleasure, experimentation, fulfilment, love and commitment. For many, gay liberation opened up new possibilities for exploring their sexualities in new and creative ways. Our sexuality was where we had been most scarred and rejected, and gay liberation offered a process of healing and redemption. But what this meant in practical terms was less clear. Being open about our sexual needs and desires did not change the power dynamics of relationships, or the challenges in sustaining them. More sex in itself was hardly revolutionary when millions of our straight friends and neighbours were doing that anyway. This was after all in the midst of what was supposed to be the sexual revolution. Experimenting with open or multiple relationships was right on, especially if they challenged power hierarchies, violence, jealousy, possessiveness and guilt, but many heterosexuals were doing the same, and it did not answer the enduring problems of how to make things work. What was revolutionary about our claim to sexual freedom?

I have had many discussions in recent years, especially among younger queer activists, where the pervasive tone is one of nostalgia for those early days of gay liberation where traditional values seemed so radically questioned, and possibilities of new ways of life beyond the restrictions of gender, family and pair-bonding seemed not only desirable but tangible. We certainly tried to live life differently, and we certainly learnt a great deal about ourselves. But I think we also learnt about our personal limits, and about the limitations of the models of sexual liberation we were trying to work with.

Like many others in my generation I was heavily influenced in the late 1960s by my reading of Freudo-Marxist theorists like Wilhelm Reich, Erich Fromm and Herbert Marcuse, who in very different, and often contradictory, ways had linked sexual liberation to social transformation.[56] According to their arguments, the repression of sexuality was a, if not the, key characteristic of capitalist society, at least in its founding moment. Unleashing sexual freedom was therefore a key to unlocking the oppressive weight of contemporary society. But what did that mean in everyday life? More sex could not easily be equated with greater happiness, and it was not always clear how sexual freedom in and of itself could be the golden road to social emancipation.

Michel Foucault, the French philosopher who was to influence my own work and wider sexual theory, remained deeply sceptical of the identity politics of gay liberation, and argued that it was not always clear why sexuality in itself could ever be a founding point of opposition to power. For was not sexuality itself deeply implicated in relations of power? And wasn't it true that the pursuit of sexual pleasure was a wider phenomenon than simply a gay need? It was also, some radicals reminded us, a mainspring of the new consumerism that was sweeping the Western world, and certainly by the mid-1970s becoming a key feature of the gay world in London. Affirming our sexuality might be an essential part of social freedom, but didn't the really radical implication of gay liberation lie in the new sorts of relationships gays could develop? Perhaps, Foucault suggested, gay friendship was a more radical challenge to the status quo than more sex, however personally liberating it seemed: 'To imagine a sexual act that doesn't conform to law or nature is not what disturbs people. But that individuals are beginning to love one another – there's the problem'.[57] These thoughts were to influence me later in the 1970s as the first impetus of gay liberation waned, and I like many others were faced by the reality of conflicting sexual needs and desires, the inevitable tensions in relationships as people took different directions, as happened with Angus and myself, and the widening gap between our political hopes and the darkening political climate by the end of the decade.

CHAPTER 4
WRITING THE REVOLUTION

WRITING AS ACTIVISM

Through all the ups and downs of gay liberation I remained firmly committed during the 1970s to working as best I could for the movement, and it became increasingly clear to me that my best contribution could come though my writing. I had always had a fantasy that I would become a writer, though of what and how was less obvious at first. My efforts at poetry were derivative and feeble, suffused with teenage angst and existential crisis. Essay writing as a student had been a chore, though I turned out to be good at it. But I quickly found I could write fluently and, I hoped, interestingly about gay issues.

I had abandoned my PhD when I went into school teaching, fed up with the loneliness and isolation of research, but my flight back into a proto-academic career at LSE on the political archives project required me at least to get another academic qualification. So, during my first couple of years in GLF I was struggling to hold together my involvement in the movement, a relentless research job (tracing the descendants of several thousand members of the political elite) and completing what became my MPhil thesis. Once the thesis was done in 1972, I felt free to explore other writing possibilities. My writing skill was likely to be more useful to the cause, I felt, than my negligible talents in something like street theatre.

Shifts in the politics of the movement encouraged me. Early in 1972 the Counter Psychiatry group, at a meeting in our house, decided to go in two different directions. Some members, with Micky as a leading member, started Icebreakers, a self-help phone line to support lesbians and gays as a conscious alternative to the more professional counselling groups then emerging. Its founding philosophy was that most gay people did not require expert advice to come to terms with their sexuality but rather needed mutual support from people like themselves. It was to prove an enormously influential initiative over the next fifteen years, and I was proud to be involved at the fringes. But I joined the other new grouping, a pamphlet writing group, which seemed more my métier.

A small group, including the artist David Hutter and the mathematician Andrew Hodges, alongside Paul Bunting, Randal Kincaid and me, began work on writing a pamphlet, which became *Psychiatry and the Homosexual*, published later in 1972.[58] The pamphlet begins resolutely: 'The oppression of homosexuality in western society is total'. Given this, it goes on to argue, it is not surprising that 'some gay people develop neurotic symptoms, which they attribute to their sexuality instead of to their oppression'. Like Icebreakers' founding philosophy, our answer was not psychiatric treatment, 'but the total acceptance of homosexuality within a just society'. The rest of the pamphlet is a brisk polemic against the medical, psychiatric and psychoanalytical institutions. It homed in on the experiences of many of our readers in encountering 'expert' opinion as they came to terms with their sexualities, and finding it badly wanting. The pamphlet proved very popular and influential at the time. What strikes me now, however, is the absolute certainty of its convictions, indeed its absolutism, which very much reflected the spirit of the early gay movement: Psychiatry, No; Liberation, Yes! Over time, attitudes became more nuanced, and many people I knew eventually trained as analysts and therapists within a variety of approaches, changing the culture of the institutions from the inside. My friend Laurie Collinson became an enthusiast for transactional analysis (TA) and built up a considerable gay clientele as a therapist in the next few years. Sometimes, it became apparent, personal problems were much more than simply a direct result of oppression.

A second pamphlet, *With Downcast Gays*, followed after I left the group, but with a similar tone. This focused on self-oppression and offered an acid critique of all those writers and icons, like the otherwise sainted E. M. Forster, who had betrayed the cause by holding to the secrecy of their gayness: 'Alas, it was his reputation that he guarded and gay people whom he betrayed'.[59] This, of course, went too far in forgetting historical context, echoing my own casual rejection of our predecessor campaigners of the 1960s, but it was very much the spirit of the time. I was eventually to find that researching and writing our history introduced all sorts of nuances foreign to the early 1970s. Writing for me was to become an exercise in understanding and explaining rather than polemical fireworks

In the meantime, I was honing other writing skills. I discovered that while I disliked it while doing it the process of collective writing could be productive and creative, and it was to prove a useful skill for subsequent endeavours. But my most vivid memory of this writing group is of sharing stories and learning from each other in unexpected ways. One stands out: David telling us about someone called Alan Turing, a founder of modern computing, who had been a close friend of

David's partner James in the wartime code-breaking operation at Bletchley Park. None of us apart from David had heard of Turing at this stage, and little was known of the wartime code-breaking operations in which he took a leading role, for they were still covered by the draconian Official Secrets Act. The story we heard from David was around the iniquities of the state in forcing Turing, following a charge of gross indecency, to imbibe damaging drugs that effeminised his body and destroyed his sex drive, culminating in his possible assassination by the secret service through eating a poisoned apple. The version that appeared in the pamphlet was more anodyne, mentioning neither his Bletchley Park work nor 'assassination'. The story made a strong impression on all of us, but Andrew Hodges, as a mathematician himself, was especially moved and intrigued by it, and this stimulated his researches for what became his eventual pioneering biography of Turing.[60] The book, the stage and television plays, and the novels and film that followed, and the massive publicity and subsequent flood of books on Bletchley Park were major factors in bringing Turing's story to public attention, and eventually led to his formal government apology and pardon for 'gross indecency' and, ultimately, to the pardoning of hundreds of others for criminal convictions for homosexual offences. I read as I write this that the Parisian authorities have just named a street after Turing. He has become an international icon. It took many years, but it is a good example of how that pioneering writing in the early 1970s did have effects, in ways that we could not possibly have anticipated in 1972.

I personally became increasingly preoccupied with writing about the moment and movement we were caught up in in 1972. Over the next few years I began researching the origins of the homosexual emancipation movement itself, and the ways in which this shaped and was shaped by the emerging gay identities. By the 1970s such identities were becoming taken for granted and naturalised, but I was increasingly convinced they should better be seen as distinctly historical creations, products of language and ideas as well as feelings and passion. I began to argue that the ways we thought and spoke about sexuality, and how we labelled and categorised it, were not simply descriptive or neutral endeavours. They shaped and created ways of seeing the world, giving meaning to the amorphous desires and possibilities of the body. Words, speech, language made sexuality meaningful. Writing was a way of changing meanings, and of making new possibilities and realities. And this was especially true of sexual identities.

TROUBLING IDENTITIES

I had spent years searching for a viable sexual identity that made sense of my own life and my relations with others. The more I researched and wrote about it, however, the more it became increasingly clear to me that the new collective identity that I so proudly proclaimed was not a permanent universal reality but was highly specific to our time and place. We had been present at its birth, we had made it through our own practices, and our actions and reactions were transparently changing lived experience all around us. We were part of a new generation attempting to change how people saw and lived their sexualities, and the assertion of identity was a crucial aspect of that.

GLF consisted overwhelmingly of young and youngish people of a particular kind, most of whom had migrated to London to escape and find their sexualities: students, dropouts, marginalised people, many of those, like myself and Angus, of working-class origins. We were part of a chronological generation that was widely, though far from universally, upending norms and values, and formed a distinctive *sexual* generation, uninhibited by the morass of traditions and values we were brought up in, though not quite sure, despite our declared certainties, what was going to replace them.[61] Gay liberation offered a smorgasbord of possibilities rather than a fixed menu.

The deeper reality, despite our optimism, was that we represented in those early days only a small fragment of a generational shift. Many of those of the same chronological age cohort as us gay liberationists were strangely immune to our enthusiasms – even those who shared our beds were often extremely hostile to the idea of being out and proud about our sexualities. And persuading other parts of our generation, let alone older ones, was extremely challenging. As an example, in the context of a developing multicultural Britain as it was emerging in the 1970s, we were overwhelmingly white. There were a handful of Black and Asian and other minority people involved in gay liberation, but they justifiably complained of casual racism, exclusion and marginalisation. My few non-white friends were usually from outside gay liberation. In the early 1980s I got to know people involved in the Gay Black Group, but they were of a younger generation, with often different preoccupations from those that dominated my experience in the 1970s, and responding to quite different currents in the 1980s. And they were much clearer about the centrality of racism and the inadequacies of the claim to a universal gay identity. During the 1970s my gay identity had subsumed all other identities, giving shape and meaning to all my activities. My Black friends made it clear that the contours of the identity we had forged in the early movement were often antithetical to the communities they came from and that remained central to their own social belonging. I gradually came to the conclusion that the sort of gay identity I had embraced so passionately in the early 1970s was vital but partial, enabling and a potential trap, which empowered action but could not be a final destination or ultimate truth. The experience of gender and same-sex sexual diversity is just too varied to be encompassed under a single and singular label. Although in the 1970s we fervently evangelised for all our brothers and sisters to come out as gay, its meaning was already beginning to be fiercely contested.

Early gay liberation spoke of liberating the homosexual potential of everyone, implying a universal potential bisexuality. Dennis Altman looked forward to the 'end of the homosexual' in his groundbreaking book, *Homosexual: Oppression and Liberation,* and of course to the end of the heterosexual too.[62] Yet in the day-to-day life of the movement and community those who identified as bisexual were regularly seen as copping out, fearful of committing to one or other side of the binary divide. A number of my women friends, on the other hand, seemed to find it easier to move between same-sex and heterosexual relationships. Similarly, a number of men I knew in the movement deliberately identified as gay, while their sexual practice was actually bisexual or in one or two cases exclusively heterosexual. It soon became clear to me that the proud adoption of a gay identity, and the inevitable sharpening of the divide between heterosexuality and homosexuality that flowed from that, was a political and cultural act that did not necessarily bear a strong correlation to what people did in bed. That did not make the adoption of an identity less important. As Kwame Anthony Appiah has recently put it, the fact that identity is contested does not mean 'it is up for grabs'. Identities, whether of creed, country, colour, class, culture, gender or sexuality, are 'lies that bind'.[63] Identities matter to people. The problem is that there are potentially so many of them!

I began to think of my own gay identity as a journey not a destination, a process not a fixed achievement. James Baldwin, my first literary hero, once remarked that identity is 'the garment with which one covers the nakedness of the self; in which case, it is best that the garment be loose, a little like the robes of the desert, through which one's nakedness can always be felt'. My new identity felt much more than a loose garment I could put on or take off at will. But I was increasingly aware that there was no guarantee where identities would end up, where the garments would billow and our nakedness be exposed. Indeed, as Baldwin suggested, trust in our nakedness was what made it possible to change our robes.[64]

The reality was that the gay label concealed a multitude of possible ways of life and identifications. So, 'gay', the adoption of which had been so liberating for me, was being increasingly seen by many lesbians in the movement in particular as an obscuring of their own identity. Lesbians from the start had been reluctant to subordinate their own struggles to the obsessions and passions of gay men, who tended to dominate the weekly meetings of GLF and emote about their own preoccupations, notably about cruising and the merits or demerits of cottaging. Many women preferred to engage more directly as lesbians and feminists with the women's liberation movement, which had helped to inspire gay liberation in the first place.

Many lesbians from GLF began meeting separately on Friday nights in 1971 to discuss their own experiences. When in early February 1972 the majority of lesbians walked out of GLF meetings to organise separately, I felt personally devastated, though I continued to be friendly with and work with women in other groups, such Mary McIntosh, Elizabeth Wilson and Nettie Pollard. Later in the 1970s a number of lesbian feminists, influenced by radical and revolutionary feminists, went much further, and developed separatist options where men, whether gay or straight, were now seen as the main enemy. For many separatists, lesbianism was more a political rather than a sexual identity, expressing the continuum that linked all women in a patriarchal world. Increasingly, they expressed hostility to gay male sexuality. In reaction, others sought to affirm that lesbianism was very much about sexual pleasure and the exploration of distinctly lesbian sexual experiences, whether butch or femme, sadomasochistic or vanilla. I was closely associated with these pro-sex activists and was bitterly attacked by separatists for my pains. I was identified as a leading 'gay male theorist', and hence by definition an enemy of separatist lesbians. The reality was a little more complex. I remained friendly throughout the 1970s and early 1980s with several lesbians who identified as separatist, including teaching some.

As a member of the *Gay Left* collective in the late 1970s I was involved in several initiatives to develop closer relations with both leftist and some soon-to-be-separatist revolutionary feminists. On one occasion I was part of a group that was asked to donate sperm to assist some women in self-insemination. I personally declined, but others did participate. Later relations became more fraught, and separatism became more absolutist for some women. One student of mine was banned from an all-women group because she had a male child (by self-insemination). These differences were major elements in the 'sex wars' among feminists in the early 1980s, which effectively marked the end of a unified 'second-wave' feminism.

The increasing identification of a distinctive lesbian experience and politics was paralleled by a machoisation of the gay male community, with the widespread adoption of the moustached clone look originally imported from the USA. This was clearly in part a collective rejection of the historic association of male homosexuality with effeminacy. It was also a sign of a growing self-confidence in proclaiming pride in male desire for other men. I was attracted to the look but knew I could never properly perform it. I had grown a beard in early 1971, and kept my thinning ginger hair ever shorter, and this remained my characteristic appearance. As leather increasingly became a marker of a particular sexualised culture I was drawn in, though I never identified with the burgeoning world of gay sadomasochism (S&M, much later to be called BDSM). I did, however, became involved in the heated debates it generated, especially around the issue of lesbian S&M. I got to know the two leading American proponents of lesbian S&M, Gayle Rubin and Pat (later Patrick) Califia on my first visit to San Francisco in 1981, and talked at length about what they were trying to do. S&M raised to my mind important issues about identity, pleasure, power and choice that I was later to write extensively about.

Gayle was to be a major intellectual influence in the development of gay thinking about sexuality. She was also an enthusiastic archivist of the evolution of sexual norms, with a vast, well-catalogued collection of press cuttings that I envied. She was a famously reluctant writer, and her doctorate on the leather scene in San Francisco took years to complete. But what she did write was enormously influential, and two articles in particular are still widely cited, 'The Traffic in Women' and 'Thinking Sex'. She and Pat were excoriated and abused by radical feminists, and Gayle in particular became a symbol of the feminist battles around female desire and choice in the early 1980s.[65] It largely destroyed her early academic career, though she remained an inspiration for many women, as well as men like myself, for opening up debate on the dialectic of pleasure and danger that was to be so important to feminist debates in the 1980s.

Pat Califia took a completely different path, and I lost touch after the two split up as lovers. But the evolution into

Patrick foreshadowed the growth of the trans movement, and controversies over drag kings, female masculinities, gender fluidity, genderqueerism and the long-term shift where gender diversity became an increasing battleground not only in the movement but in the wider culture. Transgender people had been central players in the original Stonewall riots, and a small number were involved in London GLF – a couple of people I knew transitioned in the first few years. Bob Mellors, the co-founder of GLF, also became increasingly involved with exploring gender fluidity. He became closely involved with the controversial Charlotte Bach, who developed an alternative biological theory highlighting the positive role of homosexuality and gender variety in evolutionary advancement. But despite such developments on the fringes, as older trans activists have made clear in subsequent years, trans people were made to feel increasingly marginalised in the gay movement as it developed in the 1970s and 1980s. Many gay men, though happy to socialise in a number of drag pubs that boomed as the gay community rapidly expanded in London, especially the Black Cap in Camden Town, which was our local for a while, were often hostile to more explicitly political trans activism, and couldn't see the implication for their own gender assumptions.

There was particular hostility to trans women, partly on the grounds that they risked associating gay men with the stigma of effeminacy. Many lesbians were also influenced by the radical feminist polemics against transsexuality, especially for aping and confirming gender stereotypes. The assault was epitomised by Janice Raymond's *The Transsexual Empire*, which had a lasting influence, and is still referenced today.[66] But it was difficult for anyone involved in gay liberation to escape the issue of gender fully. It was implicit in the experience of everyone in seeking to affirm and validate a sexuality that was in apparent contradiction to gender norms. Most of us gay men and lesbians had suffered slings and arrows for being in some way unmasculine or unfeminine, and even our forms of resistance, whether camp or clone, butch or femme, clearly in the end played with dominant ideas of what was appropriate behaviour. Some self-consciously toyed with new forms of gender nonconformity, particularly those around the radical effeminacy tendency within GLF. But the very confusion of performances and styles underlined my growing conviction that there was no royal road to liberation.

Some roads, moreover, were obvious dead ends. The greatest challenge to early gay liberation came not from trans awareness or even radical effeminacy but from the emergence of paedophile advocacy groupings. Two small groups had emerged out of the flux of the early GLF: Paedophile Action for Liberation (PAL) and Paedophile Information Exchange (PIE). What encouraged this link was what seemed to many in the movement the iniquitous fact that the male age of consent for homosexual activity in Britain was 21, where it was to remain until 1994, whereas the effective heterosexual age of consent was 16. Moreover, at a time when all sexual minorities were conventionally lashed together as perverts, an informal sense of solidarity between groups was perhaps inevitable.

There were legitimate questions about what a realistic age of consent all round should be when continental neighbours had ages of consent of 16, 15, 14 or lower. And for many of us in early gay liberation, sexual freedom must include – at a time when their sexuality was denied – sexual freedom for young people. With the development of gay teenage groups in Britain this was becoming an important issue for the movement.

Where it became difficult and problematic was when the focus shifted from the rights of teenagers to consensual sexual exploration to the desires of those adults who increasingly defined themselves proudly as paedophiles, and were in effect using the language of gay liberation about pride, identity and self-affirmation to legitimise their own needs and desires, even for prepubescent children, at which most people drew a line. This inevitably raised profound issues about power and exploitation. Paedophile organisations, such as PIE, by their very existence inevitably re-associated gay activists with the historic libel that linked homosexuality with child abuse. The end result was disastrous for the self-identified paedophiles, some of whom like the evangelical Tom O'Carroll ended up in prison or in exile abroad.[67] Others in gay liberation who wanted to encourage debate on consent and the rights of young people, while not identifying or practising as paedophiles themselves, also put themselves in the line of criticism. Micky, who was not a paedophile, did some research work through the National Council for Civil Liberties with some of the PIE activists on the age of consent, and got a little too close to PIE for his future comfort.

In some later writing I sought to grapple with the ethical and value issues raised by intergenerational sex. I was concerned about where the boundaries could or should be drawn – between adults and children, power and consent, rights and responsibilities. Debates over these issues, however, became increasingly difficult as the climate changed. There was evergrowing evidence of widespread abuse of children in the wider culture, and the voices of those who had been abused began to be heard. I found myself attacked in print and on the web for being too pro-paedophile, which I was not. There were sporadic panics over child sex abuse and paedophiles in the 1980s and 1990s, but in recent years these have exploded into a major crisis revolving around the abusive behaviour of priests, popular entertainers and senior public figures, as well as in the daily routine of family life. Paedophile as a term has moved from being a self-description of people who wanted to justify relations between adolescents and older men to become the signifier of the archetypical moral monster and abuser, a million miles from the liberatory rhetoric of the 1970s. The early support of paedophile activism proved a historic error, both within gay liberation and for all involved.

What such controversies underlined is that not all identities are valid or acceptable just because they are strongly asserted. I increasingly realised I was not a libertarian in any real sense. I believed strongly that all actions, practices and identities had to be located within a wider system of values and ethical standards based on equality and human rights. Sexual choices had to be more than playing around in a sweet shop of delights. Choices were meaningful and had consequences. The puzzle for the movement was how to make these distinctions while valuing pluralism and diversity. For many of us during the 1970s at least part of the answer lay in opening up to wider debates about what sort of society we wanted, which for me at that moment involved looking again at the legacy of socialism and Marxism.

GAY LEFTİSM

From the start, I was closely involved in the debates within gay liberation about the relevance of anti-capitalist positions to our sexual politics. A number of us in the early 1970s were concerned to link gay liberation with wider social analyses and political practice, and from early on I was attracted to the socialist and Marxist tendencies in the movement, which seemed to fit logically into my background and political commitments. I was already a keen trade unionist, while politically I was moving to the left of the Labour Party, but not attracted by the various Trotskyist and Maoist *groupuscules* of the ultra-left. At LSE I had become heavily involved in the local branch of my union, the Association of Scientific, Technical and Managerial Staffs (ASTMS). Under its charismatic and garrulous national leader, Clive Jenkins, this presented itself as the dynamic organisation for the new cadres of technical staff, but locally it was a strange melange of generally conservative technicians and of some of the more radical young researchers and academics at LSE and neighbouring colleges. I toiled painfully as treasurer for a couple of years, trying to restore order to chaotic finances (radicals proved poor payers of union dues), then became the branch's chair. This brought me directly into the factionalism of the *soi-disant* revolutionary left. It was a rumbustious group, bitterly divided between left Labour Party members (including two future MPs and ministers, Chris Mullin and Chris Smith), International Socialists (notably the feminist economist, Irene Bruegel, always wily and mischievous) and supporters of the ultra-leftist and apocalyptic Workers' Revolutionary Party (WRP). The WRP was famous for its celebrity members like Vanessa Redgrave and its obscure financial links with countries like Libya, and was later to be exposed for the long-running sexual exploitation of its female members by its revered dear leader, Gerry Healey. It was led in our union branch by the dedicated young researcher and lecturer Adam Westoby, a model Leninist revolutionary, who rigidly followed the party line, whatever it was at any particular time. I became chair only because I did not belong to any of the factions and could just about hold the whole thing together.

Our meetings were not a good advertisement for left politics, dominated by sectarianism, riven by ideological and tactical differences, and marked by unfraternal or sororal nastiness. I was once called in by the national executive of ASTMS and reprimanded because of the branch's involvement in the attempt to deselect the Labour MP Reginald Prentice, who later confirmed suspicions of him by becoming a minister under Margaret Thatcher. As it happened I was completely innocent of any intentional conspiracy but had been lumbered with the consequences of sectarian manoeuvrings. It confirmed my sense of alienation from both the traditional Labour Party and the revolutionary left. There was certainly no obvious interest among fellow branch members, even Irene at that point, in the sexual politics I was committed to. It was a spur to try to work through a different form of leftism.

After 1972 many radicals in the GLF began to drift towards various leftist organisations. Aubrey Walter and David Fernbach, along with their young protégé Peter Tatchell, were involved for a while with an obscure and puritanical Maoist sect. Others moved towards the Communist Party of Great Britain (CPGB) or the various Trotskyist would-be parties. Ever resistant to joining exclusive groups, I became involved instead in a succession of socialist reading groups within gay liberation. In these we would discuss key Marxist texts, often through the cheap editions available from Moscow or Beijing publishing houses and available in left and libertarian bookshops like Compendium in Camden Town (where I also bought copies of early gay liberation and feminist texts from the USA). In theory we would read the topic of the week beforehand and have an intense discussion, and then socialise over dinner or a drink. It was an earnest but convivial experience, though I am not sure now whether it generated more heat than light, slogans rather than insight. The challenge was to link our orthodox readings more explicitly to gay and feminist issues, to make these hallowed and recalcitrant texts relevant to us sexual radicals – a largely doomed project, it turned out. Some works, like Engels' *The Origin of the Family, Private Property and the State*, in theory lent themselves readily to this. Others were dutiful dead ends. We learnt a lot about the arcana of

Marxist debates but little about our sexual oppression. Even poor Engels' book, though widely hallowed as a founding text for Marxist thinking about women's oppression, had little to offer the ardent gay liberationist. One of my first writing efforts on the theme I called 'Where Engels Feared to Tread', in which I outlined the winding road of socialist writing since the late nineteenth century on gender and sexuality, and found it wanting.[68] We needed clearly to go further, I suggested in the article, to make the socialist tradition relevant to us, and for the time being at least I was still optimistic that a Marxist analysis could be flexible enough to help us.

Through 1973 into 1974 I co-convened a gay Marxist study group, which had earlier produced a few editions of cheaply produced, embryonic magazines but was essentially a reading and discussion group. It generated intense commitment and enthusiasm for all of us involved, opening new ideas, links and possibilities. The potter Emmanuel Cooper, who was to become one of my closest friends, gingerly exploring in the early 1970s the new gay politics he was coming across in London, described the impact on him of encountering the group: 'By good fortune I was invited to the tail end of a series of meetings of the Gay Marxist Reading Group, and for the first time in my life "things came together". Here politics, sexuality, work, study and discussion seemed all part of a whole, which could be looked at and analysed. I could hardly sleep for the excitement and wondered if it was all too good to be true'.[69] Out of this enthusiasm, echoed by other members of the group, came the idea for a more professional and regular journal that would explore the links between socialism and gay liberation in a more sustained and systematic fashion. The reading group was rejigged, and after some anguishing over the name we became a working collective and a publishing and political project, with the journal *Gay Left* as its focus.

The journal first appeared in the autumn of 1975, produced by a collective consisting of Keith Birch, Gregg Blachford, Bob Cant, Emmanuel Cooper, Ross Irwin, Randal Kincaid, Nigel Young, Angus and myself. The year leading up to its first appearance had been hectic as we discussed and re-discussed what we were trying to do, and as we attempted to gel as a collective. An early decision was that we would work to break down the traditional division of labour between thinkers and doers, writers and technicians. All our editorials were written collectively, based on a rough draft that one or two of us would produce. Similarly, we all worked on the production, literally cutting and pasting the galleys in an age long before personal computers or software packages. Only Emmanuel had actual magazine editing experience, as co-founder and co-editor of *Ceramic Review*, and he patiently guided us through the process. I had experience from my LSE work at copy-editing and proofing, but with other practical things I was all thumbs and sweaty palms, not particularly competent at either cutting or pasting the hard copy, but I ploughed on. Others took to the process immediately, and later became involved elsewhere in magazine production themselves. From the first we sought to evolve a distinctive and elegant design for the journal, which matured as we worked through ten issues; we wanted to look professional and to be taken seriously. And finally we worked together on the distribution, negotiating with an alternative distribution collective, developing subscriptions, but also crucially taking copies around to meetings and demos, making contacts and encouraging discussions.

The original collective consisted of nine people. The group that produced the last issue five years later consisted of eight people. In between there had been a considerable churning of membership. Angus left after the first three issues; Derek Cohen joined after the first issue and stayed for the duration, while at various times Ron Peck, Richard Dyer, Simon Watney, Philip Derbyshire and Tom Woodhouse were involved. Fifteen people in all served on the collective, but a core of us stayed with the project throughout. We were a group of men – a fact that was to prove increasingly controversial – and we were all ethnically white – something that was not especially controversial then but now would stand out as a significant weakness. We were London based, though in fact only one of us was born and bred in London; like most activist lesbians and gay men we were migrants to the big city from elsewhere in the UK – or beyond. Two were Canadian, Ross Irwin and Gregg Blachford.

Most of us were in our twenties or early thirties, of working-class backgrounds but generally highly educated. Several of us were still students, or soon became students. The rest of us were first-generation university graduates, characteristically working as researchers or teachers in schools, colleges and universities, but we also had two potters (Angus and Emmanuel), a filmmaker (Ron Peck) and a lawyer (Ross Irwin). Generally we were fairly insecure in our careers at that stage. We all regarded ourselves as on the left, though our experiences had varied enormously, from membership of small leftist groups – Bob Cant was the most experienced here, as a militant in International Socialists, later the Socialist Workers Party, then as now a leading Trotskyist group – to mild anarchism and armchair Marxism. All of us had been radicalised through our experience of the gay movement, and in our youthful enthusiasm we saw *Gay Left* as a critical intervention in left debates about sexuality.

We declared in our first editorial that we had a double aim: to develop a 'Marxist analysis of homosexual oppression' and to encourage in the gay movement 'an understanding of the links between the struggle against sexual oppression and the struggle for socialism'.[70] Whatever the twists and turns of our efforts, that remained the ambition for the next five years, though by the end, in an increasingly polarised political world, and with a hopelessly embattled left, the whole enterprise was fraying. The collective statements we wrote for each issue trace our changing perspectives. In developing these we attempted to work absolutely collectively on a specific topic, reading, discussing, arguing and, finally, writing together, sentence by sentence, word by word, in endless drafts. Putting together these statements took weeks and vast amounts of energy, probably the hardest writing experience I have ever had. Sometimes we would meet as a collective twice a week or more in each other's homes, usually over a meal that we cooked in turn.

We also had regular away weekends, usually staying in a cottage in the Northamptonshire countryside owned by a friend of Emmanuel's. Here we would have consciousness-raising meetings as well as sessions planning the next issue, interspersed with collectively cooked meals and bracing walks. It was all very earnest, and not in the least erotic for a highly sexualised group of young men. Sex was talked about all the time but, to my knowledge at least, little practised over these weekends. The consciousness raising could be highly challenging, and the discussions were often vigorous and heated, yet we always came away with a strengthened sense of the bonds that held us together. In the summer we would have a trip to the seaside. The most memorable was the first, a trip to the wild and windswept pebbly beach of Dungeness, where we picnicked in sight of the nuclear power station, long before it was made famous as the location of the home and garden of the gay artist and filmmaker Derek Jarman.

We all strove to be self-consciously theoretically engaged, but we cherished our self-image as activists, involved in wider struggles. We dutifully attended the early morning mass pickets at the Grunwick strike and lockout in North London, in which a struggle for union recognition by largely East Asian women workers between 1976 and 1978 became a *cause célèbre* for the Labour movement. In August 1977 we were involved in the so-called 'Battle of Lewisham', which attempted to halt a neo-fascist National Front march. A number of us were involved in various other trade union strikes and campaigns. Bob Cant, Gregg Blachford and Nigel Young were active in the politics of education and the teaching unions, and we covered these and other struggles regularly in the journal. We also tried to engage in debate with various leftist organisations, warning that a fragmented left needed to learn from the issues raised by the sexual liberation movements since the late 1960s: that the personal was highly political. Bob Cant recounted his own painful work with others to set up a gay group in International Socialists, and the obfuscations and resistances he encountered.[71] The CPGB on the other hand, still the strongest group to the left of Labour, though riven by ideological conflicts between Stalinists and Eurocommunists, had already adopted an important statement at its conference in Autumn 1976 on the oppression of homosexuals. In *Gay Left* 4 we carried an interview with two prominent lesbian activists in the party, Sarah Benton and Bea Campbell, who expressed the hope that the gay movement would find in the CPGB a party that was now open to gay and feminist issues.[72] A number of lesbian and gay activists did indeed get involved in the CPGB, and especially with its lively theoretical journal, *Marxism Today*, to which I later contributed.

We were anxious to avoid spouting wisdom from an ivory tower, and made various attempts to engage with our growing constituencies (the *Gay Left* print run at the end was around three thousand, with a much larger readership in Britain and a small but highly engaged readership outside the UK), holding regular readers' meetings and several conferences. Our dialogue with a growing range of readers inevitably shifted our perspectives. By *Gay Left* 5, in our collective statement 'Why Marxism?' we attempted to articulate a more flexible theoretical position, open to new trends within Marxism (the growing influence of Antonio Gramsci, for example) and other social theories – the recognition of the importance of psychoanalysis (especially via the writings of Juliet Mitchell) and later the work of Michel Foucault were particularly important. Ironically, given that we were now clearly, if not yet explicitly, moving away from any real affiliation with orthodox Marxism (if we ever had any), the front cover of *Gay Left* 5 was adorned with a slightly tongue-in-cheek photo of members of the collective posing alongside the grandiose grave of Karl Marx in Highgate cemetery. We were now publishing articles on key developing themes and theories in sexual politics that had little obvious associations with Marxism, such as the work of the French gay philosopher Guy Hocquenghem and the Italian gay theorist Mario Mielli, and closely following developments in socialist feminism. At the same time, we were attempting to reflect the growing crisis on the left as the political climate became increasingly polarised. We carried contributions on fascism, which at the time seemed a major threat with the rise of the National Front. We were also alive to the significance of the British swing to the right, not only politically but culturally (the collective statement in *Gay Left* 8 referred to the election of Margaret Thatcher, which proved to be a decisive moment in British politics).

Our developing political commitments provided the spine for *Gay Left* in its five years of existence, but as a group of gay men we were also firmly located in the developing gay community and culture, with all its burgeoning concerns. Gay politics was still at heart a personal politics, and the bridge between the personal, social and political was an abiding preoccupation. In our second editorial statement, 'Within these Walls' we cast a critical look at our own community. But we also tried to show how central the sense of community was to coming out. Angus' article 'From Latent to Blatant' movingly demonstrated that, and was a first example of highly personal articles that at the same time raised wider issues, culminating in 'Personal Politics – Ten Years On', which gave members of the collective an opportunity to reflect on what had changed since 1970.[73]

A recurrent theme was the undeniable fact that we were a collective of white gay men. We had stated right at the start that we felt we could 'best explore our sexual attitudes most truthfully in an all-male group', and in many ways we did indeed operate as an awareness or consciousness-raising group as well as an editorial collective. But our maleness and alleged exclusivity was a major source of controversy. Sue Bruley, a close personal friend of mine, launched a vigorous broadside against the collective, 'Women in Gay Left', in the third issue, followed up in subsequent issues by a series of responses.[74] Although growing numbers of women contributed to the journal (and to our later book) over the years that followed, and we worked closely with a number of women in the Lesbian Left group over specific projects (such as the 'What is to Be Done?' conference in July 1977), the collective remained all male for the duration. The reasoning behind that was partly reflected in the work we did on masculinity for our collective statement, 'Love, Sex and Maleness',[75] a defining moment for the group.

More controversially, we also entered the debates on paedophilia and intergenerational sex, pornography and S&M, which were probably among the most divisive topics we wrote on, and began to explore tentatively the impact of racism on our community and wider politics. The fact that we were all *white* men was apparently less controversial at the time than the fact we were all men, but in retrospect it appears more of a problem. The article on 'Gays and Fascism' in *Gay Left* 5 did refer to racism, and in a long letter published in *Gay Left* 10, Errol Francis specifically and strongly raised the issue, but there was no in-depth discussion of the intersection of race, ethnicity and sexuality, which was to become a major theme in the 1980s, after the journal left the scene.[76] What you can see in the pages of the journal, however, is an attempt to see gay liberation in an international context, especially in the Global South. We published articles on, for example, 'Gays in Cuba' and 'Gay Liberation in Central America', and became part of a growing network of international journals on gay politics. What is not explicitly addressed in the journal is what has now become a dominating theme: the diversity of the LGBT world, and though the issue of rights was a key if implicit concern, we did not anticipate the rise of the discourse of human rights as crucial to international queer politics. We also failed to engage fully with bisexual or transgender issues. Our sense of what constituted a valid sexual and gender politics was still in evolution.

In other ways, however, *Gay Left* was a leader in exploring gay culture in its broadest sense. Gays in film formed a continuous theme following a groundbreaking article by Richard Dyer in *Gay Left* 2, at the start of his highly influential work as a writer on film.[77] Subsequent issues carried regular reviews – for example, of the films of Fassbinder by Bob Cant – and coverage of Ron Peck's attempts to make his film, *Nighthawks*. Emmanuel Cooper began his career defining analysis of 'Gay Art', in the journal.[78] There were many other themes for which *Gay Left* provided a forum, from the emerging gay history to disco and from the meaning of camp to gay television. We were seeking all the time to expand our coverage, adapting to the rapidly changing climate, and to our own personal changes in life circumstances and political outlook. By the time we ceased publication in 1980 the kaleidoscope had been shaken again and new, yet more intricate patterns were emerging. After a final burst of energy, we produced a book, *Homosexuality: Power and Politics*,[79] which reflected a growing diversity on the broader gay left. After that, went our separate ways.

It had been a turbulent experience in many ways, politically, intellectually and emotionally. We were a disparate group, and inevitably there were many political disagreements. More dangerous for our cohesion were the personal conflicts and sexual tensions. What precipitated the final collapse was the breakdown of the long-term relationship between two members of the collective, Emmanuel and Nigel. Such tensions were probably inevitable in a group where personal life and political commitments were so closely intertwined. Yet I think we all gained much more than we lost from such close involvement. For me it was an amazing experience of personal growth, and it was a forcing house of talent for all its members. Between us, we have had a wide range of subsequent careers, and most of us continued writing: some sixty books and innumerable articles on film, culture, history, sociology, art, photography, popular culture, ceramics, IT, the media, AIDS and politics. Emmanuel Cooper and Richard Dyer became internationally recognised for their contributions to gay art and gay film. Bob Cant became a documenter of gay history, especially of the Scottish gay experience and of gay migration. Simon Watney became a passionate writer on the HIV/AIDS epidemic. Keith Birch served for many years as a trade union representative on the National Executive Committee of the Labour Party. As for myself, involvement developed my writing skills, encouraged my journeys into gay history and broadened my intellectual horizons. We may not have changed decisively the political discourse on sexual politics, but we opened up and shaped debates that continued for many years across the political spectrum. My tears when we decided to end the adventure were for the pain of break-up but also for the end of an era in our political and personal journeys.

ENDİNGS AND BEGİNNİNGS

On 7 September 1976 my father committed suicide. He had been in a precarious mental state for many years. He had a nervous breakdown in the summer of 1968 and had taken redundancy from work. For someone who had immense pride in his status as a 'skilled man', his inability to find other skilled jobs fed into his sense of failure and social emasculation, especially as Mam now became the breadwinner of the family. The following eight years were miserable for him and difficult for all of us in the family as he endured endless pills, all too few sessions with a psychotherapist and several bouts of electroconvulsive treatment, which made him hyperactive for a while before he fell again into chronic depression. His death was a release for him but left an endless burden of guilt for my mother, us boys, and all who loved him.

My own relationship with Dad had always been difficult and fraught, though in the last years of his life he had become a more gentle, reflective, even mellow, person, and took a much more direct part in my younger brother Robert's upbringing than he had in mine or Dennis'. I had spent much of my life building a wall to protect my gayness against his disapproval as I perceived it. It took his death, however, for me to realise how much he was part of my life, how similar we were and how much I loved, and missed, him.

Dad's death happened at practically the worst possible

time for me. I had been ill for the previous two months with hepatitis and was still extremely feeble. That summer was almost unbearably hot, and the week Dad died our house in Camden Town was in chaos, piled with half-filled packing cases: we were due to move into our new house in Archway the following week. Angus and Micky had to finish packing my things and transport them. I went home to Wales to be with my mother and brothers, and to prepare for the funeral, and came back to a new home in London, where I was to stay for the next twenty-seven years.

A year later my research post at LSE finally came to an end and I found myself unemployed and apparently unemployable. During the early *Gay Left* days I had been researching and writing my first two books, *Socialism and the New Life*, with Sheila Rowbotham, and *Coming Out: Homosexual Politics in Britain from the Nineteenth Century to the Present*. They were published in 1977 to considerable acclaim when I was living on the dole, despairing of ever getting another job. To make things worse my relationship with Angus was beginning to fray. We were drifting apart as he became increasingly preoccupied with his ceramics course at Camberwell School of Art, and new circles of friends. By 1979 he was involved in another relationship. I was bitterly hurt and jealous, and for a time found the pain almost unbearable. At the same time, I still felt committed to Angus and all we had believed about the importance of non-possessive relationships. We agreed to go on living together in our shared home, even for a while continuing to share a bed, and after a difficult transition we re-established a strong and intimate friendship that endured till his premature death. Dad's death, unemployment, changing relationships, all signalled new uncertainties in my life. My continued involvement with *Gay Left* and the deep friendships I had there provided a focus and a purpose, but even there the ice was beginning to crack by 1979. It was as if my personal life was being battered and reshaped at the same time we were witnessing seismic shifts in the wider society.

What had seemed in the early 1970s an inevitable movement to the left had by 1980 become the triumph of a new sort of right, marrying with what turned out to be varying degrees of success a harsh economic liberalism with a clear social conservatism, with a distinct hostility to homosexuality a key part of the mix. There had been many signs of this shift even as gay liberation and feminism seemed to be moving with the tides of history. Evangelical movements like the Festival of Light, Lord Longford's commission on pornography and the prosecution of *Gay News* for the unlikely crime of blasphemy all seemed to be sounding the tocsin for backlash and darker times, which we in *Gay Left* were struggling to understand.

Yet beneath the turbulent surface profound changes were taking place that were to transform gay life in the decades ahead. Gay liberation and associated movements jet-propelled shifts that were already underway from the 1960s, and inadvertently undermined our fervent belief that no change was possible in existing society. Perhaps, I began to suspect, the oppression of homosexuality in Western society was not so total after all. My own perspectives had developed in London and true to my father's wishes I had kept my activism largely separate from my family's life in South Wales – though after I became relatively well known as a writer I spoke several times in Cardiff at GLF, CHE and Gay Soc meetings in the university. From the mid-1970s there was an explosion of change that led to the setting up of gay groups in Cardiff, Swansea and Newport as much as cities like London, Manchester, Brighton, Leeds and Edinburgh, but even stretching into smaller towns. We saw the rapid rise of gay neighbourhoods, clubs, bars, bath houses, consciousness-raising groups, self-help groups, campaigning and social networks, phone lines, newspapers and magazines, faith organisations, health campaigns, especially from the early 1980s around HIV/AIDS, sexual subcultures, shops, restaurants, trade union factions, gay political caucuses in the major parties, legal campaigns, parenting support groups, campaigns against violence, student groupings, teachers' groups, gay business organisations and many more. Some of these had grown directly out of gay liberation groups. Members of the Counter Psychiatry group were to play a major part in setting up Gay's the Word bookshop and the community-run First Out café, both in London. Others were established as part of the wider coming out of the old queer world energised by the new generations of openly lesbian and gay people. Already by the end of the 1970s the all-embracing liberationist movement had morphed into a dense network of sometimes warring but closely interlinked, loosely organised but emotionally and sexually intertwined civil society groupings. Yet the growing presence of such a potentially powerful network of overlapping social worlds raised new questions about what direction to go in.

Gay liberation had claimed it could liberate the gayness of everyone and saw itself as part of a wider movement of social transformation. Increasingly, however, lesbian and gay politics was preoccupied with a much narrower identity politics, organised around a very specific type of orientation. The search for the gay gene or the gay brain from the 1980s was to be seen by many lesbians and gay men as an essential part of their claim to minority rights. Sexual orientation was claimed to be the necessary basis for legitimate social identity – and political success. In the USA, in particular, the idea that we were 'born this way' was seen as a necessary basis for recognised minority status.

The deeper reality, I believed, lay in the diversification of identities, the pluralism of subjectivities, and of political and cultural projects. There was no natural unity based on a given orientation. For me, how you saw yourself and described yourself was a preference, not a given orientation, a choice rather than a destiny. People could make their identities and ways of life to fit different desires, even if their sexual needs seemed fixed or personally essential to them, as mine did to me. Unity was a matter of political positioning, not of natural affinities. In many ways this way of thinking presaged the emergence from the 1990s of the new portmanteau acronym of LGBT or LGBTQ or LGBTQI – the initials varied – signalling the growing complexity of queer politics in the broadest sense. Lesbian, gay, bisexual, trans, queer, querying, non-binary, intersex . . . What unified them was less a specific orientation and more a political, cultural, even an ethical stance, an alliance that had to be constructed in the process of interaction with others. And the initials were, in principle, extendable infinitely. This was an alliance that contradictorily and ambiguously embraced both the politics of identity and the radical anti-identitarian challenge to the status quo.

This lay some way in the future for us in the late 1970s. Before that we were forced to confront an epochal crisis that threatened fundamentally all that had been gained in the previous decade. We were already, though we didn't yet know it, living and loving at the edge of a devastating epidemic – one which was to re-orientate my life profoundly. History had turned for many of us in the late 1960s with the rise of gay liberation. It was about to turn again with a vengeance.

CHAPTER 5
MAKİNG HİSTORY PERSONAL

THE PERSONAL AS HİSTORY

I was a bookish boy, reading anything I could get my hands on: novels, poetry, self-help books, women's magazines, daily, weekly and even old newspapers, and weekly and political journals. Through reading I expanded my own special private place and sustained a sense of who I really was. Of everything I read, however, history books of various sorts were my favourite from my early years onwards. My secret hobby as a young adolescent was to create imaginary countries, draw their maps and capital cities, and write their timelines. I knew that this had to be as deadly a secret as my sexuality, and I never whispered it to a soul in school, not even my best friends. I was peculiar enough already. But my youthful obsessions and reading gave me an immense if arcane store of random historical facts – dates, emperors, kings and queens, presidents and popes, shifting national boundaries and capital cities – that I never lost, and provided invaluable fodder for quizzes throughout the rest of my life.

My history reading may have begun with the romantic

heroism embodied in tales of 'our island story', but by my mid-teens I had graduated to weightier political histories. My mother gave me a copy of Lord Beaverbrook's *Men and Power 1917–1918*, bought in an Exeter bookshop after she made a family trip away when I was 15 (I had dropped hints after seeing it mentioned in the *Daily Express*, which was Dad's regular read, and which Beaverbrook owned), and later the same year I was given his predecessor book, *Politicians and the War 1914–16* as a Christmas gift from my parents.[80]

Political machinations and crises such as those unravelled in Beaverbrook's books thrilled me, and still fascinate me. I also got to know from my reading about historical schools and historians. I knew about the 'Whig Interpretation of History' long before I knew about the history of my sexuality. In school history classes as the swotty nerd, always asking questions, my enthusiasm did nothing to enamour me to my classmates, and there was certainly a heavy touch of compensatory showing off on my part, but it gave me a sense of my intellectual reach and capacities that covered over my other perceived inadequacies.

So, there was never any doubt what subject I would study at university. Professor Alfred Cobban was head of the History Department at UCL when I started in 1964, and in many ways he represented its presiding liberal conservative and gently sceptical ethos. He was a leading historian of France and of the French Revolution, and I vividly remember his favourite dictum. There are three things everyone knows about the French Revolution, he would say: that it began in 1789, it started in Paris, and it was led by the bourgeoisie. All wrong: it began in 1787, gathered pace in the provinces, and was spearheaded by the aristocracy. I wasn't quite sure at this stage what the impact of the French Revolution was, and had no sense that it was too early to know, but it was a revelation that there was any doubt about its central meaning, or whether it actually took place in the way historians had taken for granted, which seemed to be Cobban's ultimate mischievous message. His benign, pink-faced and white-haired presence hid a sharp iconoclasm, which bred uncertainty about the past in general, and about revolutions in particular.

More robust views about the industrial and social revolutions could be found in the University of London lectures on European history at Senate House of the notoriously Marxist historian Eric Hobsbawm, which we were encouraged to go to to broaden our perspectives, but with the hint that we might find them a little dogmatic. I was fascinated by the apparent certainty of his analysis and the neatness with which everything seemed to fit together, delivered in a mesmerising, still distinctively middle-European accent. I wonder now where I might have ended up if I had been under Hobsbawm's direct tutelage. I learn from the definitive biography by Richard Evans that Hobsbawm was wooed for UCL by its grand liberal provost, Lord (Noel) Annan, while I was there, and he did apply for the chair in French history at University College on Cobban's death in 1968, but though probably the most brilliant historian of his generation, his appointment was effectively vetoed by senior staff for political reasons.[81]

I quickly recognised that there were strong ideological and political perspectives and interpretations between historians rather than simply disagreements over evidence, and these were not innocent differences: they could be decisive. For someone indoctrinated in the sixth form with the certainties of G. R. Elton's 'Tudor Revolution in Government', with no real acknowledgement of the deeply conservative world view behind it, this was revelatory, but at the time I had plenty of prejudices but no fixed theoretical framework or clear ideology. I enjoyed grappling with multiple and conflicting interpretations. I became skilful at synthesising different views, weighing the evidence and coming to a judicious conclusion – a talent I never lost and a fateful barrier to any polemical ambitions I may later have had: I could always, unfortunately, see multiple perspectives on any question, to the frustration of many later interlocuters.

There was a glittering array of historical talent at the college in addition to Alfred Cobban. Joel Hurstfield was the sardonic Tudor expert, heir to the departmental tradition of studying Queen Elizabeth I, and a frequent presenter of witty television and radio programmes on Gloriana and her times. Harry Allen supervised American history in a benignly Cold War conservativism fashion. Also teaching American history was the dashing new lecturer, Andrew Sinclair, an Old Etonian and iconoclastic novelist, who cheerfully did no preparations for his lectures: he would come in with a pile of books that he would riff on during the lecture hour. Visiting professor A. J. P. Taylor, as a professional contrarian, could also offer an aria mischievously, and without notes, on any topic, and tutored me for a term. There was also a conveyor belt of younger future stars such as the political historian Peter Clarke, the Welsh medieval historian Rees Davies and the historian of welfare policy Jose Harris, on their way eventually to Oxbridge chairs. But somehow the sum was smaller than the parts. In many ways it was quite laid back. Cobban told us early on that if we didn't enjoy the lectures we should stay away, as long as we did the work for seminars and tutorials. The very pluralism and broad tolerance of the department militated against a sense of intellectual excitement and engagement, and for some of my fellow students there was no urgent invitation to mental adventure (or hard slog). I have no memory of being recommended to read books such as E. P. Thompson's *The Making of the English Working Class* as an undergraduate, though it was upending interpretations of nineteenth-century social history, which I was interested in. It was only after I began postgraduate research that it became a formative influence in my own outlook. I gravitated towards the history of political theory under J. H. ('Jimmy') Burns because it seemed to me to have an engagement with ideas and a sensitivity to shifting intellectual currents, which increasingly fascinated me, and which was elsewhere absent. I chose to work with him for my graduate studies.

Burns was an expert on Catholic social thought and English utilitarianism – an odd combination – and editor of the vast collection of Jeremy Bentham papers at UCL, and was a very sweet if not particularly directive supervisor. His supervisory philosophy seemed to be that we were all independent scholars now and could/would/should carve out our own research paths. When I went to him in a crisis of confidence in my first year and said I felt very depressed he seemed to whirl into a panic and I hastily said I would be OK, there was nothing to worry about. I had no desire to enter his particular field of research (though if I had I might have discovered earlier than other historians that the founding father of utilitarianism, Jeremy Bentham, had been a pioneer advocate of decriminalising sodomy), and had no alternative but to forge my own direction. I had a clear idea that I wanted to research some aspect of the socialist revival in Britain from the 1880s to the First World War, but I had no coherent plan of what exactly I could do. I began reading widely to find a more precise topic.

This was perhaps the most intellectually terrifying part of my life. I had been an adept undergraduate student, good at working on set essay topics. As a would-be gentleman scholar in a period long before closely monitored research training I floundered at first, and had the nervous collapse I tried to tell Burns about, depressed by the isolation, my uncertainty of direction and a deep fear of failing. But I did at last find a topic that engaged me, in the ferment of ideas in the years leading up to 1914 that were critical of traditional state socialism: syndicalism (like *The Miners' Next Step*); the theories of the Guild Socialists, who challenged Fabian socialism, including the work of writers like G. D. H. Cole and Harold Laski; other pluralist political theorists such as John Neville Figgis; and the radical cultural writers around the journal the *New Age*, under A. R. Orage. These represented a lively intellectual and political excitement that fascinated me. After quixotically abandoning the research to go into school teaching – the first of several apparently madcap decisions which have punctuated my career, with unexpected results – I did eventually produce an MPhil thesis with the title *The search for community: the role of political pluralism in English social criticism in the first quarter of the twentieth century.* I only ever published fragments of this in articles, and it lies gathering dust in the British Library and on my shelves, but unanticipated by me at the time it contains themes that underpin much of my later work, and survived my flirtation with Marxism in the next few years: concern with concepts of community, criticism of statist and authoritarian socialism, interest in cultural radicalism, and a recognition of the importance of pluralist forms of knowledge.

In the early 1970s, however, I had little sense at first of the relevance of what I was researching to my growing preoccupation with sexual politics. In my wide background reading I had come across the work of the pioneering socialist writer Edward Carpenter and the sexologist Havelock Ellis. Both were closely involved in the intellectual rethinking of the 1880s and 1890s that propelled the socialist revival, and were pioneering writers on homosexuality, women's rights and social emancipation, but I had made no immediate connection between them and my own shifting political concerns.

Everything changed as I began to take an interest in gay history and its broader relationship to the history of sexuality as a whole. I was seeking a history that was relevant to me and my personal and social experience, history as personal, and the personal as history, and my preliminary scratching around in the literature convinced me that the late nineteenth century was absolutely central to the history of my present for sexuality as much as politics. With the thesis out of the way, I returned to the 1880s and began researching the debates of the time around female emancipation and homosexuality as reflected in the work of Carpenter and Ellis.

Around this time I met the feminist historian Sheila Rowbotham at a meeting of LSE's Gay Culture Society, of which I was the co-convenor, when she came to hear a paper on Carpenter, a long-term interest of hers (she was later to write his definitive biography). We became warm friends and eventually we agreed to work on a project together. The original idea was that four of us would contribute essays on key contributors to the socialist revival and sexual politics of the 1880s and after, in part as a way of exploring parallels to what was happening around us in the 1970s. For various reasons the other contributors, Bob Cant and Gloden Dallas, dropped out, and Sheila and I went on to complete what became the first book to bear my name, *Socialism and the New Life*, focusing now simply on the personal and sexual politics of Carpenter and Ellis. My contribution on Ellis, with its attempt to analyse the merits and demerits of sexology and liberal sexual ideologies, proved to be a template for much of my later writing. I greatly admired a comment of Ellis', to the effect that he wrote about the shocking and disruptive as if it was absolutely normal and commonsensical. It was a lesson I never forgot.

More or less simultaneously to agreeing to do the book with Sheila, I got contracts for two other books that I conceived of entirely on the basis of still very preliminary research. Chris Cook, the director of the political archives research project I was working on was highly entrepreneurial and had his fingers in various publishing pies. He encouraged me to try to get book contracts and introduced me to two of his mates. The result was that I was quickly contracted to write books, and received generous advances for the time, on themes that as yet I knew very little about in detail but was convinced needed a different approach. The first was to be a general history of sexuality in modern Britain, what became my second solo book, *Sex, Politics and Society*, eventually published in 1981 as a volume in Longman's *Themes in British Social History* series. The other was for what became my breakthrough book, *Coming Out*, a history of homosexual politics and identity since the nineteenth century, published, like *Socialism and the New Life,* in 1977.

So, as *Gay Left* got underway, and I was writing heavily for that, I found myself also committed to three books on various aspects of sexual history, when up to that point I was only really in the foothills of research and had published virtually nothing on the topic. I felt that having the contracts would force me to deliver, and the advances helped my bank balance, especially when I became unemployed. I turned out to be right to take the gamble. But looking back I can only marvel now at my temerity and chutzpa, and at the courage or foolhardiness of the editors, William Miller at Quartet and John Stevenson for Longman, for taking the risk and trusting me. My career path was decisively reshaped after a couple of boozy evenings with publishers. Without clear forethought or planning, and for good or ill, I ceased being a proto-political theorist and became a researcher and writer on gay history and sexuality in general. For a while, at least, finding a secure job seemed secondary to this wider ambition.

These three early books published between 1977 and 1981 made my reputation but almost ruined what passed for my career. My much-extended research contract at LSE ended in summer 1977. Despite having two books out that year, and having edited five volumes of the project's findings to wide acclaim that largely accrued to Chris Cook as director of the project, I was unemployed and had to sign on the dole for the next year. I found it impossible to get a position in a history department, not just then but for the rest of my career. Professor Burns had said to me when I began research with him that mine was the first generation where he couldn't guarantee me a permanent job, because the expansion of the academic market was slowing down. He proved right, though not perhaps for the obvious reasons. As Ken Plummer wrote at the time, and I have frequently cited since, writing about sexuality still made you morally suspect, but especially, as I soon found out, in deeply conservative history departments. My adolescent aspiration to become a professional historian, and a professor of history, whatever that meant, came to nought. I was to be rescued by sociologists, ending up as a full professor in two successive sociology departments.

Given my subject matter, which demanded a variety of disciplinary skills to tease out the recalcitrant archive on sexuality, this was probably inevitable. University sociology in the 1970s was still an eclectic and flexible discipline, with its leading lights drawn from a variety of subject areas, from demography and geography, to philosophy, anthropology and history. Only the younger lecturers had formal qualifications as 'sociologists'. I could still find a welcome. In the end, I had no real alternative but to reinvent myself as a curious hybrid, a sociological historian or a historical sociologist, with sexuality as my central preoccupation – an ironic example of my growing conviction that identities were fluid, negotiable and relational, never quite one thing or another, though this time in relationship to my careering career rather than my fleshly desires. As a footnote, I have to add that in a long if see-sawing subsequent academic career my liberal history department never once invited me back to give a lecture or seminar, even though I became well published and have spoken in universities across the world. I had to find my intellectual home(s) elsewhere.

WRİTİNG THE HİSTORY OF HOMO/SEXUALİTY

My first ambition was to write a history that would contextualise the extraordinary changes in attitudes towards sexuality that were manifestly transforming British life, and certainly mine. I had lived through the important if limited recent legal changes in relation to abortion, birth control, divorce, censorship and obscenity as well as homosexuality in the late 1960s, and wanted to understand how and why these had occurred and how they had led unwittingly to the radical present I was living in. That inevitably posed questions I wanted to research and answer about what had happened since the grim 1950s, as I saw them, that I had grown up through, and how in turn that was related to the mythologised sexual repression of the nineteenth century. How had Britain become one of the most socially conservative countries in the world up to the 1950s and beyond, and yet by the early 1970s we were experiencing rapid changes and profound challenges to the moral status quo?

By the time I began researching, right-wing ideologues in America and Britain were already preaching about the breakdown of family values caused by the so-called sexual revolution of the 1960s, and were beginning to blame the sad decline of 'Victorian values', in the terms used later by Margaret Thatcher. That narrative did not fit into my sense of what the history actually was. My preliminary reading clearly told me that those Victorian values embraced denial of female sexual autonomy, child exploitation, punitive attitudes towards prostitution, rampant hypocrisy and repression of homosexuality, none of which I found desirable or praiseworthy. Yet the two narratives that were widely available, of a lost stability that should be re-found, and of a dark repression from which we were slowly clambering out in a teleology of progress, did not quite fit the analysis I was working towards either. The nineteenth century, as I saw it, was a battleground of conflicting values and attitudes, but our reading of them was made hazardous by the polemical power of the early critics of Victorian hypocrisy, stretching from Havelock Ellis and Edward Carpenter to Lytton Strachey and others in the Bloomsbury Group, whose progressive prose sometimes obscured the complex processes at work, and who between them had fixed in the mind an idea of a Victorian monolith of moralism. Moreover, the more I researched the more I grew convinced that understanding what had happened to homosexuality was a key to understanding our sexual history more generally. My research increasingly focused on the new concepts of homosexuality that I saw emerging in the late nineteenth century, through major changes in the law (notably the passing of the Labouchère Amendment in 1885, under which Oscar Wilde and many others were prosecuted); in sexology and medicine (as I traced it in the work of Havelock Ellis and others); and in radical political activities (exemplified through my work on Edward Carpenter and his circle). What was going on? What did these changes mean? How were they related to other changes, economic, cultural, intellectual and political? To my mind they were remarkably reminiscent of the similar ferment of my own time. A socialist revival: check. Problems in Ireland: check. The re-emergence of feminism: check. And new ideas about same-sex desire: check, check, check. In times of profound change, my reading-group exploration of Engels' *The Origin of the Family, Private Property and the State* had suggested, sexual relations were thrown into moments of radical disruption. I was living through such a time in the early 1970s. It became increasingly clear to me that something very similar had occurred in the 1880s and 1890s, and yet the existing literature barely noticed it, let alone documented it. My research increasingly focused on these shifts and become central to the story I told in my first solo book, *Coming Out*.

That title came at a late stage of the writing, though once I lighted on it it seemed obvious and right. Gay liberation was stressing the vital importance of being open about our gayness, of confronting a hostile world with our pride in ourselves, our lives and sexualities. It was a moment of affirmation, in a term used by Michel Foucault, an individual and collective act that made a difference. But I wanted to suggest this was not simply a vital gesture in the present but a historical process, whereby homosexuality had moved from oppression and denial into some sort of public presence, and one that was central now to my sense of self and identity. The actual history as I wrote it suggested a circuitous and complex process: there was no automatic progression from a miserable past to a more enlightened present. Nothing was inevitable, and it was already obvious that there was no ready agreement about our destination. But the central part of the story was that while there were complex forms of oppression – from religion, the law, science, medicine, and popular prejudice – there were also multiple forms of resilience and resistance.

Two in particular seemed to me inextricably intertwined: the development of embryonic campaigns to change the law, which I could trace back to the nineteenth century, and changing forms of identity embodied in nascent social networks and communities. I knew from my own experience that my encounter with gay liberation had transformed my sense of self and personal and social identities. I came to see that something similar was happening in the late nineteenth century in the circles around people like Carpenter, Ellis, Oscar Wilde, the criminologist George Ives and others, including working-class groups intoxicated by the poetry of Walt Whitman and the writings of Edward Carpenter. So, a study that tried to relate campaigns, social movements, and changing personal and social identities seemed logical, necessary and, for me, inevitable. It was a prism that offered the opportunity to understand profound and long-ignored changes.

There was, of course, already a substantial literature on the history of homosexuality, and the 1960s in particular had seen a new genre of reveal-all biographies and autobiographies, especially of Oscar Wilde and Bloomsbury figures like Lytton Strachey. These were overwhelmingly about men, however, and famous and iconic men at that. The former Ulster Unionist MP and supporter of the 1967 reform, Montgomery Hyde, had produced a worthy but limited study, *The Other Love*, and the eccentric Tudor historian A. L. Rowse had offered an overview of famous homosexuals that I found to be gossipy and useless for my purposes. The problem was that they all treated homosexuality, in line with the dominant ideology of the 1950s and 1960s, as at worst an exotic and quixotic deviation, or at best 'a very minor aspect' of sexual history, which is how the progressive campaigner François Lafitte, adopted son of Havelock Ellis, had described it. For me, however, it was increasingly obvious that the history of homosexuality, far from being a minor indulgence, was central to the social organisation of sexuality as a whole, and was inextricably linked to the wider history of heterosexuality. You could not understand one without the other, and my first two books tried to grapple with that relationship. *Coming Out* focused on same-sex love and its relationship to the wider culture. *Sex, Politics and Society*, meanwhile, was more concerned with the making and remaking of dominant sexual norms, values, ideologies and practices, and how homosexuality was constructed within them. The implication – though it took a while for me to make this explicit – was that both heterosexuality and homosexuality had histories that needed to be unravelled rather than taken for granted and assumed. Both, in a phrase that was to become notorious, were 'socially constructed', and each depended on the existence of the other: without homosexuality there could be no heterosexuality, and without heterosexuality there could be no homosexuality.

The key influence in my early thinking about these issues was a reading of Mary McIntosh's now famous but then rather obscure essay, 'The Homosexual Role'. I had known Mary since my first GLF meeting, and she was one of the most impressive people involved in the movement. After the women's split from GLF she became one of the most influential advocates of what became the socialist feminist strand of the women's liberation movement. Ten years older than me, she was then a senior lecturer in sociology at Borough Polytechnic in London. Much later, by a nice twist, when it became London South Bank University (LSBU), I became Professor of Sociology there, long after Mary left. After studying at Oxford, Mary had been a research student in the USA (from where she had been deported after involvement in a protest demonstration), a Home Office researcher and a sociology lecturer at Leicester University. There, she was part of a cohort of students and lecturers who were to become luminaries of British sociology, including some like Anthony

Giddens and Paul Hirst, who were later to influence my own work.

Mary was personally diffident in style, and became famous for calmly doing needlepoint in gay liberation and feminist meetings when all around her was in uproar, but she was a powerful and charismatic speaker and a popular teacher. She was to become a leading radical intellectual, involved in various feminist projects, a founding editor of *Feminist Review* and *Economy and Society*, and a member of the CPGB, though never a proselytiser for that cause. Her influence was widespread, but as an academic she never reached the heights she deserved. Her besetting problem was that though a powerful writer she hated writing and left few published works behind. What she did publish, however, were destined to be enormously powerful interventions in their field.[82]

'The Homosexual Role' is a great example of this. It was written during the debates leading to homosexual law reform in England and Wales in 1967 and deliberately published in a fairly obscure American journal, *Social Problems*, so as not to muddy the waters in the British controversies surrounding homosexual law reform.[83] But the essay fundamentally challenged the dominant argument made by reformers from Havelock Ellis onwards and central to the campaign: that homosexuality was a specific unfortunate but relatively harmless condition that some people had and others didn't. This was effectively a minoritising argument and the implication was that decriminalising homosexuality was *sui generis*; it could be achieved without effecting anything else. Mary argued, against this, that homosexuality was a social category, not an unfortunate attribute, and different societies organised homosexual activities in a variety of different ways, from institutionalised puberty rites to cross-gender practices. Western societies, however, had since the eighteenth century developed a specific homosexual role, a separate and inferior category for same-sex activities, which acted to control such practices and separate the sheep from the goats, the acceptable from the unacceptable. In the process the idea of 'the homosexual' as a separate, inferior, sad and sick type of person was born. The logic of this was that how we conceptualised and regulated same-sex practices was integral to particular forms of society and forms of regulation and control, and not simply the result of contingent prejudices or timeless oppression.

I came across the article early on in my GLF experience. It was circulated in photocopy like a *samizdat* document – I think Bob Mellors gave me a copy – and it was revelatory, providing a startling but resonant insight. Homosexuality as we knew it was a social invention, and so by implication was heterosexuality. Same-sex activities, as Mary made clear, existed in all types of society and across all historical periods, but the form with which we in Europe and America had become so familiar, that homosexual proclivities and behaviour were peculiar vices or psychological traits or personal failings of some people and not others, was a very particular historical phenomenon. The article immediately helped me to make sense of the evidence I was gathering about the shifts of meaning of same-sex practices since the nineteenth century, and it structured my central argument in *Coming Out*.

I did not slavishly follow Mary's case. She had offered evidence that an embryonic role was already emerging in the eighteenth century, and several contemporaries, notably Randolph Trumbach in the USA and later Alan Bray in Britain, focused their research on eighteenth-century London as the key moment. I recognised the importance of the evidence on this, but focused instead on the late nineteenth century, where it seemed to me recognisably modern concepts of same-sex activities and 'the homosexual' (under the guise of the 'invert', the 'urning', the 'third sex' or 'intermediate sex') began to emerge among writers like the German Karl Heinrich Ulrichs, the Hungarian Károly Mária Kertbeny (also known as Karl-Maria Benkert), the German Magnus Hirschfeld or the British Edward Carpenter, and were codified in sexological theory by a new class of sexual experts such as Havelock Ellis and Sigmund Freud. It was obvious that these did not map exactly onto concepts of the homosexual as appeared in the Gordon Westwood/Michael Schofield writings of the 1950s and 1960s and in gay theory from the late 1960s, but that in a way only confirmed the argument I was trying to develop: that ideas and concepts shifted, new meanings emerged, and shifting languages were critical to the emergence of new categories and ideas. A striking fact was that Kertbeny's invention of the homosexual preceded his definition of the heterosexual, underlining both that what we now readily call heterosexuality was the unspoken, taken-for-granted other, and that like homosexuality it had to be defined. Something new was happening.

The homosexual role, Mary had strongly argued, was a social category, not a simple description of a natural phenomenon, and its main function was social control. The obvious derivation of the idea of a role was Parsonian structural functionalism, which Mary had imbibed from her aborted American studies, and which basically assumed that all social phenomenon had a social function designed to assure social order. To this she added a touch of radical deviance and labelling theories that critical sociologists were heavily engaged with from the mid-1960s, when she became involved in the regular National Deviancy Conferences. This approach emphasised the critical importance of social labelling in defining categories such as the criminal, the prostitute, the hooligan, the drug taker and so on. It was a small step to extend this to the homosexual. I was already suspicious of any theories that suggested subjectivities and identities were a simple result of social organisation or pressure, whether from what was still mainstream American functionalist sociology or Marxist theories of economic determination, even in the 'last instance'. Rather than focus on role, important as that was in forcing a social analysis of sexual classifications, I increasingly began to think in terms of identity, which suggested to me the push and pull between social categorisation and self-creation. In *Coming Out* I tentatively formulated this as a tension between social definition and personal and collective self-definition, and the effects could be illustrated in various ways, from the complex subcultural ways of life of many homosexually inclined people to the campaigns and social movements that helped create contemporary gay life. It's fair to say I was not entirely successful in that task as I have been bedevilled for the past forty-odd years by criticism that I was arguing that the modern homosexual was a creation of the structuring and disciplinary powers, whether capitalism, the state, sexology or medicine. On the contrary, I was suggesting that we had created ourselves, though never in circumstances of our own choosing. *Sex, Politics and Society* was shaped consciously as an attempt to provide the wider context within which nineteenth- and twentieth-century definitions and self-definitions were being shaped.

One of the attractions of Michel Foucault's introductory volume to his projected *History of Sexuality*, which appeared in English translation in 1978, was that it offered a framework for understanding what the empirical evidence I was uncovering suggested to me, and that Mary McIntosh's work helped me understand.[84] I have often been categorised (and denounced) as a close follower of Foucault, and his work certainly did influence mine, but I had written all of *Coming Out* with the barest acquaintance with his work. What little reference to Foucault there was in that book was to his *Madness and Civilisation*, which makes quite a different argument from volume 1 of the *History*, which I read in French after submitting my own book. By the time I came to finish writing *Sex, Politics and Society* in late 1980 I tried to do justice to his explosive influence by discussing his work in some detail. I put it in a wider intellectual context, of Mary's work, the interactionist revolution in the sociology of sexuality generated by the work of John Gagnon and William Simon, both of who I later got to know, and my friend Ken Plummer, as well as new developments in psychoanalysis popularised by Juliet Mitchell in *Psychoanalysis and Feminism*. That book had taken many of my feminist friends by storm, and I found it invaluable as an introduction to the recovery of Freud from the biological determinism that had encrusted his work. I was stretching towards an approach that understood sexual identities as a complex interaction of bodily possibilities, psychic process and social organisation.

Foucault's work clarified some of these issues for me. It's difficult now to recall the intellectual excitement generated by Foucault's work among my generation of gay and feminist writers. I can remember discussing his arguments in London's mega-disco Heaven, shouting over the beat and battling the smell of sweat and poppers (from what we now know about Foucault's life in America this seems quite appropriate). The attraction was that it seemed to be taking radical theory beyond the increasingly tired iterations of crude Marxist economism, which sought to relate sexual change exclusively to the onward march of the economy and class conflict. Foucault had himself evoked a gestural economic explanation for sexual change by linking the genealogy of the modern apparatus of sexuality to capitalism, but that barely bothered his argument. What was exhilarating was his problematisation of traditional notions of sex and sexuality, the clear assumption that sexual categories were social and historical creations, and that the homosexual had a birth in specific historical circumstances that distinguished him (sic) from predecessor categories and social attitudes. He famously argued that the sodomite had been seen as a temporary aberration, a possibility in all sinful nature whereas the homosexual was now assumed to be part of a minority species. I had already got there myself in describing the historical shifts in concepts of same-sex desire from buggery to homosexuality, but it was exhilarating to have this confirmed by a major European theorist, who was also, if still discreetly, gay. More decisively, he linked the birth of modern sexuality to shifts in the forms and deployment of power. Power in his account was not a negative repressive force but a positive, constructive element inherent in various social relations. This freed me finally from futile efforts to find the direct causative links between capitalism and sexual organisation, which was the temptation of Marxist orthodoxy. The rhythms and turbulence of capitalism might provide the framework and possibilities, but sexuality had patterns of its own – a history of power and resistance, inextricably entangled, that produced complex sexual systems requiring their own historical investigation.

HISTORY FROM BELOW

Self-activity, active participation in the making of our own lives, was central to the gay liberation politics that was reshaping my life. It was also a critical element in the wider revolution in historical understanding and practice that was going on in the left. E. P. Thompson's boldly romantic and passionate *The Making of the English Working Class* had famously sought to rescue the struggles of the poor and exploited from the condescension of history, and of historians. And as the book suggested, the creation of a working-class consciousness and movement was an active process: the working class were present at their own making.[85] My friend Sheila Rowbotham was developing a similar approach to women's history, focusing on those 'hidden from history'. It was an easy jump to see parallels with the making of a gay minority.

I was strongly drawn to the History Workshop movement, founded at Ruskin College, Oxford, which sought to do two broad things I was deeply sympathetic to: encourage a broadening of the historical agenda to embrace the forgotten, the ignored, the denied, the condescended to and lost subjects of history; and create a history from below where new voices could be heard. Raphael Samuel, the founder and continuing inspiration of History Workshop, had an extraordinary range of interests, from the Irish in Britain, to the poor of the East End, from nationalism to the social impact of religion, from the origins of sociology to the history of socialism and communism, from family history to the history of film, and many others. He became an enthusiastic promoter of women's history and of my own first steps into gay history. The women's liberation movement in Britain had actually been sparked off following an intervention by Sheila Rowbotham at a History Workshop conference at Ruskin in 1969, and a founding conference was held in Oxford in 1970. Feminism was to be a central organising theme of *History Workshop Journal* (*HWJ*), founded in 1976. It soon billed itself as 'a journal of socialist and feminist historians', and after a period as an associate editor I became a full member of the editorial collective in 1979. The first edition of the journal had already carried my first academic article on the history of homosexuality, 'Sins and Diseases', which prepared the way for the fuller development of my arguments in *Coming Out*.[86]

In the absence of an intellectual home in a university

history department, *HWJ* was to be the focus of any sense of belonging I had as a historian for the next twenty years, especially in the first half of the period. The monthly Saturday afternoon meetings at each other's homes were convivial and intellectually demanding, dominated by the hyperactive Raphael. But though clearly respected and much loved by all of us, his views were constantly discussed and challenged by the other members of the collective, especially the strong contingent of feminists, led by Anna Davin and Sally Alexander. The feminist editors had given me strong support and encouragement in writing 'Sins and Diseases', which helped alleviate my sense of embattled isolation. The journal became a natural destination for key articles I wrote. After the first essay, I realise in retrospect, I unconsciously marked each stage of my intellectual development by an essay in the journal.[87]

My contributions were as rigorously reviewed and edited as any other submissions. The routine of reviewing articles, which came flooding in as the reputation of *HWJ* grew, was the primary commitment of the editors. *HWJ* in its early days had the policy of all articles being read and commented on by all members of the editorial collective, which inevitably meant that there were endless delays in making decisions, and a tendency to regress to the mean in final decision making. This also reduced the autonomy for editors of particular issues on what went into the journal. I was thrown into the deep end of editing an issue almost immediately upon joining the collective, and soon realised that whoever the editors of each particular issue were, Raphael would be whispering in your ear, either physically or on the phone. The collective as a whole, however, was exceptionally strong with innovative and challenging historians. I benefitted enormously from my involvement with them, and with the wider international movement for a more grassroots, democratic history.[88] I developed links with our sister journal in the USA, *Radical History Review*, who published one of my early articles in a special volume on the history of sexuality. I was also influenced by the young feminist historians in the USA who gravitated towards the journal. I found the early publications of Judith Walkowitz particularly valuable. Her account of prostitution and the 'making of an outcast group' in late nineteenth-century Britain was especially important: it echoed what I was trying to describe about homosexuality in the same period.

But Raphael was the undisputed centre of the History Workshop galaxy. He was a vivid physical presence, slight, intense, casually dressed as if he had just stepped out of an artist's garret, his comb-over hair always flopping over one eye, a frequently unlit roll-up cigarette in his hand until he gave up smoking quite late in his life. He could dominate a room by force of intellect, power of persuasion and not-so-subtly signalled deviousness.[89] Raphael's roots were in the CPGB of his youth, and he wrote movingly about the lost world of British communism. But he had left the party after the Soviet invasion of Hungary in 1956, and the rest of his life was a search for alternative forms of political action. He had been a leading light in the first New Left, starting its short-lived coffee shop in Soho, and editing one of the predecessors of *NLR*. He was an inveterate inventor of leftist groupings and institutions, though History Workshop was probably his greatest and most successful creation. History Workshop as a network of worker and radical historians was for him a social movement closely associated with other social movements of the 1970s, especially the women's liberation movement, but also embracing new union militancy, radical science, and challenges to authority in all areas of public life, especially academic history. In his wonderfully inspirational late book, *Theatres of Memory*, first published in 1994, he challenged the authority of History with a capital H as a discipline, especially as practised in university departments, for being hierarchical and hermetically sealed, stifling creativity and different ways of seeing the past.[90] He believed that history left to the professional historian was apt to present itself as an 'esoteric form of knowledge', fetishising archive-based research, encouraging intellectual inbreeding, introspection and sectarianism. For Samuel, history was not the prerogative of professional historians, and should not be left to them. It was rather a social form of knowledge, the work of many different hands embracing an 'ensemble of activities' in which 'ideas of history are embedded in a dialectic of past-present relations'. This was the domain of unofficial knowledges, whose sources were 'promiscuous', going way beyond the official documentary record and drawing not only on real-life experiences but also memory, myth and desire.

Such arguments resonated with my experiences and the experiences of many pioneering historians of sexuality. Much of the early feminist, lesbian and gay history in the 1970s and 1980s was developing outside the academy, and often against the academy, shaping alternative knowledges about the past, and creating a counter-history to challenge the silences and occlusions of the keepers of the official flame – in adult education, often through the Workers' Educational Association (where Sheila Rowbotham, Sally Alexander, Barbara Taylor and many others, including myself for a short time, taught), neighbourhood women's centres, informal history groups, and in national and local history workshops. I organised a few local gay history workshops, supported by Anna Davin and a handful of fellow pioneers, hoping to get a movement going, but it was too early in the UK in the 1970s, unlike in the USA where a flourishing community history was developing. There was not yet a base of would-be lesbian or gay historians to mobilise, though there was lots of lively interest. Raphael was not directly involved in these activities, but he remained the presiding inspiration of the wider grassroots movement for alternative histories.

Like many others I experienced the many sides of Raphael's chaotic and creative genius. I once invited him to be the keynote speaker at a conference I organised at the University of Essex in 1979 on 'History, Deviance and Social Control'. He turned up, very late, for his slot, and presented me, the by now extremely anxious and panicked chair of the plenary session, with two great piles of notes, on completely different topics, and asked me in front of a large waiting audience which talk I wanted him to give. I muttered that perhaps one on the theme of the conference might be best. He then proceeded to make up the lecture as he went along, strumming rapidly through one of the pile of notes, randomly quoting a page here and there, delivering a mesmerising talk that opened avenues everywhere and conclusions nowhere.

Notes like the ones he presented to me were characteristic of Raphael's zest for learning and mutual discovery. On his death he left behind thousands of pages of scribbled notes, now archived in the Bishopsgate Institute in London, the product of omnivorous reading and countless conversations. I was one of the many people he would phone out of the blue, usually as I was about to sit down for dinner, with endless penetrating questions, perhaps on the role of the unconscious in Freud, Auden and Isherwood's dash to the USA in 1939, the militancy of South Wales miners, the Social Democrats' split with the Labour Party, the legitimacy of the Falklands War, and I could hear him scribbling down my off-the-cuff responses on a sheet of paper in his huge scrawl, as if my haphazard thoughts were gems of insight. And though we never got personally close he went out of his way to be privately and publicly supportive. During one of my bouts of unemployment he suddenly came up with the idea that I should become librarian of the Marx Memorial Library in Clerkenwell. He remained convinced throughout the time we worked together that I was really a trained archivist, because of my work at LSE, and thought I would be an ideal foil for the various factions at the library. He promised to fundraise to find enough money to pay for me, but I had to thank him gently and decline. There was no suggestion that he had discussed the idea with anyone at the library, and in any case I had no desire to spend my life dealing with sectarian factions, and was still hankering after a university job. But it was a thoughtful and generous gesture.

I felt I embodied the contradictions in being a committed historian that Raphael was later to write so powerfully about. There was an inevitable tension between the sort of historical work I was striving to develop and wanting a conventional academic career, not least because I saw gay history as very much a political project, but at the same time I was committed to producing historical work that was of the highest scholarly standards. They were not contradictory ambitions. I could identify completely with the American historian and later warm friend, Jonathan Ned Katz, when he wrote in his pioneering *Gay American History*, which I read just as I was finishing *Coming Out*, that through our involvement in the movement 'we experienced the present as history, ourselves as history makers ... We experienced homosexuality as historical'.[91] Our historical work was a way of preserving and using memory and a way of giving voice to countless people, and thereby becoming part of and transforming the historical canon. The fundamental argument of Samuel's *Theatres of Memory* is that memory, far from being a mere passive receptacle or storage system is an active, dynamic shaping force that is dialectically related to historical thought rather than being some kind of negative Other to it. At stake in the historical endeavour is who controls memory, with all its ambivalences and ambiguity. Memory is always partial, and historians must always beware of seeking final Truth in recollections of the past. But if there cannot be a single Truth in the highways and byways of disparate memories, there are surely to be found pathways to multiple truths. Alternative histories do more than excavate a buried past, though that is a crucial if hazardous task. They also create and reshape memories that give greater meaning to the present, and do so through constructing alternative archives of emotion and by providing voice to feelings and experiences that may have been long stifled or forgotten.

Effective use of oral history is a key way of giving and preserving the voices of the forgotten or marginalised. Human beings, Ken Plummer has powerfully argued, are above all narrators and storytellers, and society can be interpreted as an endless series of stories that help make society work.[92] Sexual stories are integral to that: as old as society, they were long embodied in folk memories and oral tales, and became central to the more scientific efforts from the late nineteenth century. The narratives of the founding sexologists who attempted to define what a homosexual was are frequently constructed around the voices of the sexual subjects they encountered in clinical situations and then sought to classify and categorise. And what was gay liberation but giving voice, individually and collectively, to our lives? So, it is not surprising that oral testimony came to play an increasingly important role in a new history from the 1970s that wanted to recover the voices of the oppressed, including the sexually oppressed.

After finishing *Coming Out* I realised the next phase of my work had to be to link my developing theoretical concerns with an exploration of individual and collective memory through oral history. The challenge was finding the money and place to do it. Conventional history departments gave no indication that they might be interested. It was precisely at this moment that it became obvious to me finally that my academic future, if I had one, would have to be somewhere else rather than in traditional history departments.

INTO SOCIOLOGY

I was unemployed for a year from the autumn of 1977, but I continued working on *Sex, Politics and Society*, going daily to the British Library, still at that period located in its old British Museum base, and developing wider contacts with fellow historians. There weren't many of us at first. The period leading up to the publication of *Coming Out* was probably the period of greatest intellectual loneliness in my life, but I was slowly bit by bit making other contacts. I had read Randolph Trumbach's essay on 'London Sodomites' soon after it came out in the USA and felt here was a kindred soul. It turned out we had a mutual friend, and first met on the London Pride march in 1977. I met Jonathan Ned Katz in August 1980 on my first visit to New York, but we had already established friendly links by occasional letter. I greatly admired his documentary zeal in compiling *Gay American History*, even though I felt it could do with a brisk encounter with my own theoretical efforts.[93] As copies of *Gay Left* and then *Coming Out* circulated I gradually expanded my links across North America and in Europe, especially the Netherlands, Germany and Denmark. But it still felt a limited diaspora of historians. Among sociologists on the other hand there was growing interest in my work.

This was largely due to the efforts of Mary McIntosh and Ken Plummer. By the mid-1970s they were colleagues in the Sociology Department of Essex University, already one of the most dynamic and innovative in the country, and were building its reputation for work on gender and 'sexual deviance' as it was still generally known in academic circles. Ken and I were more or less the same age, and we moved in overlapping circles so got to know each other well. I was also an admirer of his work in developing a new sociology of homosexuality. As a student he had worked with Michael Schofield for a while (and became a lifelong friend of his), so was linked to the early empirical efforts to describe the homosexual experience in Britain, but his independent work was more obviously theoretically ambitious, and heavily influenced by gay liberation. First as his PhD then his first book, *Sexual Stigma,* he had produced a brilliant synthesis of the post-Kinsey studies of John Gagnon and William Simon, labelling theory and symbolic interactionism, which I found dazzling and an endless mine of insight. It was not the sort of sociology I could ever do, but I envied Ken's skill in generating and blending ideas with empirical evidence. He was now working on a major project exploring sexual diversity – from paedophilia to cross-dressing to S&M – using life history techniques, a project that was to feed into much of his subsequent work on sexual narratives. His research overall seemed a serendipitous complement to the sort of work I wanted to do next. Ken supported Mary and myself in bidding for a fellowship for me from the then Social Science Research Council (SSRC) to study the emergence of same-sex identities and communities in the late nineteenth and early twentieth centuries. The aim was to supplement and develop work I had begun in *Coming Out* by exploring new archival sources and doing oral history interviews with self-identified homosexual/gay men over 60 (which then seemed almost unimaginably older than me). I wanted to explore change over time in official attitudes and in how older men had seen themselves and their sexualities.

We got the money for a pilot study, and I began a year of intensive research in the supportive environment provided by the Sociology Department at Essex.

Its overall ethos put a strong emphasis on class, with a heavy reliance on quantitative methods. Mary and Ken's teaching and research opened up different perspectives. There was a small group of social historians, around Paul Thompson, already the leading British pioneer of oral history, and Leonore Davidoff, doing important work on class, gender and sexuality in the nineteenth and twentieth centuries, but my direct involvement was with Ken and Mary, and a small research group formed around us. Mary was at this point combining research on prostitution and the legal position of women with the more respectable membership of the Policy Advisory Group of the government's Criminal Law Revision Committee, which was focusing on an examination of sexual offences, especially in relation to the age of consent. Ken's work was attracting a number of highly able research assistants and former and current PhD students, including Annabel Faraday, who worked with both Ken on sexual diversity and Mary on lesbian history; Gregg Blachford, former comrade on *Gay Left*; John Marshall, later editor of *Gay Times*, both working on aspects of the sociology of gay men; and others. We developed a strong group identity, the main focus of which was the development of a book project that became *The Making of the Modern Homosexual*. This turned out to be a key text in the emergence of social constructionist analyses of lesbian and gay identities.

My period at Essex gave me two specific opportunities to develop my own historical work. The more traditional archival work that I did gave me privileged access to hitherto closed records at the Public Record Office and the Home Office, including records of sodomy cases more than a hundred years old, access to Oscar Wilde's medical examinations at Reading gaol, the original records of the Boulton and Parke 'Men in Petticoats' trial in 1871, and the manuscript of Sir Roger Casement's so-called 'Black Diaries' – transparently genuine and not the government forgery that some, especially in Ireland, still claimed. More challenging for me at first were my adventures into oral history.

Although many gay men, and some lesbians, had been interviewed for various projects over the years, and their testimonies had appeared in many forms, from early sexological works to the writings of people like Michael Schofield, Donald West and Ken Plummer, a systematic attempt to document the lives of a wide range of self-identified homosexual men – my particular brief – had not yet been attempted in Britain, and there was some nervousness from our funders, the SSRC, about it. At the time there were none of the university ethical guidelines that are now obligatory, but I followed closely the approaches and safeguards that Ken had evolved for his diversity project. I also had to learn the technicalities of recording the interviews. Technical skills had never been my strong point, and I had to battle in my pilot interviews with the usual crop of problems: batteries failing, mics not working, poor-quality recordings. And, of course, I had to find the interviewees, older gay men. I boldly took a small advertisement in the personal columns of *The Times*, which the editor personally had to approve, and surprisingly got three or four replies, of which I interviewed two. Some names were suggested to me by friends in the gay movement – I did some snowballing through these – and some men approached me as news of the project spread. In the end I collected the testimony of approaching thirty men.

As the ultimate published version of the interviews, *Between the Acts*, shows, I managed to garner a wide cross-section of stories across class, geographical, occupational and life experiences, with ages ranging from early sixties to late eighties. For some men it was the first time they had spoken about their sexual lives to anyone. One man was so garrulous, like an unblocked tap, that as I was leaving after a three-hour interview he was still shouting details of his life as I was walking up the street, with him trotting along beside me. Another told of his pain after his partner died many years before in the 1930s, and never being able to speak of his grief to anyone – I was the first person in forty years he had ever talked to about it. I felt privileged to be given these testimonies and I wanted to do justice to their narratives in book form.

The problem was that once again my career, and my ability to complete the project, tottered. I was funded by the SSRC on a one-year pilot project, to prove that there was sufficient material to justify a longer-term project. We certainly did that, but unfortunately, just as the funding came up for renewal, the Conservative government under Margaret Thatcher came to power, in June 1979. One of its first acts was to introduce a budget, cutting public expenditure, and among the budgets cut was that of the SSRC, long a bugbear of the New Right in the Conservative leadership. Funding of my project was chopped immediately, and once again I was out of work, with a few weeks' notice. I was completely disheartened and my first instinct was to abandon the project completely. I never did go back to it in full, though I was able to incorporate its findings into later work. The interviews languished for several years in their files, and I found it too painful to go back to them. Eventually, however, I felt guilty that I was letting people down. I asked Angus to help me edit the transcripts, and after he found it more and more difficult to find time as his ceramics career became more demanding, in the late 1980s I asked a young gay colleague in my new career as an academic administrator, Kevin Porter, to help me. We finally produced a workable text and *Between the Acts* was published in 1990.

Despite the by now predictable setback in my own career, the Essex work was to prove very influential in shaping the future direction of lesbian and gay history and sociology in Britain and beyond, and that was largely because of the unexpected impact of our book project, *The Making of the Modern Homosexual*. The book had grown out of our regular seminars and another project Ken and I were involved in, working on an Open University television programme on methods for sexualities research.[94] Overall, the various essays in the book were exploratory and often tentative in argument, but they offered a whole programme for future research and debate.

CONSTRUCTİNG CONTROVERSİES

We had intended to be provocative and to challenge easy assumptions about the meanings of homosexuality. Unfortunately, the book also inadvertently touched a quivering nerve in the nascent lesbian and gay studies movement, especially in the USA. An early signal of this came with a sharp polemical attack on the book, and on me personally, by the gay anthropologist Stephen O. Murray in the *Journal of Homosexuality*. He denounced us as a Marxist grouping with shoddy scholarship (calling us in the process the 'Sussex group', suggesting a certain confusion about the geography of England, and a scholarly shoddiness of his own), who were attempting to obliterate the distinctiveness of gay history and the continuity though time of a gay identity. At the centre of the critique was a furious rejection of my argument that homosexual identities were time bound and historically specific. This proved to be a trailblazer for a heated controversy that became known as the essentialist/constructionist controversy.[95]

Part of me was completely baffled by the vehemence of the response we evoked. Constructionist approaches were commonplace in sociology and arguments about the invention of class, national, ethnic or racial categories were at the forefront of social and cultural debates. And anyway, none of us, I think, saw ourselves as constructionists in the strict sense. It was a convenient if slightly mechanistic label to describe a historical approach that was alive to context, languages and meaning. Yet when applied to homosexuality such approaches produced fury and denunciations that seemed to me completely disproportionate. None of my writings denied the struggle for identity and rights; on the contrary they were explicit attempts to explain why such campaigns had developed at certain times in specific historical condition. And far from seeing identities as the products of regulation, the usual accusation, I sought to explain the processes of self-creation, taking different forms at different times. But what I couldn't in good conscience do was argue for a continuous gay identity through all cultures, societies and history. It patently wasn't true. It wasn't true of any other social category, and there was no reason to think it could be true of homosexuality. This was the burden of my critique of John Boswell's landmark book *Christianity, Social Tolerance and Homosexuality* in 1980. From its subtitle, 'Gay People in Western Europe from the Beginning of the Christian Era to the Fourteenth Century', to its final words it took for granted the transhistorical existence of a gay identity remarkably similar to the gay male identity that was by now hegemonic in American cities (the 'modern homosexual' whose history Mary, Ken and I had been tracing). I never met John, or had any direct communication with him, though I respected his enormous scholarship, language abilities (he claimed knowledge of seventeen languages) and commitment, both to his gayness and his Roman Catholicism, which is a constant subtext of his writings. We had a number of friends in common. But I found his essentialism challenging and frankly wrong, especially in light of the proliferation of so many varied queer identities in later years. He never indulged in the passionate polemics of other defenders of essentialist arguments, and his critique of constructionism was cast in the form of medieval philosophy, attacking us as 'nominalists' in a famous essay.[96] In practice, the various versions of his essay on this showed his position was more flexible than everyone tried to pretend at the time. But his attack on constructionism was to provide the benchmark for the controversy into the early 1990s.

In many ways I could understand the passions unleashed by what now seems an arcane and somewhat abstract debate. The argument that gays constituted a fixed permanent minority had been central to the development of homophile and gay liberationist politics, especially in the USA, despite the flirtation with ideas of polymorphous perversity and universal bisexuality in the days of GLF. They gave a sense of legitimacy to individuals struggling to affirm their identities, and an argument that fitted exactly into wider American discourses on minority rights. As the backlash against the gay revolution developed in the later 1970s and was supercharged by the eruption of the HIV/AIDS epidemic in the early 1980s, the cry that we were 'born this way' as a legitimisation of our claims for recognition resonated in a way the more nuanced arguments of people like myself could not as readily do. Yet to me this seemed a flimsy basis for a radical sexual politics. In and of itself claims of a biological essence to homosexuality could be deployed as readily as an argument to eliminate this curious minority phenomenon as to promote gay rights, as the later reaction to arguments about the existence of a 'gay gene' or 'gay brain' demonstrated.

This debate was at the height of the AIDS crisis in the 1980s, and the crisis undoubtedly fed into a reaction against constructionist arguments. Eve Sedgwick, author of *Epistemology of the Closet*, had clearly been influenced by constructionist arguments, and was warm and supportive of me when we met, but she expressed anxiety that in an era of AIDS it was a hostage to fortune to offer the radical right the idea that gayness was socially formed. In its place she suggested the need to adopt what she called, after Gayatri Spivak, a 'strategic essentialism', using an argument based on protecting minority rights even if you believed that the 'minority' was a historical fiction.[97] I was not against this. I had several times used arguments based on natural rights in specific political situations, and it was in essence not far removed from what Mary McIntosh had done in the late 1960s in publishing 'The Homosexual Role' outside the UK. My worry was that in taking a pragmatic position, you abandoned the struggle over values that was at the heart of the culture wars in the USA and beyond that, as the AIDS crisis dramatised.

I became increasingly convinced as the 1980s progressed that the only principled way of challenging the New Right consensus against the so-called 'gay agenda' was to engage with those debates around values that they had attempted to make their own, and in particular to defend our sexual choices from first principles. Same-sex desire and love were valid not because they were fixed by biology, which might or might not be the case – who could tell? – but because they spoke of basic human needs and personal truths. For me this opened a whole new agenda around rights, choice and justice, which I first touched on in *Sexuality and Its Discontents* in 1985, and wrote more fully about in *Invented Moralities* ten years later. In terms of my personal, political and intellectual trajectories that decade or so was to prove decisive.

MAKING LINKS

By the 1980s there was the beginnings of a boom of lesbian and gay writings, from fiction and poetry to books on cinema and art. Gay Men's Press, later known as GMP, and founded in the late 1970s by GLF pioneers Aubrey Walter and David Fernbach, had developed a credible list, while a profusion of feminist publishers, including the market leader Virago, The Women's Press, Sheba and Pandora were publishing lesbian writings. Mainstream publishers were now also eager to enter the fray. What disappointed me, however, was that there was no great burst of historical writings in Britain. The major exception was Alan Bray's *Homosexuality in Renaissance England*, which had begun, as he makes clear, as a rebuttal of my arguments in *Coming Out* but ends up as a radical challenge to the myth of the eternal homosexual. It is a work of intense, detailed scholarship on seventeenth-century London that helped to redefine early modern studies on sexuality.[98] I was friendly with Alan, though he always guarded his private and professional lives fiercely. Like Boswell, with whom he established a strong friendship despite sharp disagreements about historical interpretations, he was a deeply committed Roman Catholic, who struggled to combine his gayness with his faith commitments.

I think his day job as a senior tax civil servant in the Inland Revenue also defined a great part of his historical practice. He was a meticulous scholar who taught himself Latin to be able (like Boswell) to read original texts on same-sex friendship. I once travelled across the Atlantic with him to a conference in Toronto, and he spent the whole journey painfully translating Latin pieces. The labour was productive for him. It was to contribute to his brilliant but austere posthumous book, *The Friend*. This is in effect a defence of Church recognition of same-sex intimacy and love up to the nineteenth century rather than an attempt to impose contemporary gay meanings of same-sex partnership or 'gay marriage', as John Boswell had done, on an unknowable past, and certainly appears to celebrate celibacy over sexual pleasure. This reflects his own personal journey and took him a long way from the London Blues nights at the London nightclub Heaven, where I used to see him regularly.

For a long time Alan probably felt as isolated intellectually as I did. It was to be another decade and a half before the emergence in the early twenty-first century of a brilliant group of young 'Queer British historians', who deployed a range of interdisciplinary skills from literature to geography and cultural studies to illuminate queer life, and sought to distance themselves from the old guard, including myself.[99]

Until the new century I continued to find my main collaborative friends outside Britain. I already had good relations with Dennis Altman, who I first met through *Gay Left* in the mid-1970s. From his first book, on gay liberation, he had an uncanny ability to be a witness and acute commentator at all the key moments in subsequent queer history, from 'the Americanization of the homosexual' to the sex wars of the 1980s, though the HIV/AIDS crisis to battles over human rights and same-sex marriage. From the late 1970s I was closely involved with Dutch colleagues in a series of conferences in the Netherlands, and with collaborators in Germany and Scandinavia.[100] Cheap transatlantic travel from the late 1970s enabled me to build close relations with a range of fellow gay activists and scholars in North America. Randolph Trumbach taught me a lot about the inexhaustible treasure house of the sexual archive and the merits of patience in interrogating it. He was also a good companion in walking the New York waterfront. I stayed with him in Manhattan in August 1980 and through him met a number of lesbian and gay scholars, including the social anthropologist Esther Newton and the psychologist Charles Silverstein, co-author with Edmund White of *The Joy of Gay Sex*. On this same trip I built an intimate friendship with Jonathan Ned Katz, who was working on his new compendium, *Gay/Lesbian Almanac*. The following year, on my second visit to New York City, he showed me the final draft of the book: carefully swathed in rolls of protective plastic, he pulled it out of his kitchen fridge. His theory was if his brownstone burnt down his fridge was the most likely container to survive. This was a lesson I never forgot: keep multiple copies of your manuscript![101]

In these years and through these contacts, the main lineaments of what became LGBT/queer history were being laid down. There was above all a concern with the complex meanings and contexts of identity, and how these related to the vast range of expressions of same-sex and gender-variant behaviour. It was already clear that there was no single destination, and challenges to a single narrative structure were built into the work that had already appeared. Carol Smith-Rosenberg and Lillian Faderman had shown that same-sex relations between women (the 'female world of love and ritual') had a different trajectory to that of men, while Martha Vicinus was exploring the lives of single women and sexual relations between women. As the developing work of John D'Emilio and George Chauncey was to show, gay identities that seemed so resonant in the 1970s had to be made, not assumed. And the AIDS crisis in particular in the 1980s dramatised the plurality of different ways of being, and underlined that the world of (homo)sexuality was bisected by differences around race and ethnicity, class, religion, geography and age, which were to become fruitful areas for analysis and controversy in the decades to come. Identity could no longer be seen as a fate or destiny; it was a site for exploration and challenge.

If identity and its discontents were a major organising principle of the new history and sociology, another theme was beginning to appear: the contingency of heterosexuality. The temptation of a new lesbian and gay history was to explore it in its own terms, as a separate field. But that could never tell the whole story. Jonathan Ned Katz again proved a pioneer by writing a book on *The Invention of Heterosexuality*, which appeared in 1995,[102] but it was implicit in our early work that the stories of normative sexuality and heterosexuality were essential to any useful narrative on queer history. The modern organisation of same-sex desire is a product of a transformation of sexuality as a whole. This is now a central theme in contemporary critical sexuality studies, and its understanding has inevitably taken time to mature and is still ongoing. But already by the early 1980s it proved a necessary step as the AIDS crisis unfolded. A potentially cataclysmic crisis in sexual relations, it needed acute historical and sociological analysis to shape both the official and activist responses. Fortunately, the tools for this task had already been forged through the early development of a critical body of historical work on (homo) sexuality that I was privileged to be part of.

1. War time wedding 1944

2. Babes in arms 1948

3. With Santa, Dennis and Dad 1949

4. Student 1965

5. *With Angus 1972*

6. *Portrait by David Hutter 1972*

GAY LEFT

A Socialist Journal Produced By Gay People
Number 5 Winter 1977 Price 40 pence

GAY LEFT has come out. In this bigger bumper issue, Why Marxism, the Images of Homosexuality Season at the NFT, Lesbian Invisibility, Gays and Fascism, Gay Theatre past and present, Politics and Ideology, Approaches to Gay History, the Future of the Gay Movement, and much much more

7. Gay Left 1977

8. On the march, with Emmanuel Cooper 1977

9. Gay News book award 1978

*10. Angus as
potter mid-1980s*

11. Mark and Jeffrey 1992

12. Civil Partnership 2006

13. With Mam 2008

14. With Mariela Castro, Cuba 2013

15. *Conferencing in Mexico, November 2015*

16. *Exhibition in memory of Angus, Ruthin, Wales, 2018, with Mark and Ziggy*

CHAPTER 6
LOVE AND LOSS

SAN FRANCİSCO: AUGUST 1981

I paid my first visit to San Francisco in August 1981, just as the first warnings of the outbreak of mysterious illnesses among gay men were appearing in the *New York Times* and the gay press. For my generation San Francisco had become the mecca for gay men looking for liberation and new ways of life, replacing Amsterdam as the destination of choice for those wanting to escape the still-stifling sexual restrictions of Britain. It promised greater relaxation and intimacy than the frenetic pace and threatening spaces of the mythical birthplace of gay liberation, New York, which I had visited the previous summer. It was less intimidating than the vast, amorphous, polycentric Los Angeles, which a friend of mine from gay liberation had once travelled to in hope and desire, and had been so befuddled by the profusion of destinations he could travel to in the city that he had not left the airport and took the first available flight home.

From the late 1970s cheaper air flights had made regular trips to the east and west coasts of America both easy and increasingly desirable. San Francisco, Carl Wittman's refugee camp for homosexuals, had a special aura that particularly appealed to me. San Francisco had its tradition of cultural radicalism going back beyond the hippies and flower power of the 1960s. It also had a strong claim to be up alongside New York as the pioneer of gay liberation, with activists proclaiming 'gay is good' and trans people resisting police raids in the years before Stonewall. It was also increasingly famous as the focus for effective and sophisticated pro-gay interventions in more conventional local politics. Harvey Milk had been the first openly gay man to hold an elected position in the USA when he became a supervisor in the city. His assassination in 1978 had aroused a huge spontaneous outpouring of grief and resistance, presaging an increasingly polarised sexual politics. And it was the home of unprecedented sexual experimentation and freedom, wittily and enduringly portrayed in Armistead Maupin's *Tales of the City* stories. Originally written for newspaper serialisation, the first two novels had appeared by 1981, and I was already devouring them when I went there for the first time. I had a vague hope that, like the central gay character Michael ('Mouse') in the first novel, I would meet the love of my life in the Safeway at the tip of Castro. The tragedy was that San Francisco as the prototype and very model of laid-back sexual liberation was already shadowed by violence, political reaction and illness, and was soon engulfed in cataclysmic loss.

On the surface at least, little had yet changed that summer of 1981 in the sexual vibrancy of San Francisco. I spoke to a number of people about the newspaper reports and they were clearly worried, but did not yet see a deadly threat, and there was more than a suspicion that this unknown set of illnesses was in some convoluted way part of a plot to contain the gay revolution, perhaps concocted by the CIA. Most of the time the looming disaster was little more than a background echo. I spent a lot of time getting to know local activists, and exploring gay history and theory with them. Gayle Rubin was still researching her PhD on the leather communities of San Francisco, which had all but disappeared in gentrification by the time the work was finished many years later. More immediately, she was working on her defining article, 'Thinking Sex', which became central to emerging critical lesbian and gay studies, and was to be at the heart of the Barnard Conference on Sexuality controversies over sexual pleasures and danger in 1982. The conference heralded the so-called 'sex-wars' among feminists, pitching pro-sex feminists against the anti-porn radical feminists who up to that point were defining feminist debates on sexuality.[103] I also met Amber Hollibaugh, who had earlier contributed to *Gay Left* about the 'White Nights' riots in San Francisco following the acquittal of the killer of Harvey Milk. She was an inspirational speaker and activist, and her exploration with Cherríe Moraga of butch–femme and intersectional relationships in the lesbian community was to be trailblazing and highly influential.[104] Both Gayle and Amber were to be key figures in advocating pro-sex alternatives to the rigidities of radical feminist theories of sexuality. They were members of the San Francisco Lesbian and Gay History Project, established in 1978, alongside Jeffrey Escoffier, Estelle Freedman, Eric Garber and Allan Bérubé, all of whom I met for the first time that summer.

I felt particularly close to Allan, a warm and generous man who embodied the values I saw and sought in radical gay history, especially his embracing of history as a grassroots activity, giving voice to people hitherto excluded from History with a capital H. A university dropout, he had been enthused by reading Jonathan Ned Katz's *Gay American History*, and had become an engaged community historian who saw history as a form of activism. By 1981 he had an enthusiastic following in the Bay Area for his slide shows of lesbian and gay history, and I envied his ability to communicate passionately to a wide community audience who felt he was telling their history.

His first slide show, 'Lesbian Masquerades', was based on stories he came across about women who passed as men. Presented to an emotionally charged audience in a crowded San Francisco Women's Building in 1979, he received a standing ovation, a response echoed in many other subsequent performances. Much later, his work was re-interpreted as an example of trans rather than lesbian history, vividly confirming that the way we tell and make history has no fixed or pre-determined meaning, even as we weave meaningful narratives from it. But whatever the stories we tell one another, they have to have a grounding in empirical detail to make them live and breathe, and Allan's history worked because it resonated with the experiences and knowledge of ordinary lesbian, gay and trans people.

In 1979 a neighbour gave him a box of letters and photographs written by a group of gay men who served in the US military in the Second World War, and who continued to write to each other after they had been sent overseas or to different bases in the US. Through these Allan began to trace the development of friendships, networks and a sense of common identity against institutional rejection that was to eventually feed into the dramatic transformation of gay identity from the late 1960s. The slide show he put together, 'Marching to a Different Drummer', was shown more than a hundred times at community meetings across the USA in the following decade. It also provided the basis of the research that underpinned his widely read and influential book, *Coming Out Under Fire: The History of Gay Men and Women in World War Two*, published in 1990. Looking at my copy recently I re-read

Allan's dedication, thanking me 'for doing the work so early on that made it possible for me to begin imagining that I could write this book'. I was deeply moved, and reminded yet again how such connections across distance were what made the birth of LGBT and queer history possible at all.

On this first visit I was staying in a gay hotel near the Castro, the focal point of the burgeoning gay community, with my travelling companions that summer, Micky and Philip Jones, who I had worked with at LSE, both among my closest friends. That gave plenty of opportunity to explore the highly charged erotic aspects of the community in the streets, shops, bars, bookshops, bathhouses and backrooms. In that village-like atmosphere it was possible to see our gayness as a whole way of life, where our sexualities were simply aspects of ordinary everyday activities, and where our lesbian and gay identities were proudly affirmed at the same time as being taken for granted. Yet it was difficult to avoid an undercurrent of anxiety about an upcoming firestorm. The Milk murder had undermined any easy optimism about automatic political progress, and as was happening back home the broader political context was moving sharply to the right. California was proving the laboratory not only for sexual experimentation and personal exploration but also for a new conservatism.

Its former governor, Ronald Reagan, had recently assumed office as US President in January 1981, backed by the New Right, and there were ominous signs that a new form of anti-gay politics was developing nationwide as part of the new conservative coalition. Anita Bryant, the queen of orange juice advertising, had pioneered a first effort at a virulent anti-gay politics in Dade County, Florida in the late 1970s. California itself had seen a massive defensive mobilisation against the Briggs Initiative, which sought to ban lesbians and gay men from teaching in Californian schools. The campaign against this had first brought Harvey Milk to prominence. Despite the defeat of the initiative in the 1978 elections, it provided a marker for the potential political and cultural effectiveness of anti-gay mobilisation. This became a vital aspect of the emerging Moral Majority movement (neither moral nor a majority as the postcards I bought in San Francisco observed), and an increasingly powerful part of the New Right. An online definition I recently came across nicely sums up its objectives: 'The Moral Majority was "Pro-life" and supported Bible-based morality, Classroom prayer, "Family values", "Free enterprise" and Israel; they opposed Communism, the Gay agenda, Pornography and Sex education'.

Sexual issues were increasingly a central part of right-wing politics in a way they had failed to become for the left, despite the fact that the new social movements that had emerged in the 1970s were broadly progressive when they were not explicitly revolutionary. The attack on the so-called 'gay agenda' by the right was not only a direct challenge to the values I most closely adhered to; it was proving an effective wedge issue to undermine all progressive values.

And it was precisely at this historic moment that a new disease or set of diseases, affecting above all, it seemed, gay men, emerged. It was inevitable from the first, as was dimly becoming clear in that summer of 1981, that what we soon came to know as AIDS was likely to be more than a routine health challenge. Little did we know then that it was destined to become a catastrophe for the communities where it first manifested itself, with San Francisco to the fore, and the harbinger of a worldwide pandemic. And at the heart was the question of gay sex, and how it was lived.

For many in the rapidly expanding lesbian and gay communities, for women as well as men, sexual freedom was the very definition of what the gay revolution was about: freedom to have multiple partners, to experiment with different types of relationships, to explore sexual needs, to engage in hitherto taboo practices, like the lesbian S&M that Gayle Rubin had become an articulate advocate for. I was fascinated by the dynamic new sexual scene and happy to throw myself into it. But I was also aware that American gay writers were beginning to sound the tocsin. Larry Kramer's *Faggots*, published in 1978, had already denounced promiscuity among gay men as mindless and out of control. Andrew Holleran's *Dancer from the Dance* portrayed an emptiness behind the glittering fast sex lives of gay men in New York and Fire Island, also in 1978. Even in a less frenetic gay culture in Britain, heated controversy about gay male lifestyles had broken out in the columns of *Gay News*, with the film critic Jack Babuscio leading the defence of sexual experimentation. I worried about a certain callousness and carelessness in large parts of the gay scene alongside its warm sense of community, and picked up many of these debates in the book I began working on soon after my visit to San Francisco: what became *Sexuality and Its Discontents*, finally published in 1985. By the time it appeared it was obvious that AIDS had cast an unprecedented searchlight into all our preoccupations, and had become an existential threat to the ways of life we had so painfully built up since the 1960s.

'LOVE AND PASSION, STILL IN FASHION'

Margaret Thatcher's victory at the 1979 election heralded a new politics of the right in Britain that threatened all that I had taken for granted: the social democratic settlement of 1945, which had shaped my life chances; the collectivist values that had become so embedded in my own; and the sexual breakthroughs heralded by the eruption of lesbian and gay and feminist politics in the 1970s. Thatcherism as we came to know it was still an evolving set of policies and practices, but it was already clear, especially to those of us influenced by the contributions of Stuart Hall in the pages of *Marxism Today*, that it was a hegemonic project in which a revivified sexual conservatism (summed up by the Thatcherite phrase 'Victorian values') was a central part of a broad radical right agenda. Prior to the Falklands War in 1982 it was not at all clear whether the experiment could get a grip on the massively resistant state and civil society. But her victorious seizure of the crisis and the collapse of the traditional left following the Labour Party split had by 1983, following a massive general election victory, made a more radicalising dynamic possible – at exactly the moment when AIDS emerged in Britain as a real, not potential, threat.

My personal circumstances had stabilised a little in the early 1980s. From late 1980 I was involved in a new relationship, though I won't identify him further as he has asked to remain anonymous in this book. He introduced me to a new group of younger friends mainly drawn from people of African-Caribbean and Asian descent, and through him I developed an increasing appreciation of anti-racist and what later was to become known as intersectional politics. Over many heated discussions I came to see that my early analyses of sexual identity were highly culturally specific and obscured the diversity of sexual subjectivities, even in Britain let alone across global distances. When not in university (in Cambridge) my new partner moved into our Archway house. Angus and I at last stopped sharing a bed, and we built a new room in the roof space as our bedroom. For a while I found myself commuting three ways between London, Cambridge and Canterbury, where by now I was based. I had a new job.

After the abrupt termination of my Essex research, I had two part-time teaching jobs: lecturing in history at Bulmershe

College, a teacher training school near Reading, and lecturing on sexualities and society at the University of Kent at Canterbury. Both looked promising for future positions. Halfway through my contract at Bulmershe a full-time lecturing job came up, covering my areas of teaching, and I was warmly encouraged by my head of department to go for it. My nemesis came from an unexpected source. A friend and colleague decided to apply as well, phoning me just before the closing date to say she was only doing it for the experience, and reassuring me she wouldn't get it. I wasn't so sure. On the day itself I managed to make a spectacular hash of the interview, and my friend sailed through, with the support of the external advisor to the panel, a leading feminist historian. I had no problem with the decision itself, but I was devastated at my inability to seize a golden opportunity that seemed mine for the taking. I felt an abject failure, and never went back to Bulmershe, cutting myself off from friends there. Many years later I unexpectedly met my former head of department at a meeting. I was by then a university dean, he a senior educational bureaucrat. Neither of us mentioned this personal debacle.

This was the crisis of my career, and one of the few times in my life when I got cataclysmically depressed over a sustained period. If I couldn't get a job in Bulmershe, a small college that few had heard of, where I already taught a course apparently successfully, could I get a job anywhere? Were my research and books as much of a career killer as they now seemed? For the first time I seriously considered giving up on an academic career. The odds seemed just too firmly against me, especially in a darkening political and cultural climate.

Then miraculously I got a full-time lecturing post at the University of Kent, thanks largely to the support of Mary Evans, director of the new MA in women's studies there, and her partner David Morgan, who was the dynamic and innovative chair of sociology. The position was to replace Professor Ray Pahl, best known then as an urban sociologist, who was going on partial research leave for three years. Ray himself was deeply sceptical and wary of me at first, and opposed my appointment, but we eventually established a surprisingly warm relationship that continued after I left Kent. I co-taught one of his courses with him, on micro-sociology, and much later our research interests coincided as we both wrote on friendship, but my main brief was to teach the sociology of sexuality at undergraduate level, and on the new MA.

On the advice of my friend, Ros Coward, I had taken the precaution of having a coaching session on how to do interviews before the formal interview at Kent itself, at the very least to try to restore my confidence. Despite my scepticism it proved surprisingly useful. As a result, for the first time I felt I was able to take command of the interview and project myself. Before this I had flunked most interviews for a job I wanted. After, I got almost every job I went for. More crucially, I felt for the first time that here at Kent was a team that was keen to support my intellectual interests and positively wanted me to contribute to their courses. I subsequently learnt that my appointment hadn't been that straightforward, with the old guard representatives on the interview board very hostile, no doubt seeing my research interests as frivolous, and not really sociology at all. But to my lasting gratitude David got it through.

My appointment, from the beginning of 1981, coincided with the beginning of my new relationship. Despite the three-way commuting, the nearly three years I spent at Kent were among the happiest and most satisfying of my academic career. My undergraduate course was already successful and popular, the MA was a pioneering effort in Britain, and I developed a close sense of identity, both with many students and with other teachers on the course, particularly Mary Evans, already a renowned feminist scholar, who directed the programme.[105] I found my involvement with the MA immensely challenging and stimulating, and I learned a huge amount through it. However, as one of only two men on the faculty, the fact that I was teaching what was becoming the most divisive topic for feminists as the 'sex wars' raged became controversial for some students. If I had continued at Kent I would probably have had to give up on it, despite by this time being one of the best-known historians/sociologists of sexuality of my generation. But true to form, Kent gave up on me first: I was only ever on a temporary contract during Ray's leave, and the hope held out early on that a new permanent post could be carved out for me was thwarted by the government cuts to university funding in 1982. Kent suffered badly from these and had to lose rather than gain posts. I managed at last to get my PhD qualification while at Kent, based on the work I had done for *Sex, Politics and Society*. And I now seemed to have been fully recognised as a promising sociology teacher, which shaped the rest of my career. But by the summer of 1983 I was back on the job market, bruised for a second time within five years by government economic and financial policy and budget cuts.

1983 was one of those years that echoes in the memory, and not only or primarily because of my erratic career. It was a year that brought the political and personal into noisy concordance. The June election had seen the crashing defeat of Michael Foot's Labour Party, with its divided leadership and disastrous catalogue of utopian aspirations (not for nothing was its election manifesto described as 'the longest suicide note in history'). The party escaped by a whisker being pushed into third place by the SDP–Liberal Alliance. Something had ended in British politics, and the Thatcherite agenda was clearly ascendant. My career aspirations seemed nothing compared to this disaster. But what particularly marks 1983 for me was that it was the year when the HIV/AIDS threat began to loom ever larger in Britain – and in my personal life.

In *The Swimming-Pool Library*, the novelist Alan Hollinghurst portrays 1983 as the year everything changed, a before-and-after moment in gay history. The narrator comments, 'My life was in a strange way that summer, the last summer of its kind there was ever to be. I was riding high on sex and self-esteem – it was my time, *my belle époque* – but all the while with a faint flicker of calamity, like flames around a photograph, something seen out of the corner of the eye'.[106] AIDS is never mentioned in the book, but its shadow looms over the story. The melodrama suggested by that quote eerily echoes my personal timeline. I was closely following the path of the epidemic through American contacts and in the American and, increasingly, British gay press, and trying to understand how it related to sexual history and changing sexual mores, the history of epidemics and other sexual panics in the past. But as yet I had no direct personal experience of the unfolding disaster.

In the USA by the end of 1983 about two thousand people had died (by the time of writing this in 2019 some seven hundred thousand Americans have died of HIV infection), but there was still considerable controversy about its causes and likely consequences. In the UK there had been only a handful of cases. Terrence Higgins had died in June 1982, reputedly the first British person to succumb to what was still known as GRID – gay-related immune deficiency. I did not know him, but his young lover, Rupert Whitaker, was a friend of my partner's. A retrovirus given the name of LAV (lymphadenopathy-associated virus) had been identified in France as a likely infective agent, and in the USA the HTLV-III (human T-cell lymphotropic type III) virus was unveiled as the likely cause. It wasn't until 1984 that researchers resolved that they were the same thing, and HIV became the accepted acronym for the virus, with AIDS the official descriptor of the syndrome. So, there was an air of uncertainty about the set of illnesses, and uncertainty breeds fear and loathing. Although numbers were still tiny in Britain the tabloids were already in full homophobic flow, while hospitals insisted on barrier nursing, hairdressers refused to cut suspects' hair, refuse collectors wouldn't pick up rubbish and undertakers were refusing to bury the dead. Conservative commentators seized the moment, drawing apocalyptic moral lessons in what in the next few years became a torrent of hate-filled writing. Even in the gay community there was continuing doubt about the significance of the emerging epidemic. HIV deniers, including some I had known in leftist organisations, sang their song for many years to come. For those in the front line, however, the reality was overwhelming – and terrifying. In the summer of 1983 it became increasingly obvious that Geoff Horton, Angus' lover, was at risk from whatever this syndrome was.

Geoff was a medical doctor and had hitherto been healthy and active. But he had come back from a holiday in Turkey with Angus earlier in 1983 looking ill, constantly exhausted, his psoriasis out of control, with mysterious lesions soon appearing on his body. I knew enough already to realise what this indicated, but for a while no name was whispered. But by the autumn he had almost died several times of pneumonia and other illnesses, each time pulled through by hospital treatment and a strong will to survive. Angus temporarily abandoned his ceramics, giving up his studio to care for Geoff. He survived until the spring of 1984, and was among the first twenty people to die with AIDS in the UK.

Geoff's was the first AIDS-related funeral I went to.

Angus wore a multicoloured jumper Geoff had given him, to celebrate a life, not mourn a death. Many more funerals, some traditional church services, others creative attempts to reflect an individual life, were to follow in the years ahead. By the end of the decade I knew countless people living with the syndrome: former lovers, close friends, colleagues, my students. Angus himself had been diagnosed just as Geoff was dying.

This direct encounter with illness and death was to shape my life for the decades ahead: my sexual interactions and relationships, my friendships, my research and writing, my career path. It taught me many things, some of which I am still filtering. But above all it taught me the power of love. In a lecture I gave at Brown University in Providence, Rhode Island in the mid-1980s, a young faculty member asked why I always wrote about sex, not love and relationships. I thought this a bit unfair, as my own self-criticism was that I rarely wrote about sex in favour of identity, subjectivity, social attitudes and the like. But looking back I can see that from the mid-1980s I increasingly wrote about intimacy, friendship and love. The hardest lessons I tried to distil and make sense of were learned in the AIDS crisis, starting in 1983.

FEAR AND LOATHING

The Thatcher government did many things I detested but its greatest sin of commission and omission from my perspective was its silence on HIV and AIDS until the epidemic seemed in danger of getting out of control by 1986. I felt a growing bitterness that while I would regularly see closeted Tory MPs dancing their nights away in the gay megaclubs in London, like Heaven and Bang, none were prepared to distance themselves from the wilder extremes of radical rightists echoing the worst excesses of American Moral Majority rhetoric. Prime Minister Thatcher, despite having favoured partial decriminalisation of the law on homosexuality in 1967, and having close gay associates, including notorious paedophile Peter Morrison as her Parliamentary Private Secretary, was quite happy to make numerous anti-gay comments. Some of her wider supporters went much further. All this rhetoric culminated in the passing of the notorious Section 28 of the Local Government Act in 1988. The more immediate concern in the years after 1983 was the neglect of the threat posed by HIV until the crisis year of 1986, the moment that AIDS was for the first time being presented as a threat to the heterosexual world as well as the gay world.

It was becoming clear to me that while much of the tardiness was due to ideology and political opportunism, there were deeper forces at play. I began to argue that we were in the midst of a partial and unfinished sexual revolution, a staging post in what I later called the 'great transition' between traditional authoritarian patterns of sexual regulation and newer, more individualistic and tolerant forms. Ironically, I gave a presentation of a paper on this theme on the day Margaret Thatcher resigned, 22 November 1990. My point was that despite her political success in wielding together a hegemonic project from diverse forces, the sexual politics of the 1980s was shaped by much more than her individual political will. The AIDS crisis acted as a trigger for deep uncertainties about rapid sexual change to become focused on scapegoated Others, with gay men a specific target. It was noticeable how a steady increase in public acceptance of homosexuality dating back to the late 1950s was dramatically halted in the mid-1980s as the epidemic developed. Fear entered into the soul of the lesbian and gay community, and something amounting to terror scoured the emotional response of many people in the wider community, as the work on the affective impact of AIDS by Matt Cook powerfully demonstrates.[107] One of Angus' oldest friends from drama school days just dropped him when his diagnosis was confirmed. She loved Angus, she said, but couldn't risk her child.

At least two gay-identifying men I had known well suddenly discovered their heterosexuality and got married to women. Others declared their celibacy. I learned from a friend with HIV recently that he had not had sex since 1999, loathing his own body and scarred by the feared reaction of others. But there was also another side to the response. The growth of self-help organisations like the Terrence Higgins Trust, Body Positive, The Lighthouse, the Landmark and many others from the mid-1980s, whose growth and impact I was to explore in a research project with Peter Aggleton in the early 1990s, revealed a positive and creative response from the community itself. There was a genuinely mixed, fearful and resistant flux of emotions as we confronted the unknown.

For some in the community there was a sense of guilt that we had brought this disaster on ourselves. Had our 'high-risk' behaviour caused the epidemic? Did the use of poppers by gay men cause unknown mutations in the body? Was anal sex inherently unhealthy, weakening the immune system? Had we encouraged a cultural backlash with our outlandish behaviour? While it was obvious that frequent changes of partners without protection was likely to maximise cross infection, I was always clear that HIV/AIDS was a natural disaster that could not be blamed on particular groups of the population. There were no guilty or innocent victims as Princess Anne once seemed to suggest; there were simply many thousands of people – survivors, not victims – living with HIV. And one of the reasons why so many did survive the early panics and discrimination was because of those self-help organisations. It turned out that the community-building work of the 1970s had not been in vain. The development of a culture of safer sex was a powerful individual and collective symbol of that: a massive change in personal practice developed from community-transmitted knowledge of what was likely to be risky behaviour.

One of the anxieties in the community from the start of the epidemic had been that it would lead to the re-medicalisation of homosexuality. A major achievement of the first ten years of gay liberation had been the way it had seized the definition of homosexuality away from the traditional diagnosticians of sexual aberrance and deviance. This was one of the themes I explored in my book, *Sexuality and Its Discontents*, which I had struggled with writing in the early years of AIDS. It reflected in its narrative and arguments the changing course of the epidemic. Conceived as the final volume of what I called an 'informal trilogy' alongside *Coming Out* and *Sex, Politics and Society*, it was an attempt to show how contemporary sexual politics, and the epidemic in particular, had been shaped by the sexual discourses that had defined the binary, hierarchical sexual and gender orders since the nineteenth century. One of the implications was that what constituted the truth of sexuality and gender was not a product of nature but a highly contested historical, social and political struggle.

The history of the previous decade now confirmed and reaffirmed to my mind the relevance of this argument. The 1974 success of campaigners at the American Psychological Association to remove homosexuality from the list of disorders in the bible of clinicians, the *Diagnostic and Statistical Manual of Mental Disorders*, had not been a triumph for a scientific rethink. It was a quite blatant triumph of political struggle, in effect saying that the right to define the nature of same-sex activities belonged to the people who lived them, not the medical or scientific establishments who categorised them. HIV/AIDS represented an obvious medical emergency that demanded proper scientific knowledge and targeted medical intervention. But it was equally true from the start that the mysteries of the retrovirus and the opportunistic diseases it led to could not be solved without the active collaboration of the communities most affected, like the gay community; and history had fortuitously produced an active and sophisticated community of identity and interest that was ready and able to respond.

It soon became clear to many activists that here was an epidemic where those most at risk had to take the lead in combatting it. In practice, in Britain, this took the form of community-based organisations, and a growing alliance between grassroots activists and the professional doctors, epidemiologists and researchers (many of whom, of course, were themselves lesbian or gay) who made up the public health tradition. It was this alliance that was to propel the Health Secretary, Norman Fowler, to persuade a reluctant government, and even more reluctant prime minister, to adopt a more proactive policy in 1986–87.[108] The resulting campaigns and policies, with their emphasis on fear-inducing imagery and risk avoidance strategies, aroused huge criticism, both at the time and since, from all sides, but there can be little doubt that this bizarre, pragmatic alliance between AIDS activists, the medical establishment and government had the ultimate effect of ensuring that the epidemic in Britain was better contained than in many similar countries.

And it did not ultimately inhibit, as some feared, the continuing autonomy of the AIDS activist movements themselves. The sharply perceptive and polemical writings of people like Simon Watney, alongside the more sober, empirically grounded works of the *Social Aspects of AIDS* series and similar works, created new forms of knowledge about the epidemic that both reflected and reshaped evolving community values and norms. The fightback against AIDS had started among the communities most affected and most excoriated by the panic. The government mobilisations against the epidemic had, however, been spurred by the fear of a heterosexual epidemic. In the process, those at highest risk were in danger of being forgotten. The launch at the end of the decade of the 're-gaying' of AIDS campaign, led by Gay Men Fighting AIDS in response to the downplaying of the differential impact of the epidemic on gay men, testified to the inspired self-activity of many in the lesbian and gay community.

THE LONG MARCH RENEWED?

Sexuality and Its Discontents received the (American) *Socialist Review* book award in 1985, as a recognition, in part, of its effort to relate the sexual crisis to a wider political analysis. My concern was still how to combine commitments to gay liberation with a radical, socialist analysis, on the assumption that one was not possible without the other. My perspectives were, however, evolving. I increasingly came to believe that the totalistic and absolutist politics of the 1970s were highly problematic. There was not going to be a big bang moment when social contradictions and confusions could be magically resolved. Nor, on the other hand, in the darkening political climate, was there much hope that a progressive sexual agenda could gain any purchase in the short term. That seemed to rule out both the revolutionary and the reformist approaches. This was disastrous when it was obviously the reactionary agenda that seemed to be catching fire, and this posed troubling questions about the viability of the analysis and political practice of the left in general, and of myself in particular.

I had rejoined the Labour Party in 1981 and for a while was drawn into the fraught battle in my constituency, Islington

North, to replace the local MP, who eventually defected to the Social Democratic Party. The campaign was led by local Labour activists but with a heavy input from various factions of the Trotskyist left, most of whom would deny to your face that they were 'entryists' even though you knew that they knew that you knew their true affiliations. I got on well with some of the individuals but was increasingly alienated by their conspiratorial politics. Nevertheless, the result of these activities from 1983 was the election of a new young Labour MP in North Islington, drawn from the Bennite left but with a policy of 'no enemies on the left' – Jeremy Corbyn. I neither warmed to him then nor in subsequent years, especially when he emerged from relative obscurity to become leader of the Labour Party in 2015.

I was increasingly drawn after the disastrous election of 1983 to efforts to recreate the Labour Party as a wide reformist movement that could appeal to a broader constituency. For this reason I supported the new party leader Neil Kinnock's modernising efforts to rebuild the Labour Party, despite his less than enthusiastic embrace of pro-gay politics at the time. Kinnock, of course, like myself, had come from the Welsh mining valleys, and I felt an almost instinctual identification with what he was trying to do, even as I distanced myself from his 'Welsh boyo' style and caution about sexual politics.

The Welsh pragmatism and low-key scepticism about millenarian politics that I saw in him was increasingly my politics too. It shaped my attitude towards the great miners' strike of 1984–85, which was to prove the defining and final battle of 1970s industrial militancy. From the start I had my doubts about the National Union of Mineworkers' (NUM) refusal to hold a ballot before striking, not just on democratic but on simple tactical grounds: it gave the moral initiative immediately to the government, which used it successfully to underpin and strengthen state power. The struggle of the striking miners was heroic but doomed. I knew from my brothers in South Wales that there was great scepticism among other trade unionists about the would-be revolutionary leadership of Arthur Scargill, and a weary stoicism rather than an insurrectionary enthusiasm among the striking miners themselves.

Of course, from a gay perspective there was an important other angle. I knew many of the people, like Mike Jackson, Nigel Young and Jonathan Blake, involved in the Lesbians and Gays Support the Miners group, and was proud and supportive of their work with striking miners, especially in the Dulais Valley of South Wales, mythologised and immortalised much later in the film *Pride*.[109] I laughed and wept with nostalgia and inspiration when I saw the film, and celebrated the NUM's support in the Labour Party for gay rights that followed. But I couldn't escape a sense of melancholy and loss. When in the face of crushing and inevitable defeat the Rhondda miners proudly and defiantly marched back to work in March 1985, everyone knew it was the end of coal mining in the Valleys, which had shaped them and me. Lewis Merthyr, with its sister pit Tymawr, had ceased work in July 1983, and was soon to become the site of Rhondda Heritage Park. Within a couple of years the last pit had gone in the Rhondda, and the hillsides could finally return to green, but with the future of its inhabitants uncertain. Few regretted the end of a dangerous and exhausting job, but an industry was destroyed with no obvious replacement, and a whole way of life was fundamentally threatened.

I had in 1978 initially resisted the arguments of Eric Hobsbawm's Marx Memorial lecture, 'The Forward March of Labour Halted?', but it was difficult to avoid its logic after the historic defeats for the traditional Labour movement of 1979, 1983 and 1985.[110] I was increasingly drawn to the analysis being developed in the pages of *Marxism Today* by Hobsbawm, Martin Jacques, its editor, and particularly Stuart Hall on the nature of the crisis and the evolution of Thatcherism as a coherent hegemonic strategic response. Stuart's often collective work at the Centre for Contemporary Cultural Studies (CCCS) at Birmingham University, especially *Policing the Crisis*, first published in 1978, resonated powerfully with me, especially in showing how 'mugging' was socially constructed in the course of the 1970s as a mechanism of an increasingly coercive and racist state to reinforce social order.[111] It was an obvious extension to see how the reaction to 'homosexuality' could be deployed in the same way. Hall's eclectic deployment of the theoretical approaches of Louis Althusser, Michel Foucault and Antonio Gramsci in this and other works coming out of the CCCS influenced my own analysis in *Sex, Politics and Society* and later *Sexuality and Its Discontents* of the regulatory and coercive potentiality of the liberal reforms of the 1960s, and the anti-gay mobilisations in the USA and Britain in the wake of AIDS. His developing analysis of the ups and downs of Thatcherism from the late 1970s into the 1990s made *Marxism Today* essential reading. I got to know Stuart reasonably well during the 1980s, though we never became particularly close. He examined my PhD, and later I worked with him for a period with Barbara Taylor on an abortive attempt to set up a sort of socialist review of books, which never really took off despite some pleasant Saturday afternoon meetings.

Stuart was a wonderfully warm and charismatic speaker and a penetrating political thinker who influenced a generation of left activists seeking an alternative to the determinism and narrowness of traditional left thinking. He brought a focus on racism and its deployment in the New Right authoritarian populism to the heart of socialist thinking, and was supportive of feminist and gay liberation analyses. His writings on identity fitted well into my own sense of its fluidity and contingency, and its characteristic hybridity. And while he was an effortless theoretician, he wore his theoretical sophistication lightly, unlike some of his contemporaries. I liked his avoidance of theoreticism: theory, he famously said, is a detour on the way to something else. He wrote little, however, specifically on issues around sexuality and gayness, despite his own involvement for a while in a gay men's discussion group at Gay's the Word bookshop in London. This was partly compensated by the work of a number of his former students at the CCCS, like Frank Mort and Lucy Bland, whose historical work I admired.

Marxism Today itself published little specifically on sexuality and gender. Of its leading intellectual figures, Eric Hobsbawm had long distanced himself from countercultural and what later became known as 'identity' politics. In my own few direct dealings with him I found him warmly distant and sceptical. Martin Jacques, the editor, was more ruthlessly concerned with what was directly relevant to contemporary political preoccupations. Apart from occasional reviews, my contributions to the journal came in response to the AIDS crisis and its aftermath. In January 1987 I published an article in the journal (with the title supplied by Martin), 'Love in a Cold Climate', where I argued strongly that AIDS had 'come to symbolise an age where fear, prejudice and irrationality battle against reason, responsibility and collective endeavour. At the moment it is by no means clear which will triumph'.[112] Martin proved to be a brutal but highly effective editor, turning a potentially dry piece into one of the most influential I ever wrote. Compared to the icy logic of Hobsbawm's essays and the passionate clarity of Stuart's, Martin's own writings were often surprisingly dull, which didn't stop him getting a lucrative contract as a columnist for the Rupert Murdoch-owned *Sunday Times*, then being boycotted by trade unions.

But he was a brilliant editor and ideas entrepreneur, who was to help reshape political debate on the left. He was a polar point in the debates within the CPGB about its future direction.

Though a number of colleagues and friends from the women's and gay movements were members of the CPGB – such as Mary McIntosh, Elizabeth Wilson, Angela Mason, Sarah Benton and Bea Campbell – I remained deeply sceptical about its historic legacy. I was never remotely tempted to join. I could never identify with its history of rigid centralism, its long subservience to Moscow, and its traditional cultural conservatism, even as it strove to remake itself. Nevertheless, I regularly participated in the annual Communist Universities from 1978 into the early 1980s, which were festivals of ideas and debates, including around sexuality. I spoke a number of times, but it became increasingly fraught as the divisiveness of the American sex wars, with radical feminists denouncing socialist feminists as being essentially male, reached even this bastion of the old left. A special place in hell was reserved for gay men by the lesbian separatists. I had the dubious pleasure of being denounced at a conference session by the Black lesbian radical feminist activist Linda Bellos as a malign influence. The whole episode, especially the escalation of radical feminist denunciations of other feminist women as well as gay men, is captured in Elizabeth Wilson's novel about the impact of feminism on women's lives, *Prisons of Glass*.[113]

Despite my caution about the CPGB, I was drawn to the Eurocommunist thinking around *Marxism Today*. It promised a complete break with the Stalinist past, and a more open, democratic and pluralistic politics. Paradoxically, several of my own friends continued to identify with the old guard, the 'tankies' (those in the party who had supported Soviet military intervention in Eastern European socialist states), for reasons I have never really fathomed, and they remained anxious and resistant as the paper moved ever closer to abandoning conventional communism. This trajectory became clearer after the publication of the 'New Times' edition of the journal in October 1988. It had been preceded by an away-weekend conference that I attended, which proved one of the most dynamic and important of my life. As Martin wrote later, the special edition that followed:

> was, in a multitude of respects, a tour de force. It sought to understand the profound changes in society, culture and the economy, to which neo-liberalism was a response and to which it sought to lay claim. Post-fordism, globalisation, the state, the changing nature of the culture, post-modernism – this being the era of 'post-' this, that and everything – and much else besides were put under the analytical searchlight. It was *Marxism Today*'s boldest project of all and attracted enormous publicity.[114]

It's interesting now to note that in the litany of transformative events, there is no mention of the shift in gender and sexual relationships that preoccupied me and many of the younger members of his staff, like the young Suzanne Moore, soon a leading feminist journalist, and Chris Granlund, later a highly renowned TV director. There is no doubt, however, of *Marxism Today*'s growing influence on the mainstream centre-left. The traditional far left tended to see the New Times concept as a sell-out to Thatcherism, but the reforming elements in the Labour Party saw in it an invaluable political framework. It offered a recognition of the importance of a project to widen the appeal of the left to broader social and democratic forces, which Kinnock supported in the 1980s, and which was to reach fruition in the Tony Blair leadership of the Labour Party from the mid-1990s. I certainly saw its relevance to my own political trajectory. By then *Marxism Today* was long gone: it ceased publication in 1991, apart from a special edition in 1998 to denounce the New Labour government under Blair for surrendering to neo-liberalism, which ironically many on the left had long condemned *Marxism Today* for. The core group around *Marxism Today*, including Jacques, Hall and Hobsbawm, resisted embracing Blair. I in the end did not.

That was a long way off in the early 1980s, and I was still casting around for political and theoretical frameworks that could make sense of my particular concerns. A significant influence on me during the early to mid-1980s was the work of the Argentinian political theorist Ernesto Laclau and his partner, the Belgian theorist Chantal Mouffe. I was invited to participate in their Discourse and Theory discussion group held monthly at City University. While I found Chantal much clearer, I struggled for a while with the language and conceptual complexity of Ernesto's analyses. He was totally unaware of the opacity of his style, and I once surprised him by saying that the chapters he had written in his book with Chantal, *Hegemony and Socialist Strategy*, were among the most difficult things I had ever read. But I was attracted to the sharp break with orthodox Marxism and economic and class determinism that their book represented. Rather than seeing the working class as the predestined historical vehicle for social transformation, they emphasised the importance of building a movement for change that linked the new social movements, including feminism, gay liberation, anti-racist politics and green politics, with other popular forces. But rather than assuming a necessary linkage between the various social groupings as in orthodox Marxism, their emphasis was on the ways in which the various antagonisms and conflicts of social life could be articulated with one another to create a hegemonic project around notions of radical democracy.

Although written in a different register, this fitted well to my mind with Stuart Hall's analyses (he was a regular attender at the Saturday discussions). While Hall focused on conjunctural analyses, Laclau and Mouffe were laying the outlines of a different political strategy. They were to become enormously influential on many left intellectuals across the world, from Greek radical economists to Argentinian Peronists. Back home, Chantal was much later to become an ardent supporter of Jeremy Corbyn as a prophet for a left populism. I am not sure this was what anyone would have expected at the time, and I certainly could not follow her there.

All of this in the early 1980s contributed to an increasing fraying of any sense I had of affinity with Marxism or the hard leftism of the Bennite tendency in the Labour Party. Through Ernesto I had been recruited onto the early steering committee of the Socialist Society, set up to provide a space for dialogue between the Labour left and the wider far left. I organised a meeting at the University of Kent, which produced an enthusiastic if eclectic response from academic staff, but which led nowhere, and I later participated in the first national conference. Here I met Raymond Williams for the first and only time, chairing a session he spoke at. He was charmingly avuncular and distant. Tony Benn also spoke, with his usual passionate intensity, and gained a standing ovation. I stood and applauded like the rest but felt increasingly alienated from the hero-worshipping of, to my mind, such a hopeless prophet. Soon after this I dropped out of the Socialist Society and out of any remaining fantasy that there was a natural affinity or realistic hope of agreement between all those who described themselves as on the left.

A large part of the problem was that the debates on the left that I found so intellectually absorbing (not least because of my earlier engagement with political theory) were not fully, if at all, addressing my lived experience in the midst of an epidemic that was increasing in intensity and redefining my personal and emotional life. More and more, I sought to define myself in terms of the fundamental values that gave meaning both to my personal life and to my wider allegiances. 'Socialism' as we had known it no longer seemed sufficient. Trying to think through a way forward that expressed my experiences more accurately than a catch-all description or ideology, I began work in the late 1980s on a series of essays on basic social democratic values, which formed the starting point for my book *Invented Moralities* – finally, after many ups and downs, published in 1995. Of all my publications, this was my 'AIDS book', an essay in what I described as 'radical humanism'. It was a book shaped and given meaning by the despair generated and magnified by the epidemic and the political and cultural response to it, tempered by the resilience and hope I found in those living with HIV, and most notably in my own immediate circle from Angus.

'PRETENDED FAMİLY RELATİONSHİPS'

AIDS gave the anti-homosexual agenda an electric charge that was manifest in a range of interventions from people in high places in Britain. The former Tory Solicitor General, Sir Ian Percival, otherwise forgotten to history, saw in AIDS evidence that 'so many had strayed so far and so often from what we are taught as moral behaviour'. The Evangelical Christian head of the Manchester police, Sir James Anderton, opined that the spread of AIDS was a result of 'degenerate behaviour', and that 'people at risk are swirling around in a human cesspit of their own making'. The eventually unsuccessful action against London's Gay's the Word bookshop by HM Customs and Excise in 1984, for stocking allegedly obscene books, including advice on safer sex, was widely seen as evidence of a shift from policing crime to policing people – and especially lesbian and gay people in the wake of AIDS.[115]

The clearest example to me of the callousness and cynical indifference of government policy was the introduction of what became infamous as 'Section 28'. This was on the surface a minor clause added to the Local Government Bill trundling though Parliament, introduced by a right-wing Tory backbencher, and ostensibly a response to the attempts by lesbian and gay activists in local government to advance 'positive images' of same-sex relationships. Its immediate spur was the publicity given to books directed at children like *Jenny Lives with Eric and Martin* and *The Milkman's On His Way*, whose author David Rees we knew a little and had stayed with us a few times. These were seen by the conservative right as dangerous corruptors of youth and a threat to the family. Behind this was the continuing fear of AIDS, and the tightening grip of homophobia that propelled it. In the wake of the sense of emergency that the government interventions on the epidemic in 1986–87 generated, public hostility towards homosexuality reached a peak. According to a British Social Attitudes Survey shortly before the clause was introduced, 75% of the population agreed that homosexual activity was 'always or mostly wrong', with only 11% believing it to be never wrong.[116] Dame Jill Knight, a leading proponent of the clause, rediscovered the threat of GLF, and its by then fifteen-year-old manifesto to justify her actions. 'This all happened after pressure from the Gay Liberation Front [which had died in 1973, so there couldn't be that much pressure]', she declared later. 'At that time I took the trouble to refer to their manifesto, which clearly stated: "We fight for something more than reform. We must aim for the abolition of the family". That was the motivation for what was going on, and was precisely what

Section 28 stopped'.[117] It is difficult, however, to see a cause and effect between mildly informative texts on sex education and the actual wording of the clause, which forbade the promotion by local authorities of 'homosexuality as a pretended family relationship'. The carelessly ambiguous and catch-all nature of the wording of the clause – Did it include schools or not? What did the promotion of homosexuality involve? What was a 'pretended family relationship'? – betrayed a wider anxiety about sexual and cultural change. And in one sense it was effective. Although no prosecutions under Section 28 were ever brought, it did effectively inhibit any further local government or school initiatives for fifteen years.

But like all such fear-driven moral panics, it had contradictory effects and unintended consequences. In the immediate wake of its introduction it produced a political furore in parliament, which I found myself inadvertently drawn into. I was at a conference in Amsterdam during the House of Lords discussion of the clause in mid-December 1987, my travel and accommodation financed by a British Council grant. A peer angrily wondered whether this was evidence of a publicly funded body deliberately promoting homosexuality. I was a bit taken aback, if flattered, to learn that my name had been mentioned in the parliamentary report on radio. Was I such a threat? The developing opposition mobilised liberal as well as lesbian and gay opinion, with the arts establishment to the fore. I chaired a forum for *Marxism Today*, published as a discussion in the paper, which brought together various people, including Matthew Parris, gay former Tory MP and political commentator, the novelist and critic Adam Mars-Jones, and the activists Angela Cooper and Femi Otitoju. Between us we covered a range of opinions, from blaming gay militants to attacking moral conservatism, but all united in opposition to the clause.[118] Labour and other ostensibly progressive politicians, including Neil Kinnock, were at first more ambiguous in their response to the clause, fearful of hostility from traditional supporters, but eventually rallied round.

It proved a decisive marker in the gathering challenge to moral conservatism: in retrospect we can see that this was the high-water mark of the sexual agenda of the New Right in Britain. In reality, Margaret Thatcher herself was ultimately more interested in advancing economic individualism than in opposing sexual change, though it didn't seem so at the time. In practice, once you proclaim the sovereignty of individual choice in economic matters it becomes difficult in the end to erect barriers to sexual and relationship choice. Despite the moral conservatism she publicly advanced, and the criminal delay in addressing the AIDS crisis, in historical perspective we can see that Mrs Thatcher in reality presided unintentionally and counterintuitively over a major growth in LGBTQ self-organisation and an ever-expanding gay world, opening the way to major advances in the late 1990s and the new century.

More obviously, the threat posed by Section 28 galvanised the sense of common interests in the lesbian and gay community, and energised activists. From late 1970s the movement had weakened under the impact of political defeat and AIDS, and men and women often seemed to have different priorities, though many lesbians worked closely with gay men in combatting the epidemic. The struggle against Section 28 mobilised people in new ways, above all by reaffirming that, despite differences, there were common imperatives in resisting government actions and what was increasingly described as homophobia. Lesbians famously took the lead in some of the most symbolically significant acts of resistance: the lesbian invasion of the BBC *Six O'Clock News* and the abseiling into the House of Lords during the Section 28 debate.

More significantly in the long term, Section 28 led directly to the founding of Stonewall, fronted by well-known actors like Ian McKellen and Michael Cashman, and involving experienced activists like Lisa Power, which was to become by far the most successful campaigning group produced by the movement. It developed the lobbying skills that had characterised the old HLRS, avoided the bureaucratic tendencies that had beset CHE, and by rejecting mass membership in favour of a top-down lobbying structure ensured it would not be troubled by the sectarianism and fissiparousness that had enfeebled earlier attempts at a coherent national campaigning organisation.

Stonewall came to represent a new stage in lesbian and gay activism. Unlike the HLRS it was an openly lesbian and gay organisation that was committed to active organisation for rights and justice. It represented what I began to identify at this time as the moment of citizenship, where the focus was on legislative campaigns to achieve formal equality. Ostensibly ranged against it was the more rumbustious grassroots activism and advocacy of direct action of OutRage!, founded among others by Simon Watney and Peter Tatchell, which I saw as representing the moment of transgression, aiming to disrupt the symbolic order and focusing on dramatising injustices. These two moments, of belonging and recognition on the one hand and challenge and subversion on the other, seem to inhabit different, polarised spaces. But, I began to recognise and argue, they were actually two aspects of a single movement. Without the sober-suited elaboration of the meaning and practice of full citizenship the movement lacked all sense of direction and precise goals. But without the grassroots energy and dramatic interventions of the dissidents and transgressors, the movement lacked soul and passion. I found myself supporting both. They were necessary to each other.

Beyond the activism, by the end of the 1980s it was obvious that the wider LGBT communities were becoming increasingly embedded in British civil society, despite, or perhaps because of, all efforts to marginalise or contain them. Single again, after 15 years or so of close couple relationships, I was probably in these years of the late 1980s more deeply involved in the gay commercial scene than ever before or since. Gay bars and clubs were booming, and becoming much more overtly sexual, despite AIDS. With the rise of gay villages in Manchester and Soho and elsewhere, and the consolidation of networks and social activities, it was more possible than ever before to lead an openly sexual and pleasure-driven life. The sense of living on the edge of a volcano heightened rather than squashed the sort of hedonism I had seen in a soon-to-be-threatened San Francisco at the beginning of the decade. Yet at the same time, the grinding impact of the epidemic had reshaped the priorities of many people living with or side by side HIV. The widespread adoption of condoms and safer sex practices by gay men, including myself – it was estimated that quite rapidly by the mid-1980s the majority of gay men had adopted safer sex routines with little positive support from the state – was a triumph of grassroots self-education and community activism. The rise of an AIDS service sector of and for gay men, women at risk, Black and other minorities, people living with haemophilia, drug users and young people, including helplines, information services, hospices, social and respite centres, befriending and buddying opportunities, research, fundraising and treatment activism, was a testimony to people's ability to resist and survive even the worst effects of the epidemic.

İN MEMORİAM

Angus' life with AIDS exemplified for me the devastation wrought by the epidemic, and the resilience of those struggling with it. The artist and filmmaker Derek Jarman once remarked sardonically that you don't live with AIDS, you die of it. And for Derek as for Angus this was true. AIDS was still a death sentence, and they died within months of each other. If they had lived another three years they would have benefitted from the new triple-combination drug therapies that transformed the life possibilities of many, many thousands, and perhaps survived. As it was, Angus struggled with the various drugs then available to treat the range of opportunistic diseases, from tuberculosis to meningitis, that punished his body. Early on, he was prescribed AZT (azidothymidine), one of several experimental therapies that never fulfilled their promise and had toxic effects.

Angus had been devastated by Geoff Horton's death, and a few weeks after the funeral tried to take his own life. On that day, I was driving to Southampton, where I then worked, in torrential rain, and my car suddenly stopped on the motorway, the engine flooded with water. I had an instant feeling that something was wrong with Angus, and after a long day trying to contact him, we found him in time, unconscious but alive. Gradually he returned to his pottery, and a year after Geoff's death, Angus had a solo exhibition of his pots, 'The Whole Works', dedicated to Geoff's memory. This signalled a new burst of creativity, with a distinctive new inflection in his work.

He had trained from 1976 at Camberwell School of Arts, which was going through a period of exceptional innovation and excitement. There he learned from inspirational teachers and made lifelong friendships with fellow students. Ceramics became for Angus more than a craft: it was a way of life. Through clay he found he could explore his identity, his sexuality, his loves, his sense of joy. Starting with conventional forms, most frequently the teapot, he wrought mysterious and vivid objects, using brilliant colours and often written messages on the pots to challenge conventional meanings. As well as teapots he played with the shapes of boxes, cups and saucers, altar pieces, spoons and rings. But as the epidemic entered directly into his life, with Geoff's illness and death, and his own diagnosis, Angus' work became increasingly monumental and serious, the colours more muted, often evoking pre-Columbian mourning statuary.

By the early 1990s he had a growing international reputation, exhibiting in Europe, the Americas and Asia. He also became an inspirational teacher, and a fine writer. His was an engaged and committed life, and whatever he was doing, his courage, adventurousness and dedication to the possibilities of his craft persisted. Through clay Angus had found his voice, and he made it sing. But by 1992 the struggle against frequent illnesses and growing frailty finally forced him to give up ceramics.

My relationship with Angus had many ups and downs in the twenty-two years we knew each other. But I was always clear that whatever happened in our intimate entanglements, our friendship was a commitment to the end. With Micky and Mark, my new partner, I helped care for him during his final illnesses, and we were with him when he died, in June 1993.

His funeral was a celebration of his life and achievements. His mother, sisters and brother (the same brother who had threatened Angus in 1971) had only learned of his AIDS diagnosis a month before and had dashed down to see him, just in time. They were now among the mourners, alongside his friends and colleagues. In death there was some sort of reconciliation. At the service I read W. H. Auden's 'Lullaby' – 'Lay your sleeping head, my love' – which had been among my favourite poems since school days, and which Angus had asked me to read at Geoff's funeral nine years before. For me, the poem celebrates the contingency and fragility of our lives but also the transforming power of love.

A few weeks later Mark and I, both exhausted by nursing Angus through his final illness, went to New York and then San Francisco for a break. San Francisco was suffused in loss, and many of the bars, clubs and baths had long closed. A number of the friends I had made in 1981 had died or moved on. The Castro area was more subdued, almost middle-aged, more into leisurely bar lounging and shopping than fucking. Mark and I spent a memorable afternoon in a bar at the edge of Castro listening to Joni Mitchell's *Blue*, with its iconic track 'California', an album of belonging, love, loss and survival. The gentrifying impact of the financial and Silicon Valley tech revolutions were already changing the whole South of Market area with high rises springing up everywhere, but the gay scene survived. The number of leather bars in the Folsom Street area had substantially dropped from the thirty or so when I first went there, but the annual leather fest was still booming. Despite everything, San Francisco felt welcoming and still defiantly and affirmatively a queer city. 'Barbary Lane' (actually Macondray Lane on the side of Russian Hill), the locus of the central characters in *Tales of the City*, had become a tourist destination, and we could mourn with the fictional inhabitants as the epidemic took its toll. Mourning *and* militancy defined the culture. We had left behind our prolonged adolescence in the furnace of the epidemic.

In the San Francisco Museum of Modern Art we found a powerful and deeply moving exhibition consisting of a number of installations by the Canadian artists' group General Idea that focused on AIDS, death and love, which was to inspire the closing chapter of my book *Invented Moralities*. The central installation, which lent its title, *Fin De Siécle*, to the whole exhibition, was a homage to Caspar David Friedrich's early nineteenth-century painting *The Death of the Hope*, which showed a ship fatally trapped by towering icebergs. This sense

CHAPTER 7
İNTİMACY MATTERS

LEGİTİMATİON THROUGH DİSASTER

My stint at the University of Kent had ended in the summer
of 1983. I had a book, *Sexuality and Its Discontents*, half-written,
and I was soon commissioned to write another, *Sexuality*. This
proved to be my most successful book ever, going through
five editions between 1986, when it was published, and today.
Though a short book, *Sexuality* proved to be an influential
text on the meanings and makings of its subject. But another
university teaching job eluded me.

At the last minute I managed to get a post at the University
of Southampton as a research fellow on a fairly esoteric project:
on the information needs of family studies, which was funded
by the British Library. This wasn't the most obvious job for
me as I wasn't an expert on information science, and family
studies, in so far as it existed in the UK, tended to be a reserve
of conservative thinkers. It wasn't clear to me how I, as an out
gay writer on the history and sociology of sexuality who had
been critical of traditional family values, would be welcomed.
In practice, I found myself working closely with a number of

leading experts on aspects of family life, and prominent feminist academics generally critical of the traditional family, who had no greater idea of what the project was about than I did, and I had the space to devise something workable. I managed to rescue a not particularly well-designed project and produce two short books on sources for family research, which pleased the steering committee, my boss, our funder and even some of my feminist friends. In the end this turned out to be a valuable experience, despite the personal disasters the project coincided with. But by the end of 1985, with the funding at an end, I found myself in a familiar situation: sans lover, sans job and apparently sans prospects. Colin Pritchard, my very agreeable and sympathetic boss, gave me a frank supervision, suggesting I might consider changing career: perhaps re-train as a social worker like him, do a period in the field, and then come back as a senior social work academic in a few years' time.

I was not enthusiastic, not least because I was not convinced the social work profession would be any easier for an out gay man in the current climate than my past career adventures. A few years earlier a social worker acquaintance had asked me if I thought a slight impairment I had been born with in my left hand had caused my homosexuality. The tangled knot of half-baked theory, prejudice and anxiety that incident revealed marked the end of a brief friendship, but nothing that had happened since had persuaded me that social work would be a congenial home. Quixotically I decided to get out of conventional university work altogether and go into academic administration instead. My friend Philip Jones had forewarned me that an assistant registrar's position was coming up at the Council for National Academic Awards (CNAA), where he worked. The CNAA was the UK's leading validation and accreditation agency, responsible for supervising academic standards in polytechnics. The work looked interesting, managing research and development projects on higher education; it was based in London, unlike my previous three jobs, so no commuting; it was well paid; and it offered me an escape from the uncertainties of chasing a university position. At last there seemed to be a chance of at least job and income security, and an opportunity to rethink my personal and career priorities as the epidemic reached a crisis point and my love life fell apart.

I turned out to be a surprisingly good administrator and threw myself into the various roles I was given. Though some of my friends found it bizarre, I enjoyed the routines, the work rhythms geared to regular committee meetings, and the chance to make a difference in the polytechnic sector, which I admired for its openness and creativity compared with the old universities I had worked in. It offered less of an existential worry than an ordinary academic position and having to face a blank sheet of paper every day when beginning writing. I thought, for a brief while at least, when everything else about my life seemed in flux, that this was the way forward. I remember telling a casual lover, who had read some of my work, that my writing was behind me: I had written enough. For a brief moment I believed it. A new career as a professional educational bureaucrat beckoned.

For good or ill, this turned out not to be, at least in the ways I had fantasised. Events in the outside world continued to disrupt my expectations. The 1987 election victory for Thatcher was a high-water mark for what the critical High Tory journalist Peregrine Worsthorne called 'bourgeois triumphalism'. In its wake the CNAA, widely seen as a bulwark of liberal educational values, was drastically reorganised under government pressure, and new ultra-conservative figures were appointed to leading positions in the council and the committee structure through which the CNAA operated. I somehow survived the 'restructuring', where we all had to re-apply for our jobs, and was given responsibility for social sciences and research in the new dispensation. More worrying, I found I now had to work with a new chair of the Social Sciences Committee, which supervised our activities – a right-wing economist and government advisor, who had worked closely with leading Tory ministers.

He was an erratic and quixotic figure, very much a clubbable and Oxbridge college lifer possessing absolutely no experience of the polytechnic sector, with its commitment to second-chance access and strong links to local governments, many of them under Labour control. His first initiative was that members of the Social Science Committee should have sherry and a three-course lunch with wine before our meetings – quite different from the utilitarian sandwiches we were used to, and a budget buster. He clearly hoped to instil high table manners in the demotic polytechnics and the committee members who supposedly represented them. I found myself worrying about what sherry to order (he found the first efforts of the Great Northern Hotel, which hosted our meetings, too sweet) and how to keep everyone awake after a prolonged lunch. He clearly never read his papers, diligently prepared by me, and his major interest was in detecting liberal bias in the curricula we were supervising. His *idée fixe* was that Marxists had infiltrated the polytechnics and courses were bent to their ideological prejudices. He forced through a number of new appointments to the committee of what were to my mind low-grade academics but whose anti-Marxist ideological colour was impeccable. I had to battle with considerable guile for my own more credible nominees.

I did my best over the next couple of years to make the whole thing work, largely by avoiding associating too closely with the chair. He was not interested in the day-to-day work of the committee and its panels, and certainly not in me and where I came from. I, with help from other colleagues, managed to stop him doing too much harm. The social science offer in polytechnics continued to expand, and the high tide of Thatcherism began to recede. But I increasingly felt I had to get out. My appetite for working with the unadulterated right was limited. And once again the writing bug was biting me, especially as I was increasingly being asked to give papers overseas, and being invited to write more books, not least about AIDS and the sexual crisis. Fortunately, I was offered a Simon Senior Fellowship for a year, 1989–90, in the Sociology Department at the University of Manchester, to work on what became *Invented Moralities*. This provided a magical and unexpected opportunity to rethink where I was going.

For once, the wind seemed to be blowing under my wing – and ironically, tragically, the obvious reason for this was the continuing AIDS crisis. I now had several things going for me. In the first place, I had become an experienced academic. I had worked in several universities as a teacher and researcher. I had written a number of well-received books, published many articles, given papers at conferences around the world and had an international reputation. Universities were beginning to expand again and senior positions were being advertised to lead on the government's Research Assessment Exercise (RAE), to promote and support research in each university in preparation for formal measurement. Suddenly I looked marketable.

Secondly, I had demonstrated I was quite flexible in my educational interests, and not just in 'family studies'! I had managed research and development projects on a range of educational topics at the CNAA, and was also running a research project[120] on completion rates in postgraduate research – another apparently esoteric subject, but one that exercised university and polytechnic departments at the time, as too many PhD students were failing to complete their theses on time. In addition, I now had several years of administrative experience from my CNAA work, and of educational policy development projects. I was persuaded I could now seriously think of applying for jobs at senior levels, as a full professor and head of department.

But thirdly and decisively, my research on sexuality in general and homosexuality in particular suddenly no longer seemed irrelevant to mainstream research and teaching. On the contrary the continuing AIDS crisis made it highly relevant. I had already written a number of articles on the crisis, and was working with leading researchers on the social impact of the epidemic, as opposed to the biomedical aspects of HIV/ AIDS. And my peculiar mixture of history and sociology no longer seemed so quirky. My exploration of the contingencies of identity was highly relevant to attempts to understand the apparently baffling fact that many people affected with HIV did not seem to fit easily into the pregiven sexological definitions. Biomedical experts were saying that the HIV and AIDS epidemic gave unprecedented insights into hidden identities, but what it actually did was to shine a searchlight into sexual practices often totally at variance with socially defined identity categories. My work also offered insights into the processes of sexual regulation that shaped the public response, how and why the health crisis had become a crisis of sexual meanings, and the ways in which this had translated into a panic culture around homosexuality. And my ongoing work on sexual values was concerned with the implications of living in a climate of uncertainty that was supercharged by fears of HIV and AIDS.

As Dennis Altman suggested, the epidemic had led to a 'legitimation through disaster'. Government and medical responses, when they began to gather speed, in what one historian called a 'war-time emergency'-type situation, required new expertise: in basic scientific research; in aetiological research; in the medicine of sexually transmissible infections; in treatment of rare diseases; on the practices of care, and palliative care especially; and on the history and sociology of health crises, sexuality and relationships. I had considerable expertise in a number of these fields.[121] While I was on the Manchester fellowship I decided to test the water in applying for senior positions, and on my second attempt I was offered a post at Bristol Polytechnic, later University of the West of England. From autumn 1990 I became head of social science research and Professor of Social Relations in Bristol.

LOVE AGAIN

More or less coinciding with this change in my material fortunes, I began a new and enduring relationship with Mark McNestry. We met for the first time on New Year's Eve 1989, at a party in the Market Tavern, a pub in Vauxhall, south London, near New Covent Garden. He flirtatiously told me he had read my books. I was flattered and attracted but nothing more happened on that occasion as we were there with separate groups of friends. We got together a couple of months later. A mutual friend, Paul Hoddinot, gave Mark my phone number so he could invite me to give a talk at the Psychology Society at Birkbeck College, where he was a mature student. I duly gave a talk on the perverse in sexuality. Perverse or not, we began what turned out to be the most sustained, fulfilling and long-lasting relationship in my life, still ongoing as I write thirty years later. It was a transformative moment.

An obvious difficulty was that he was eighteen years younger than me, and for a number of years we struggled with the implications of this. We were at different life stages, and came from different generations, with all that implies in a rapidly changing sexual culture. But we also had many things in common from the start, apart from mutual attraction and emotional ease with one another.[122] Like me he came from an old mining community, his in the North East, and shared the same values. Both of us were also still working through the trauma of AIDS. As well as studying for his psychology degree, Mark was a volunteer at the Landmark AIDS Centre in south London, which provided treatment and support for people living with HIV and AIDS. After graduating he worked for the National AIDS Helpline, then on a National Health Service (NHS) HIV prevention project in Greenwich as a community development officer. Here he began innovative work around supporting safer sex practices among sex workers and men who had sex with men, many of whom did not identify as gay. He was able to bring NHS funding to a local gay centre, the Metro, encouraging a genuine community-led response to the crisis.

At the same time, I was beginning work with Peter Aggleton, also then at Bristol, researching the grassroots community-based responses to HIV and AIDS. Our common preoccupations complemented one another, but there were potential conflicts and problems. Mark's original ambition was to work as a university researcher on aspects of HIV. Such a post came up with Peter, on a different project from the one we were doing together. Mark was ideally qualified for this, but he absolutely refused any attempt on my part to pull strings, or even mention our link. He was always sensitive to the suspicion others might have that I was covertly advancing his career. He was fiercely independent. Although I was considerably better off than him, he always insisted on paying his way, even scrupulously buying an old Renault 5 car from me that I was happy to pass on to him for free. In effect he sacrificed his own research career rather than compromise mine. He subsequently focused on other community development work, moving into urban renewal projects, and eventually had a successful career as a consultant. I felt deeply guilty that he was so willing to put my interests before his but eternally grateful for his scruples. Our relationship deepened as we worked through all this.

Mark and I tried to live as we advocated, especially in relation to safer sex practices, working through ideas of mutual responsibility, honesty and trust. Above all, Mark laboured with me and Micky to support Angus in his various illnesses and final days. The emotional entanglements were complex and sometimes difficult. I knew I was asking a huge amount from Mark so early in our relationship to expect him to support me in caring for a former partner to whom I was still closely attached. But Mark did it unstintingly till the end, and held Angus' hand and spoke gently to him as he faded away.

My personal experiences in these early years of the 1990s profoundly shaped and reshaped the book I was working on, *Invented Moralities*.[123] Chunks of it were worked on as I sat by Angus' bedside in the HIV ward at Middlesex Hospital during his various illnesses. Its tempered positivity was shaped by countless experiences of endurance I saw all around, and by what I was learning from and through my relationship with Mark. As I completed the book in the year after Angus' death I saw this as my AIDS book, a reflection on prejudice, suffering, care, love and survival.

The theme of the book was the importance of thinking about sexual values in the age of uncertainty we were inhabiting. My argument was that the Moral Right had hegemonized the debate on values, especially in the USA where a phrase like 'family values' encoded a number of ideas: hostility towards the advances made by women, desire to protect children from the tide of permissiveness, opposition to sex education, deep hostility towards homosexuality, underpinned by the fear and loathing generated by AIDS. My fear was that progressive forces, especially in feminism and lesbian and gay politics, had essentially evacuated the field, seeing any attempt to engage in the debate about values as a surrender to the conservative agenda. A number of friends and colleagues berated me to this effect. I felt strongly, however, that it was essential to engage in the debate, not to elaborate a new moral code or ethical system, but to find ways of living with the consequences of the changes that were sweeping the world of sexuality amid a continuing panic and the sense of an ending generated by the approaching *fin de siècle*. In a world without secure foundations, outside the (false) security proffered by a unifying belief system once provided by religion, in a universe ruled by contingency, the temptation on both left and right to invent and impose absolute moral systems was immense. I was alarmed especially by the ways in which an appeal to Science with a capital S was again being used as a substitute for real debate in the gay liberation movement after years of scepticism about the role of science. This was particularly manifested by the sudden popularity of attempts to find causes of homosexuality in pseudoscientific theories of a gay gene or gay brain. While fitting comfortably into dominant concepts of gayness as a pregiven biological phenomenon, defining a minority gay identity, this did nothing to challenge the still-dominant, if crumbling, sexual and gender orders that were central to the continuing crisis. Just as the pioneering sexologist Magnus Hirschfeld's espousal of science and biological explanations for homosexuality in the 1930s to support emancipation had not stopped Nazis from adopting the same arguments to persecute homosexuals, so the theories of a gay gene or gay brain did nothing to advance our liberation. It was the former Chief Rabbi of the UK, Lord Jakobovits, who welcomed the new theories because they could lead to the elimination of homosexuals before birth through prenatal screening.[124] Falling into the hands of a dubious science was an avoidance of thinking about values. As I wrote in the preface to *Invented Moralities*, 'debates over values encapsulate our uncertainties about how we should live'.

The main theme of the book is how to live with diversity. Rather than find prescriptive answers that would tell us how to behave, I attempted to offer a framework for thinking about the issues in a democratic and collaborative way. Many forms of life can be moral or ethically valid, especially with regard to sexuality. It is not so much what you do but how you do it that should matter, rejecting a morality of acts in favour of an ethics of relationships. Central to this are ideas of care, responsibility, respect and love, but these virtues should not be reduced to any particular forms of domestic arrangements or sexual practices. They express values that can inform a variety of lifestyles and what John Stuart Mill called 'experiments in living'.

My next project, and ultimately book, flowed easily from this position: I began to do preliminary work around what were increasingly being called 'families of choice', informal but often strong and resilient networks of friends and often members of families of origin that provided the emotional support for many LGBT people, like an extended kin network rather than a nuclear family based on heterosexual marriage. This conformed very much to the context of my own domestic and emotional life. Mark and I were clearly a committed couple at the centre of overlapping and intersecting networks of friends, and increasingly recognised and affirmed by our original families. But we lived separately for the first eight years or so of our relationship, he in a shared flat in south London, while I continued after Angus' death to share our house in north London with Micky. This worked in practice because

Mark and I spent much of our time together, commuting by bike or car across London most days, while also having space to ourselves if we needed it. On the surface at least it conformed to what sociologists were identifying as a new pattern of couples 'living apart together'. It wasn't until the end of the decade that we bought a flat together, though I kept my house-share with Micky for another few years. It was 2003 before we eventually moved into a new house together, while Micky, increasingly affected by ill health, moved into our former flat, in the same street as us, so we could continue to support him.

This journey was not unique to us. In the wider LGBT world there was a distinct shift by the 1990s, with an increasing preoccupation with domestic life, and with the formal links that could embed it, including the idea of civil partnerships and same-sex marriage. The early gay liberation movement, like the women's liberation movement, had been highly critical of the conventional family formed by marriage, seeing it as the root of women's oppression, sexism and heterosexual privilege, which by its very form isolated and excluded lesbians and gays. Like many in my political and gay generation I had been an enthusiastic critic of the cloying, normative nature of the bourgeois couple. The question many activists were now debating was whether too many of us were living in something very like that. Was this the ultimate sell-out of gay liberation ideals? On the contrary, I increasingly believed that the fact that so many queer people were finding it increasingly possible to establish open, caring relationships was an index of how far we had come from the closeted, often furtive and guilt-ridden relationships characteristic of a period in the not-too-distant past. Far from being 'pretended' relationships, these were the real thing, and part of a long-term trend towards more flexible and fluid domestic arrangements. The very nature of family life and the relationships entwined in them were changing in

Western societies, and this was bound to open up questions about gay relationships and our relationship to family life.

An obvious example was the increasing interest in my generation of lesbians and gays with parenting. I personally, and the same was true of Mark, never felt the need to have children: it was enough, and emotionally satisfying in its own right, to have an avuncular interest in our growing number of nephews and nieces. But a number of our lesbian and other feminist friends did now decide to have children. The wider social anxieties that lesbian families in particular could arouse had been evident since the 1970s, when lesbian mothers often had to fight difficult battles through the courts for custody of their children. Issues around custody, fostering and adoption by lesbians and gay men became increasingly critical in the 1990s, and posed challenging questions about the legal status of same-sex parents. This was to become a major propellant for support for civil partnerships and same-sex marriage.

But it became increasingly clear that families as an arrangement of domestic practices, values, personal interaction and mutual support through time and generations did not necessarily involve children, and the HIV/AIDS epidemic dramatised this from the start. Friends, lovers and ex-lovers, as well as many volunteers and buddies, had been crucial since the beginning of the crisis in providing care and support through illness and loss, especially in the absence of social support and ignorance in the caring and medical professions about gay male ways of life. I once went with Angus to see his new GP, to whom he had been referred by the hospital for day-to-day care. I introduced myself as a friend and carer. The doctor looked startled and bemused and stammered, 'Do you mean a paid carer?' But of course more was involved than simply caring for someone. We knew many individuals who found they had no rights as next of kin when a partner died, lost visiting rights in hospitals, were excluded from funerals by parents, lost shared accommodation and were denied rights of inheritance in the absence of a will. What did this say about 'family values'? As with parenting experiences, the experience of AIDS amplified the complete absence of relational rights for lesbians and gay men.

By the early 1990s relational rights had come to the heart of community preoccupations. They were less dramatic than the questions of sexual identity and sexual freedom that had preoccupied us from the early 1970s, and of course these were still highly relevant in many people's lives. Coming out was a continuing process, identity an ongoing negotiation, and sexual freedom and choice a permanent challenge in an age of uncertainty and heightened risk. Yet the fuss over Section 28 and its attack on 'pretended family relationships' had signalled the way the wind was howling.

I was encouraged to undertake a more systematic study of lesbian and gay intimate relationships when the Economic and Social Research Council (ESRC) announced a competition in 1994 for research projects to examine changing population and family patterns. I decided I would put in a bid to research same-sex and family-like relationships, at least to raise the flag and put on paper my belief that those pretended relationships were valid and important examples of changing social patterns. I also couldn't forget that the removal of an SSRC grant in 1979 had destabilised my career. Would getting a grant this time from its successor body help break a taboo? Much to my surprise I was awarded the grant just at the time I was changing jobs, and took it with me to what became London South Bank University (LSBU), a former polytechnic in south London.

The new post was the first time I had been headhunted for a job and took it with a mixture of pleasure and nervousness.

I knew many of the people there, some of whom I had worked with at the CNAA, others of whom I knew for their work on families and ongoing work on sexuality and HIV/AIDS. Intellectually it seemed ideal. However, the school I was joining had a reputation for fractious relationships and the university was well known in former polytechnic circles for being anarchic and ungovernable. I was persuaded that the newish vice-chancellor, Gerry Bernbaum, was tackling this, not least by Anthony Giddens, who was external adviser on the appointment, and was eager to support Gerry build up its research reputation. I was one of nearly thirty new research professors appointed by Gerry, with a brief to develop a full-scale research strategy and enhance the university's standing. My position as a full professor, with little teaching or administration, was a luxurious one for me, and promised great opportunities to expand my own research and writing as well as leading a talented if fissiparous research culture. And I would not have to commute long distance anymore!

It did not turn out quite as expected. Within a few months Gerry began a major reorganisation of the internal structure of the university, partly to clear out people he felt were not up to the job – a classic action for a new vice-chancellor anxious to impose his will, I quickly discovered. He asked me if I would become head of a new school, combining sociology and social policy, politics and education. I did not fancy a future as a university manager – what would happen to my research? – and turned him down. A little later he asked me again, and again I demurred. But Gerry was a difficult man to say no to and on the third asking, after Mark and I came back from conferencing and lecturing in Mexico – would I have to forego such pleasures in future? – I agreed, on condition I would only do it for three years. It was the beginning of fifteen years of increasingly senior university management positions, as head of school, dean, executive dean and finally as university head of research, none of which I had planned or expected. Once again I found myself rethinking my professional identity, now as a senior academic manager, with the opportunity to build something up and achieve something in the public world. Writing often felt like spitting in the wind. Here I could shape something practical. But I was also aware that things could go badly wrong, and that this was a political as well as an academic challenge.

On taking the first post as head of school I was immediately faced by a poorly planned restructuring and a financial crisis, and my life was engulfed by endless meetings, difficult staff relationships, suspicion of my role as a vice-chancellor's nark, and a major task of building a sense of identity and coherence for the otherwise disparate and anarchic school. I was kept going by adrenaline, Mark's support and a new-found ambition to make a success of it. But in a curious way it was also a spur to my research. I wanted to lead by example, and prove that a busy academic life was not an inhibition to good-quality research. At the same time, I needed a space to keep my mind alert amid the myriad administrative and personal challenges that came my way. My various writing and research commitments, and eventually the families of choice project, offered that opportunity, though at continuing domestic cost. Mark felt, rightly, that our lives were overwhelmingly dominated by work, with weekends for me frequently consumed with doing the writing I could not do during the week. I was living many of the changes and tensions of domestic and intimate life I was attempting to research and understand. The research became a reflexive project in which my own life became an active participant, and what I learnt in the research fed back into my life.

I was fortunate in setting up the project with two excellent young researchers, Brian Heaphy and Catherine Donovan.[125] We were committed to listening to the stories emerging from the nearly one hundred interviews we undertook, and trying to make sense of them. We were also fully aware that the research was potentially highly controversial in the wake of Section 28, and a still-rabid press. I was offered media training by the ESRC to be able to deal with likely intrusion by the tabloid press, and I was caught out in one media scam. A *Daily Mail* journalist attended unannounced a workshop I spoke at about same-sex relationships and parenting, and my off-the-record thoughts were headlined in the paper shortly after: shock-horror, gay militants were pressing for rights of adoption and fostering, and some even wanted to give birth to their own children. But we were also aware that there was a growing head of steam behind the shifts we were documenting. Two of the five key equality challenges identified by Stonewall included 'equal recognition and respect for same-sex partners' and 'equal recognition and respect for lesbian and gay parents and their children'. Changes in the queer world were beginning to shape campaigns and, ultimately, government policy.

The book Brian, Catherine and I wrote together, *Same Sex Intimacies*, was eventually published in 2001.[126] It was the first attempt in Britain to document what one of our interviewees called the 'queer construct family'. We sought to show the different ways in which people whose lives had been lived at odds with the dominant social and sexual norms had nevertheless been able to create meaningful intimate lives for themselves, defined against what we called the 'heterosexual assumption'. The central theme that emerges is one of agency: people had a strong sense that they were inventing positive forms of life for themselves and their significant others, though not always, or ever, perhaps, in freely chosen circumstances. They emphasised the importance of choice in relationships, while recognising that choice was limited in multiple ways by circumstances and the nexus of power imbalances that entwined us. These new 'life experiments' were not so much alternative structures of domestic life as fluid forms within which non-heterosexual people were 'doing family': day-to-day domestic interactions, mutual support, caring activities, looking after children and so on; family as performative rather than pregiven, negotiable rather than prescriptive. Within this overarching picture we were able to explore the potency of the 'friendship ethic', which we saw as underpinning everyday life; ideas and ideals of home; the rites and rituals that sustained partnerships; the significance of sexual relations; the new 'gayby' boom and attitudes to parenting; and the expanding notions of citizenship that recognition of new forms of relationships would involve.

If agency was the main theme, other key themes also emerged. Our interviewees were deeply committed to values of equality and democracy in intimate life, seeing these as central commitments in building sustainable relationships. Anthony Giddens had noted similar attitudes in his book *The Transformation of Intimacy*, and he had seen lesbian and gay people as pioneers in the development of disclosing intimacy based on these, precisely because they were outside the traditional familial structures built around inequality and gendered authority.[127] We did not try to argue that what we saw in non-heterosexual intimacy was unique to queer life, but we did observe that many of the people we interviewed believed very strongly that they had greater opportunities to build lives freer of heterosexual inequalities than their straight peers – as did we.

There was also a strong belief that freeing yourself of prescriptive roles and rules, of having to do something because that was what conventional morality directed, opened the ways to bonds of intimacy that were more flexible but possibly stronger precisely because they were freely chosen: notions of duty were largely avoided, but replaced not with a vacuum but with a strong sense of mutual obligation. You cared for a friend or partner not because you had to but because you wanted to; a chosen commitment, freely given was the essential basis for intimate life. But there was a key exception: where children and other dependents were involved people believed there was an absolute duty to care for them. Our findings here corresponded very closely with those of Janet Finch on changing family obligations more broadly.[128] As with aspirations towards egalitarian and democratic relations, our interviewees were not living in a different world from their heterosexual friends and family, but it was clear that living outside the patterns of compulsory heterosexuality did allow them to explore more freely, and advance more quickly to embrace emerging shifts in intimate life.

Given these shifts it is not surprising that our interviewees had a strong sense of the injustices that continued to shape their lives. They wanted equality and recognition above all. This fed into the growing debate about the merits of civil partnerships and same-sex marriage. Very few of the people we interviewed in the late 1980s actually favoured marriage for themselves. They felt it to be too patriarchal, 'aping heterosexuals', and too restrictive for complex lives. But practically everyone firmly believed that if heterosexuals could marry, and have full parenting rights, so should they. Here was the core of a new discourse of rights and a citizenship agenda that were to underpin the major legislative and cultural shifts that surfaced in the last years of the 1990s and the early noughties. Ten years earlier many commentators, in the wake of AIDS, had written graphically of a panic culture, of *fin de millennium* malaise and a mood of 'sexual anarchism'.[129] As someone who had experienced and written about this mood myself, it seemed a nice irony that by 1999 the grassroots preoccupations of the queer world were actually more about the loves and travails of ordinary life than about obvious transgression and radical disruption. Yet these preoccupations were actually to be more transformative than anyone could have imagined a few years earlier.

GETTING BETTER?

In the 1970s and 1980s each coming out by a prominent writer, actor, pop star, politician or celebrity of any sort had been an event, often preceded by hints or speculation in the tabloid press, a confession by the celebrity, often under pressure, a few days of lurid gossip and then a move onto something or someone else. It was soon quite obvious that a pre-emptive declaration of your sexuality was a less fractious way to go. The coming out of actors like Ian McKellen or Michael Cashman in the wake of Section 28 was exemplary, especially as it helped propel Stonewall into public presence, and as a signal of new times openness often led to an establishment embrace: McKellen was invited to Downing Street as a representative of the LGBT community, and was later knighted, while Cashman became a member of the European Parliament and later a Labour peer. They were building on the lonelier efforts of pioneers in the previous decades. Maureen Colquhoun was a Labour MP who was effectively outed in 1975, and had her career ruined: she was deselected by her constituency party in Northampton North in 1977. Gradually, things began to change in the party. A few years later, in 1984, as the AIDS crisis galloped apace, Chris Smith, Labour MP for Islington South, showed much courage when he voluntarily came out as gay. At a rally in Rugby he stood and said, 'I'm Chris Smith,

I'm the Labour MP for Islington South and Finsbury and I'm gay'. He was given a rapturous standing ovation. By the time he became the first openly gay cabinet minister in Tony Blair's first government in 1997, gayness was on its way to being normalised in high political circles, and eventually several out lesbian and gay ministers were to serve in the Blair governments. As gay liberationists had always argued, being open about your sexuality, in increasing numbers, was a necessary and potentially decisive factor in changing attitudes and defeating prejudice. The outing controversy of the early 1990s, in which gay militants threatened to disclose the sexuality of closeted homosexuals, revolved around the hypocrisy of lesbians and gays in positions of power who were publicly homophobic and willing to legislate against their own. It was an attempt to show the ways in which LGBT people themselves could be complicit in their own oppression.

But as I had painfully learnt in the 1970s, with my family and some friends, coming out was not a single event, but a continuing process. In the worst years of the AIDS crisis and after, a sort of unconscious embarrassment and prejudice, even among my most liberal friends and colleagues, all too easily manifested itself: in the questions never asked about your partner or domestic arrangements; in the subject matter of your books never being referred to – what Christopher Isherwood called 'annihilation by blandness'. And the most shameful thing was how easy it was to be complicit with this. Despite the fact that I was well known as a gay academic, and lived openly with Mark, there were occasions when I just did not bother to force a conversation on 'difficult' matters. This was even, perhaps especially, true with my given family. When I first took Mark home to visit my family in Wales I knew there were questions they wanted to ask – about our age differences, about whether this was a genuine not exploitative relationship – but they couldn't, and nor could I pre-empt them by talking about these things myself. The habits of secrecy, discretion, mutual avoidance of difficult issues, shyness and embarrassment were just too strong. It was too easy to justify not bringing things to the surface because it was a 'private' matter, forgetting the lesson we had learnt in the 1970s that the only way of confronting shame, guilt and anxiety was to make a fuss about it.

At last by the mid-1990s there were signs that making a fuss was changing the political climate. The Labour Party in particular had adopted a raft of pro-LGBT policies, after years of campaigning by dedicated activists and ordinary members in trade unions, local parties, local authorities and national conferences. It was difficult to pretend that the new commitments were at the heart of party policies for government. The Labour government that took office in 1997 at first carefully balanced a vague sympathy for lesbian and gay rights with pro-family policies that nodded towards the conservative agenda of the right-wing press rather than a feminist or pro-LGBT programme. Yet, often despite themselves, the Blair governments were destined to become the most successful in British history in advancing LGBT rights.

For once, political hope had been justified by the breakthrough of 1997. I had sat through so many election nights since 1979 when tentative hopes of progressive change had been thwarted on the first appearance of an exit poll, followed by a drip feed of disastrous results. I became an ever-keener supporter of Labour Party 'modernisation' to make the party relevant to an obviously changing electorate and economic, cultural and social climate. But the election night disaster in 1992, when Neil Kinnock's leadership seemed to be on the brink of success, proved to my mind that the Labour Party had not changed enough, and that it had to abandon its traditional left posturing, which failed to resonate with the electorate. You couldn't change the electorate but it might be sensible to understand it better. Britain was changing radically at street level, and a successful party needed to understand and steer these changes. This seemed particularly obvious at the level of sexuality and intimate life.

The long, unfinished revolution that was transforming everyday life, through the unregulated, unguided practical agency of millions of people, needed to be recognised and affirmed. The Conservative prime minister, John Major, surely recognised this in some hazy fashion, and he made gestures towards it. 1994 had seen the first tentative steps towards reforming the age-of-consent legislation by reducing the age for sex between men to 18 (compared with 16 for heterosexual sex). But this was neither pleasing for his reactionary backbenchers nor appeasing to a growing LGBT campaign for legal equality. These measures were, in any case, soon drowned in the disastrous impact of his 'Back to Basics' campaign, where his apparent attempt at public moralising and his evident nostalgia for an age of quiet good manners and gender and sexual traditionalism, which had never existed, was soon lost in the flood of revelations about the private misdemeanours of his ministers.

Tony Blair, the young leader of the Labour Party, seemed to be much more in tune with what was happening on the ground. His speech in the House of Commons in 1994 on the age of consent marked him as the first prospective prime minister to embrace full gay equality. I was prepared to tolerate his nods to the more socially conservative electorate and the reactionary press as tactical moves in the interest of getting a Labour government committed to the absolutely fundamental condition of legal reform. In any case, unlike the assumptions of many of my former Marxist comrades, he seemed to stand for a reforming agenda that understood the globalising and de-traditionalising forces that were transforming everyday life. So, for once the all-night television stint by Mark and myself watching the general election results in 1997 gave unadulterated pleasure and hope.

It took time, a great deal of patience, and hopes deferred but never quite lost before the Labour government's agenda for LGBT rights unfolded. There was a great deal of resistance from the House of Lords and conservative mobilisation, noticeably around repeal of Section 28. There was unnecessary deferring to the conservative establishment, which slowed full acceptance of LGBT people serving in the military. And too many of the changes depended on relying on decisions from the European courts to soften up public opinion, as with the legalisation of a common age of consent. Perhaps there was no real agenda, just the unfolding realities of the facts on the ground that pushed for pragmatic adaptations. The rhetoric of supporting the family sounded empty when it became increasingly obvious that people were voting with their feet and developing increasingly diverse ways of doing family life. And for the first time since the 1960s there was an increasingly effective LGBT lobbying organisation, Stonewall, cannily led by the former GLF-er, Angela Mason, with friends in high places in the new political establishment. When Angela moved to a key position in the Cabinet Office's Women and Equalities unit the scene was set for dramatic and historic changes. Between 2000 and 2005 an unprecedented programme of reform transformed the legal status of LGBT people on the British mainland: repeal of Section 28, an equal age of consent at 16, the abolition of the offence of 'gross indecency', the right to serve in the armed services, equality in adoption, the right of trans people to change their gender designation, equal employment rights, and the Civil Partnership Act, which in effect gave lesbians and gays equal marital rights, but called it something else. By the time the Labour government left office in 2010 the full legal citizenship of LGBT people had been largely achieved. This was added to in 2014 by the legalisation of same-sex marriage by the Conservative–Liberal Democrat coalition government, with surprisingly little resistance compared with what was happening in the USA and other European countries. I remain convinced that this portfolio of changes is one of the greatest achievements of the Labour government. The fact that it is not an achievement the leadership of Blair or Gordon Brown flaunted is an index of how it was achieved: partly under the radar, liberalism by stealth rather than proclamation, a very British compromise instead of grandstanding principle. But the result was also a very British revolution. From being a laggard in Europe, Britain (minus in part Northern Ireland) now had one of the most advanced legal codes and a sexually diverse culture. London had become a focus for LGBT life in a way that Amsterdam, San Francisco and New York had in earlier decades, with other lively gay scenes in Manchester, Edinburgh, Brighton, Cardiff, Leeds and elsewhere. The possibilities of leading a fulfilling LGBT life had been transformed.

The revolution that Blair presided over was dismissed by some of my friends on the left as a 'passive revolution', a Gramscian term for a top-down reorganisation of social forces that aims to stifle radical change rather than lead it. The same sort of argument had been made, including, I have to confess, by myself, about the reforms of the 1960s, the only comparable set of changes in British history. This fed into a developing queer critique of the reforms as essentially assimilationist, making concessions to LGBT people as a way of binding us into the status quo, taming radical aspirations to sexual transformation and tying us into heteronormative values. Much of this new queer militancy came from the USA, and there were efforts to echo it in Britain, but interestingly the militancy of OutRage! did not reject reforms. Peter Tatchell, as the best-known confrontational queer militant, always supported same-sex marriage. Queer theory was quite another thing. I never felt at home with its arcane language or the feeling it gave out that nothing worthwhile had been thought before Judith Butler wrote *Gender Trouble*. Some American queer theorists identified an insidious problem called 'homonormativity', the development of ways of life that simply replicated and reinforced conventional values, where serving in the police and military or seeking to get married was the final sign of hopeless sell-out. Even worse, another perverse value shift, what Jasbir Puar called 'homonationalism', tied LGBT people into imperialism and aggressive nationalism, leading to the 'pinkwashing' that obscured neo-colonial and racist intent.[130] As the critique of neo-liberalism developed in the 2010s these sexual reforms were sometimes re-read as accommodations to the whiplash of economic imperatives and their ideological accompaniments, substituting government of the self for external moral control, but with the same ultimate goal: to tie individuals into the necessities of global and globalised capitalism, to give us the illusion of freedom while we freely practised our servitude.

Such critiques seemed to me profoundly wrong-headed. I certainly believed that rampant commercialisation distorted human relationships in everyday life, and that global inequalities combined with religious absolutisms fuelled anti-sexual fundamentalisms, but I was sceptical that there was any inherent logic or necessity linking the needs of global capitalism and the success of sexual and gender agency and growing campaigns for human sexual rights. It was surely possible to see flaws and limitations in the reforms and to recognise that there was still a massive challenge in transforming civil equality into the full sexual and intimate citizenship that some of us were attempting to define, without ascribing everything to neo-liberalism. Above all, the various critiques seemed to me to ignore a profound reality: they obliterated the role of the LGBT communities themselves in defining and shaping the nature of the changes. They passed over the collective and individual self-activity of the thousands, millions even, of people who in their everyday practices, for good or ill, were remaking the sexual world. This was not a top-down, passive revolution; it was a grassroots-inspired, active transformation.

How this agency was expressed and represented was, inevitably, quite another matter. The complicated growth of diverse and varied LGBT social worlds under the surface of difficult social, cultural and political circumstances in the 1980s and early 1990s burst into vivid life during the latter part of the decade. Queer life became part of an increasingly affluent, liberal and cosmopolitan culture, especially in the cities. Every possible taste was now catered for, and it was possible to live an almost completely queer life, especially if you were young, pretty and mobile, as so many seemed to be. A reasonably well-off gay man could move from a flat in Soho or a warehouse conversion in Manchester to gay cafés and restaurants, drink in a gay bar, listen to gay-oriented music, go to a sex bar and spend the night clubbing, celebrate the annual Pride without too much hassle from the police or state authorities, and travel to welcoming queer-friendly resorts all over the world. At the same time, an undercurrent of violence provided a salutary limit to too much self-expression, manifest in random queer-bashing on the streets, or abuse online, and there were gross disparities in the treatment and inclusion of various groups: women, trans people, people from Black, Asian and minority ethnic (BAME) communities, older LGBT people. A pleasure-oriented culture allowed little space for sustained campaigns or upfront militancy. It was difficult to say that the LGBT worlds constituted a single social movement in the way that made sense in the 1970s, even though homophobia, biphobia and transphobia were still rampant, including in school playgrounds.

And yet it seemed to me there were common values that held these worlds together, that manifested themselves in the annual Prides that Mark and I continued to go to throughout the 1990s. They offered an alternative set of values to the hyper-individualism that the Thatcherite revolution had both encouraged and celebrated, and which was part of a global phenomenon of individualisation as rapid change and market forces undermined traditional identities and belongings. By the 1990s Britain was probably a more individualistic culture than ever before, a combination of Thatcherite deregulation, the weakening of classically collectivist structures like trade unions, the diminishing authority of traditionalist organisations like the churches, and the displacement of external moralities by more personalist ethical systems. I welcomed aspects of this as a refreshing and necessary rupture with the social conformism and closed value system that dominated the national culture in the 1950s and early 1960s. But I was all too aware of the limits of these changes. The greater individual freedom I felt, and I believed benefitted those like myself, located forever on the margins, was made possible in and through my experience of the movement, of the struggle against HIV/AIDS, and my friendships and close relationships. Here I felt the collective strength to affirm my individuality. Not rampant individualism, but a sense of individual empowerment and agency made possible by a wider sense of belonging: becoming a fully realised individual through involvement with others. After a convoluted and tortuous journey I was reaffirming many of the central values I imbibed in the Rhondda of my youth.

BONDING

I never thought I would marry. When I first came out it was impossible anyway for me to marry another man, and unlike many early gay friends I never contemplated marrying a woman as a cover or social necessity. As the years went by, and I re-educated myself through the gay liberation movement and close contact with my feminist friends about the perils of familial life, marriage seemed ideologically wrong and personally restrictive. Throughout the 1970s I was involved in endless discussions about future possibilities, and I can't remember same-sex marriage being mentioned once as a desirable possibility. As arguments for same-sex marriage developed from the late 1980s, notably first in Denmark and other Scandinavian countries, the USA, Belgium and the Netherlands, then across most gay-tolerant countries, I watched with interest as a historian and sociologist but felt personally detached – very much like the people we interviewed for the families of choice project.[131] Then the opportunity arose in Britain with the passing of the Civil Partnership Act, much sooner than I had anticipated (historians are much better at forecasting the past than foretelling the future). How would/ should Mark and I respond?

By the time civil partnerships became available at the end of 2005, Mark and I had been together for fifteen years, and if anything our relationship had intensified over that time. Since 2003 we had at last started living together permanently. At the same time Mark had given up his post as chief executive of a community development trust, done an MA in urban regeneration and started as a freelance consultant working from home. The shared house was increasingly the focus of all the major parts of our lives, accentuated when I took a sabbatical from the university to work on a new book in 2005–06, and following my early retirement a couple of years after that. Most parts of our lives were intricately and inextricably intertwined – and we survived!

We debated for a long time whether we should formalise our relationship now that it was possible. Against was our strong feeling that we already had a strong commitment to each other and that we didn't need a legal contract. Related to this was a continuing anxiety that to in effect marry would entangle us in legal arrangements that could all too easily simply echo traditional structures. We had built our own relationship against such structures and had no desire to replicate them. On the other hand there were strong pragmatic reasons for going ahead. I was older than Mark and was anxious that he should be recognised as my next of kin in the event of illness or early death. The AIDS crisis had underlined the necessity and justice of such considerations. There were also genuine material benefits to having a civil partnership, especially in relationship to pension and property rights. For all such reasons, as a friend said to me, we would be foolish not to take advantage of the opportunity.

Transcending all these arguments was a more profound one: we now had the possibility of avowing our private commitment to each other in a public fashion as heterosexual people had from time immemorial. Many people had fought long and hard for this right for same-sex couples, and we could not ignore it. Both of us had long been committed to affirming openly our identities and sexualities. Whatever my initial doubts about same-sex marriage I was now convinced that it was not only an important act for individuals and couples; it was also an engine for changing the very nature and symbolism of marriage itself: no longer a sanctification of reproductive necessity but increasingly a freely chosen act of commitment and love open to all sexualities and genders. It was a public recognition of privately made decisions.

Mark and I decided on a quiet ceremony on his birthday in March 2006. We had had a large family birthday party just a few months before, so we didn't feel the need for another big do. Neither of us told our families until the night before, giving them no time to dash down to be with us. We didn't want a fuss. With us were our friend Jane as 'best woman', and our friends David and Philip as witnesses. We had lunch together afterwards, and the waiters, having discovered why we were there, painted 'Congratulations' on our dessert. Then Mark and I flew off to Valencia for a holiday together.

On the surface nothing obvious had changed. Our new legal status did not alter our day-to-day relationship. And yet we both felt everything was different. The pleasure our families, on both sides, took in the civil partnership was a signal of a wider recognition. As Mark's father wittily, and characteristically, said, 'once you were outlaws; now we are in-laws'. Against the odds, unexpectedly to many of us, civil partnership and subsequently same-sex marriage had become a key staging post on the road to full and equal citizenship.

CHAPTER 8

ALL THE WAY HOME

PARTY TİME

The various worlds I have lived in and between seemed for a long time impossibly separate, incommensurate, painful to negotiate between, never the twain shall meet. In practice, for many years I fudged the choices, perhaps like most people muddling through. But as time passed I realised something more profound: that we all live in many worlds, we all have to confront the challenges of our differences; that absolute commitment to one direction or another is not an answer.

Reflecting on his struggle to find a form for what became his novel *Border Country* Raymond Williams wrote, 'What interests me most . . . was a continuing tension, with very complicated emotions and relationships running through it, between two different worlds that need to be rejoined'. That rejoining can be a lifetime's challenge. But just as there are moments of conflict between different possibilities and aspirations, there can also be moments of reconciliation where we recognise our differences, respect our chosen pathways, and still like and love each other.[132]

My sixtieth birthday marked such a moment for me. Mark

organised a party to celebrate it in November 2005. I didn't want a 'surprise' party, an idea that filled me with horror. I had agonised with Mark for several months about how to mark this point in my life – should it be small and exclusive or extensive and lively, or somewhere in between? We had finally agreed the venue and whom to ask. In the end we landed on large and inclusive, representing all sides of my/our lives: both our families, still rooted in the old Rhondda and Durham coalfields, friends, colleagues, former students, gay and straight, young and old.

We hired an old river boat in the West India Docks, surrounded by the glossy towers of the new financial district of Canary Wharf, just across the Thames from where we lived. The boat was berthed next to the Museum of London Docklands, commemorating a rich industrial and commercial world that had gone. It had echoes for both of us, with our roots in old, once-industrial areas of Wales and the North East, of a lost world, but in the heart of a brash new world. The old and the new, the past, present and future, all in one hyper-urban landscape glistening with late modernity. And there were many surprises for me after all, climaxing in a big firework display I had not expected, launched from the boat, erupting in a sky traced with many other fireworks: it was Bonfire Night, and for the first time in my life I conquered my old fear of fireworks and was able to enjoy them.

But the best surprise was something less glittering and evanescent, but which had a profound effect on me, and marked a critical moment when many elements came together to transform possibilities and change perspectives. It was a celebration of my birthday, yes, but it turned into an affirmation: of my relationship with Mark, of our gayness, and of our mutual belonging in intersecting ways of life.

A friend who was present sent an account of the party to the American feminist critic and poet Eve Kosofsky Sedgwick a few days after, and accidentally copied it to me. He wryly mentioned my 'very working-class family'. I was well versed in the languages of class and his remarks didn't need much spelling out. But whatever his motives he unerringly missed the point. There were no obvious hard and fast distinctions at the party. The fact that members of both our families, young, middle-aged and old, were there intermingling and enjoying themselves with us, our gay and straight friends and colleagues was for me the pleasure of the evening. I had spent a lifetime trying to reconcile the different parts of my life, so the fact that our families were there enjoying themselves with me, with us and our friends was a transforming moment. It was a recognition of who and what we were from those closest to Mark and me, and a coming together for the first time of all the bits of our lives that had for too long seemed fragmented and forever different and mutually unrecognisable.

My mother, now in her mid-eighties, was completely at ease as the matriarch of the clan, keeping an eye on things, even having a little bop with grandchildren and younger friends. My brothers and their families mingled easily with the other guests, as did Mark's parents and siblings and their offspring. It was not so much that old anxieties and prejudices had disappeared. They no longer seemed relevant in that moment, at that time. The lives, identities and ways of being that had once been separate and separated – Other, like strange foreign countries – now seemed pretty ordinary. We were dancing together, to a soundtrack prepared by Mark of the songs that chronicled my life, in a different world.

ALL CHANGE?

My sabbatical gave me some space to think about past, present and future, and to find a way of encapsulating this in a book. I called the resulting work *The World We Have Won: The Remaking of Erotic and Intimate Life*, published in 2007. The organising conceit was that the book described and analysed the changes in sexual and gender mores and manners during my lifetime. It wasn't such a solipsistic obsession as that description might suggest. 1945 represented the birth of a particular vision of the country that had shaped me and which I continued to share. I had benefitted in every way from the education opportunities opened up by the 1944 Education Act, from the welfare system developed in the late 1940s, by the growth of affluence in the 1950s, and by the expansion of free university education in the 1960s. My life had been transformed by the cultural revolution from the late 1960s, and I had played a part, alongside millions of others, in reshaping everyday intimate life. I had witnessed a vast change in the demography of Britain, with the unfreezing of old class rigidities, new social mobilities, and a new informality in dress, behaviour and social discourse, as well as a vastly expanded Black and ethnic minority population – from barely a handful when I was born to 14% by 2011 – who had helped remake the culture in new and creative ways.

Like the rest of my generation of 1945-ers, the post-war baby-boom generation, I had lived through a social and cultural transition of immense significance. Many, perhaps most, people had taken this for granted, I suspect, though it soon became apparent that there was a sizeable chunk of the population who were not reconciled to social change, as the Brexit crisis was soon to confirm. I've never ceased to be amazed at how my parents' generation so easily lived through calamitous economic collapse, war, post-war austerity, rapid social and cultural change, technological revolution, and somehow survived and made worthwhile lives. For members of my own generation the challenges had been equally profound but possibly less obviously dramatic. In any case, the revolution remained unfinished, leaving many scars around which grievances could fester: acute social tensions, continuing poverty, class, status and gender inequities, deeply rooted racism, and an undercurrent of violence in interpersonal relations and society, to mention only the most obvious. The decade after I finished *The World We Have Won* saw the accentuation of economic, social and cultural uncertainty, which fed into the rise of a new and much more reactionary politics that resonated back to the 1930s rather than to a progressive future. The challenge in writing the book was how to balance what I believed to be real gains in terms of growing toleration, pluralism and genuine conviviality between different groups within British society, with the rise of new absolutisms whose lifeblood was fear and loathing.

The title of the book obviously referred to Peter Laslett's classic *The World We Have Lost*, which from its publication in 1965 helped revolutionise our understanding of an English past of individualism and family life (though Wales, Scotland and Ireland were always subtly different from the English mainstream).[133] But whatever the author's intention, the phrase also inevitably invoked a regret for a world that had gone irretrievably, and I felt the need to say something different. I deeply disliked nostalgia, the ache to find a more harmonious past to compensate for the disappointments and desolation of the present, but by the turn of the millennium a melancholic tone seemed ascendant in many circles I was familiar with. All around me I could feel a sense of loss, from people on the left as much as on the right. For traditional conservatives it was easy to understand, if not agree with, a lament for an order of moral certainty, social discipline, sexual restraint and family order that seemed to have slipped away, even if, as most people knew, it had never really existed in their lives. But what has been described as a post-imperial melancholia among many people on the left I found more difficult to comprehend or empathise with.[134] Some tried to elaborate a radical justification for nostalgia (and melancholia), but the pervasive sense of loss that some leftists wallowed in following on the collapse of the Soviet Union and the triumph of neo-liberalism seemed to me to ignore the achievements of the democratisation of everyday life, including sexual and gendered lives, since the 1960s. Against such settled pessimism I wanted to offer not so much optimism as a cool, realistic assessment of the balance sheet of gains and losses in the years since 1945.

In doing this I was describing a journey without a pregiven destination apart from a confused and confusing present. I didn't find, and certainly did not seek, a hidden destiny (the growth of freedom, the triumph of liberalism, universal tolerance) working its way through history. Yet it was difficult to ignore that from a liberal, progressive, freedom-loving perspective there were positive gains that needed to be cherished. Some might prefer to see these achievements as a ruse of history, using the illusion of greater personal autonomy to obscure the ever-elusive coils of power, but I was by now highly sceptical of such thinkers. On this issue, at least, some commentators on the intelligent right were nearer the mark. The conservative American historian, Gertrude Himmelfarb, made what still strikes me as a perceptive insight even as she deplored the consequences of the loss of Victorian values. Comparing the so-called 'sexual anarchy' of the late nineteenth century with the 'sexual revolution' of our time, she commented that 'a century ago the "advanced souls" were precisely that, well in advance of the culture, whereas now they pervade the entire culture. This is the significance of our "sexual revolution": it is a revolution democratized and legitimized'.[135] In other words, the changes had become increasingly embedded, normalised, sustained by a wide span of public opinion.

I was also at the same time acutely aware that the new freedoms I welcomed were still a precarious achievement, and on a global scale the years since I published *The World We Have Won* have shown that what has been gained can also be lost, even in the ostensibly most advanced countries. As I write in the fourth year of the Donald Trump presidency in the USA there is a continuing threat of an attack by federal and state administrations on abortion rights, the rights of trans people, and a wider challenge to social liberalism from an increasingly conservative Supreme Court. Even more threatening is the way in which homophobic and transphobic discourses have become common instruments of state in countries across the globe, from Africa to South America, and parts of Asia to Eastern Europe and Russia. As Ken Plummer argued in *Cosmopolitan Sexualities*, in many parts of the world the gains and losses were finely balanced, and we can't take the outlook or outcome for granted.[136]

As I reach the end of this book it seems appropriate to draw up my own balance sheet as it reflects on my own journeys between different worlds, and especially the world of my childhood and family belonging, which I had left at 18, but never rejected; the LGBT world, which had provided my sense of identity and commitment since the 1960s; and the wider international, globalising world, which provided increasingly new possibilities and which I got to know through travel, scholarship and increasingly global connectivity.

LEFT BEHİND?

'Labour country' was no longer what it was. The Rhondda was still nominally faithful to its old loyalties. But the local Labour Party had become increasingly sclerotic and devoid of ideas, and in the European elections of 2019, Labour had been beaten into third place in the Rhondda by the Brexit Party and Plaid Cymru. In the general election that followed in December 2019, Labour won but with the Brexit Party achieving one of its highest percentage of votes in the UK. Was this a once-in-a-lifetime political realignment or a reflection of a one-off political crisis? It was too early to know for sure, but there were straws in the wind. My brother Dennis, a long-serving Labour councillor, gave up his seat in 2016, disillusioned by the national leadership and local drift.

The Rhondda, like many other old industrial areas in Wales and England, was caught between a world of work that had irretrievably gone, new employment that was usually less secure than old mining and heavy industry had been, and massive cultural and social change that was only partly absorbed. Perhaps the Rhondda wasn't so much left behind as drifting gently on the rapids, with no obvious people in charge. On regular trips to see my mother and family, usually now with Mark, I found the Rhondda as warm and welcoming as it had ever been. It was also infinitely more materially affluent than it had been when I was growing up, though relatively the Rhondda Cynon Taf area was one of the poorest in the UK. New roads through the Valleys had made travel much quicker and had ended the old sense of isolation. Regular foreign travel was the norm for my immediate family. A number of houses in my mother's street now housed students from the University of South Wales in Pontypridd and the universities in Cardiff. The old school system, the pride of Wales that had made my life in London possible, had savagely declined in performance, but the Welsh government (under a Liberal Democrat minister) was working hard to revive it. The rail service to Cardiff and beyond had survived and, though rackety, was a busy commuter line to jobs outside the Valleys, with the promise of a new metro system to come. The Rhondda itself was effectively post-industrial, a run-down commuter town. Supermarkets sat on the sites of old collieries, and as in many towns in the UK, the old high street in Porth, Hannah Street, was in possibly terminal decline. The array of grocers and fruit and vegetable shops, Home and Colonial and Thomas & Evans grocery stores, independent butchers, clothiers, three chapels, two banks, a cinema and two Bracchis (Italian-owned and -run cafés that were common in my youth) that once ordered the street had been largely replaced by cheap takeaways, estate agents and boarded-up shops. The heavy drinking culture of my youth had largely gone. Many clubs and pubs had shut alongside their declared enemies, the chapels. But here was now a heavy drug culture, including a heroin problem. Some of this is captured in the vivid stories set in the Rhondda and neighbouring valleys by Rachel Trezise, whose wry, comic voice brings to life a culture of poverty, sexual abuse, adultery, teenage drinking and drugs, but also a liveliness and resilience among young people despite (or because of) few opportunities and sparse aspirations.[137]

That liveliness and resilience and an inbuilt exuberance had always been a vital part of the culture of the Rhondda. The problem for a queer boy like myself growing up in the 1950s and 1960s was that the everyday preoccupations that represented the life of most men by their nature seemed to exclude me. So much has changed! The Rhondda, once so macho and aggressively heterosexual to my youthful eye, can now boast a former priest and openly gay man, Chris Bryant, as its long-serving Labour MP. He has been personally popular and generally well liked, and is now one of several openly gay MPs, members of the Welsh Assembly and councillors. And the world of Welsh rugby has produced and embraced its own out gay icons: the international player Gareth Thomas and the international referee Nigel Owens – something unimaginable at any earlier time.

Family bonds remain at the heart of the culture, as in my own case, but they seem less institutional and the product of necessity in a culture of scarcity, and more personal: they have to be worked at rather than assumed. When my mother died, a cousin said she feared our family ties would loosen, and we would see less of each other. This was a tribute to the ways in which my mother made it her life's work to keep us together. In practice, we have held together, but for many people family links are contingent, not certain. Sexual manners have certainly changed, and my mother observed, tut-tutted and accepted all the flux she was confronted with. She rarely intervened in the difficulties of our relationships and she knew much more than she ever revealed about our would-be secret lives.

More widely, sexual behaviour is less tethered by the old restrictions but nevertheless follows unwritten rules. Fewer people marry early, as in the past, and cohabitation is normal, but in the Rhondda formal engagements are celebrated with often elaborate parties and rituals. There is an inner order that suggests almost pre-industrial patterns. It is as if the marriage patterns of my youth were but a temporary imposition on a deeply rooted secular pattern. Though still clearly apparent, gender differences are less rigid and ingrained than in the past. Most women work, if only to sustain the family economy. The taboos about women going to pubs without men has long gone. Women's autonomy is now generally accepted, even though in practice women still take responsibility for most caring activities – as is true throughout the nation. Homophobia can still be witnessed in casual speech, especially in banter between men, but the deep shame that marked my childhood and early adulthood has largely faded. Because of greater openness most families now contain or know someone who is gay or lesbian, and it is increasingly difficult to view us as strange or exotic creatures, especially given the collapse of chapel culture and the omnipresence of explicit media and social media images. I was told a story of two men caught by the police in a cubicle of a local public lavatory, apparently taking class A drugs. Their defence was that they were there to have sex, not to do drugs. The hierarchy of sins and misdemeanours has changed radically.

MY TRİBE

The LGBT world has provided the alternative framework of my life since the 1960s. As I have attempted to trace in this memoir, it has changed dramatically since I first encountered it, when it was relatively extensive in a place like London, but covert, secretive, closeted and very much a subculture, discreetly segregated from the host society though symbiotic with it. Post-gay liberation a different word became common to describe a rapidly expanding and diversifying world: the emotive, evocative and elusive term 'community', which had a powerful pull for me, rooted as I was in the culture of the Valleys. Raymond Williams noted that it was one of the few words that is never used unfavourably, and indeed it has been used widely across the political spectrum, in the most unlikely circumstances, often cynically. James Baldwin expressed the essence of the idea: '[I]t simply means our endless connections with, and responsibility, for each other', which underlined the sense of mutuality and belonging, and hence of empowerment, that has always been central for me. It suggests something counterposed to the cold instrumentality and impersonality of hyper-individualism and the commodification of a market economy. Community offers a repository of meanings for its members, a home for traditions and forms of recognition, and a vocabulary of values through which individuals shape their understanding of the social world, and their sense of identity.[138]

The community I was born into provided all these, but could not accommodate all my needs and desires. Communities can imprison as well as enable, and I needed to break away to affirm a different identity. The gay world offered me a new space. It was of course quite different from the community I came from. It had no fixed geographical location, though some areas – London's Soho and Earls Court, Manchester's Village, West Yorkshire's Hebden Bridge – attracted large LGBT populations for a variety of reasons. My own borough in London, Southwark, has become one of the queerest in the UK, rivalling Brighton in numbers of declared LGBT people, and same-sex couples and civil partnerships in the 2011 Census. But this was serendipitous rather than carefully chosen. My LGBT life has been defined more by diasporic consciousness than by physical location. What constituted the key elements of that consciousness has sometimes been less clear, even to someone like myself who had spent most of my career grappling with that very issue.

In *Coming Out* I set myself the task of exploring the emergence of a 'homosexual consciousness', and I was clearly referring to that mixture of identity, identification, subjectivity and ways of life that were recognisably present and thriving in the world around me. But I was always aware that there were other people who experienced same-sex practices but had different identifications and subjectivities from myself – were they not also homosexual, queer, gay . . . ? What bound me to them? It was not an identical identity. It was not a fixed sense of self. It was not a common political consciousness. It was not even necessarily shared sexual interests, given the wide range of sexual desires, fantasies and activities I encountered from day to day. Could it be a shared unconscious, repressed in many cases, actively played out in my own? But how did that relate to the very different histories I was discovering among women?

Was there any essential link between my desires and values and those of the paedophiles on the fringes of the movement, some of whom identified as gay even as they fantasised about young girls as well as boys? And the LGBT world was getting ever more diverse as bisexual and trans people began to assert their claims to recognition much more forcefully from the late 1980s. By the 1990s, even as many refused it, the term 'gay' had become a universal signifier, as much used in urban communities in east Africa, or teeming cities in Latin America or Indonesia as in Anglophone and European countries, and even used by the Pope. It was increasingly clear, however, that it did not necessarily mean quite the same thing everywhere. I knew I could walk into any 'queer' or 'gay' bar in any part of these worlds and feel an instant personal recognition with the people there. They were part of my tribe. And yet what made up that tribe remained fluid, with the boundaries continuously shifting. Sexual cultures remained infinitely varied even within the relatively small space of London. I continue to be amazed at the diversity and variety on a global scale, even though I have been paid to understand them. I became fascinated by this dialectic of identification and disidentification, similarity and difference that characterised the LGBT worlds. This was so much more than the accidents of obscure and speculative genes haphazardly combining.

So, what is this 'gay community' I continue to feel a part of, and which interpellates my sense of self, my subjectivity? Some have detected a quasi-ethnic coherence, and certainly it was possible to see similarities with, say, the Jewish community, which has somehow combined continuity over time, intermingling traditions, the unity of the Book and an embattled history, while being constituted of different religious and political commitments. Like a faith community, the LGBT world had developed many common rituals and celebrations, like the annual Pride parades or International Days Against Homophobia, Biphobia and Transphobia (IDAHOBIT) in many cities across the globe, that provide a sense of common belonging. Some of these echoed ancient bacchanalias when the world was turned upside down, where transgressive behaviour became the norm for the party. Essentially, though, they are invented traditions, though no less potent for that. The LGBT community has many of the characteristics of social movements, buried in everyday life and organised around the common experiences of grievance, insult, prejudice and oppression. It was noticeable how a stronger sense of common experience and purpose sprang up in response to existential threats, like the HIV/AIDS epidemic, or legislative attacks like Section 28, or the homophobic Soho pub bombing in 1999. At other times, however, once the euphoric excitement of building the gay liberation movement passed, so did the sense of a single movement.

Which is why in the end the word 'community' still seems relevant. It is a community of a particular type: a critical community, which sees the status quo in one way or another as unacceptable and intolerable. The LGBT world continues to problematise the norms of the culture, is open to new experiences and makes new subjectivities possible. It is a sexual culture, a distinctive social world, a focus of identities, a repository of ethics and values, a forum for social capital and a stage for activism, campaigning and politics. It is not exclusive, it has ill-defined boundaries, embodies many old and invented traditions, and is constantly evolving.

I rarely now visit the clubs. My dancing ability was poor enough to clear the floor even in my younger days; now I am old enough to be able to opt out without shame. The (remaining) bars are places to meet old friends before doing something else rather than spending whole evenings. I rarely if ever visit the vast and ever-expanding gay-oriented internet, which to a large extent has displaced the bar as a sexual marketplace. Yet of course the sexual aspect of the LGBT community is only a tiny part of what it means – from campaigns to choirs, business to trade union networks, political lobbies to faith groups, local groups to national organisations, LGBT media to online forums. It has become a tangle of hundreds of groups, networks, organisations and institutions, embracing all aspects of the lesbian, gay, bisexual, trans, intersex, asexual, polysexual, non-binary, multisexual, genderfluid, queer plus plus plus worlds.

Its very growth and successes, however, have generated powerful hostility. As I type this *The Guardian* reports new research suggesting homophobic and transphobic hate crimes, including stalking, harassment and violent assault, have more than doubled over five years.[139] Transphobic attacks have trebled during the same period. It is difficult not to see such statistics as related to a rise in ultra-nationalist and racist, antisemitic, jihadist and Islamophobic violence during the same period, in part generated by the rise of authoritarian populisms and the fevered political crisis generated by Brexit. It was noticeable that the areas most likely to vote Leave in the Brexit referendum in 2016 were also those parts of the country least likely to support LGBT rights and same-sex marriage. The deep social conservatism of many parts of the country where people feel 'left behind' seems to have harboured a nexus of feeling, where hostility to the so-called metropolitan liberal elite has also morphed into continuing hostility to sexual and gender change. In the most extreme cases this has taken a violent form.

So, despite remarkable change and formal equality, the struggle for LGBT rights has not ended. But instead of mass mobilisation against it as dreamt of at radical moments in the early 1970s or the early 1990s, the community now hosts a mass of civil society organisations with a wide range of different objectives, burrowing away at different issues. I have spent a large part of my time working with the main organisation of and for older LGBT people, Opening Doors London (ODL). Mark and I were involved in the early moves to set it up in 2007–08 as an initiative of Age UK Camden. After its reorganisation in 2016 as an autonomous charity I served as chair of the trustees for the first four years. ODL is a mix of advocacy and services, social interventions and caring support. In any one month we offer forty-five to fifty social activities, from coffee mornings to cinema evenings, walking groups to art gallery visits. We have a befriending service for isolated, housebound or disabled people, and we provide training programmes for other voluntary or statutory services to learn of the social and caring needs of LGBT people. It is a relatively small organisation in comparison with something like SAGE in the USA or similar organisations in the Netherlands and elsewhere, but it serves a vital role in London and beyond in supporting the needs of older LGBT people. Members range in age from 50 to 95, and embrace a huge variety of social and cultural experiences. Some have been out as gay since the 1960s. Others have recently come out in their sixties, seventies or even eighties. For me it represents what the LGBT community has become: a density of identities, desires and needs, experiences, problems, possibilities and hopes. And crucially, we can no longer simply talk of London, or British or even European or American networks. LGBT experiences have gone global.

GLOBALLY YOURS

International links had played a vital part in the growth of LGBT consciousness since its earliest moment in the late nineteenth century. Its modern history had been turbo-charged from 1969 by the American explosion following Stonewall, though each country it influenced usually took its own path, building on but also transforming its own historical antecedents. Britain has been no laggard in building on its own gay history, and from the start of my own work I sought to demonstrate the roots of our own identities and subjectivities, but always in a broader international setting. Pioneering writers on homosexuality in the late nineteenth century, such as John Addington Symonds, Havelock Ellis and Edward Carpenter, self-consciously drew on such international literature as there was, and personal links with non-British friends and contacts. Throughout the twentieth century this accelerated. The novelist Radclyffe Hall, like many others, was part of an international coterie of lesbian artists and writers, while later homophile activists like Antony Grey, for example, were sustained by strong links with European and American reformers. Cities like Paris, Amsterdam and Tangiers, as well as the obvious American cities, offered alternative visions of how we could live, work and understand each other, just as aristocrats on the Grand Tour of the eighteenth century looked to the glories of Rome or Venice. My own writing and activism from the 1970s onwards would have been impossible without my friends and co-thinkers in Australia, America and Latin America, and Europe. As my personal circumstances changed in the early 2000s I was able to participate more fully in the global dialogue.

My sabbatical in 2005–06 helped make up my mind that I should retire early from LSBU. I was by now an executive dean, and had successfully launched a new faculty, supported new courses, recruited many promising new staff and developed the research culture. I had also published several books and numerous articles in my period as a senior manager. However, I was feeling burnt out and wanted a new challenge. I was encouraged by the vice-chancellor to apply for one of the deputy posts to him, despite my initial scepticism that this was not right for me. I didn't get it for reasons that were never made clear, and this decided me to go. I gave in effect two years' notice, and in the meantime became Director of Research, preparing LSBU for the next national RAE. We did much better than expected in that, and I continued for a while as a research professor, preparing for the next. But in 2008 I was largely free of administrative entanglements for the first time in nearly fifteen years. I was still relatively young (63), had a comfortable pension, and at last I could write full time and travel more. That at least was the fantasy. Life turned out to be a bit more complicated.

Micky by now was in an advanced stage of Parkinson's disease, with increasing cognitive difficulties, and after a fall was confined to a wheelchair. We had to sell his flat and find a residential care home for him, and for the next five years until his death in 2013 Mark and I took responsibility for his affairs. By now Mark and I also had a dog, Ziggy, a lively black cockapoo, who added greatly to the joy of our lives but needed constant attention. Fortunately, Mark and I were both now largely working from home, so Ziggy had us around all the time. Despite such distractions, I began a sustained period of writing: new monographs, revised editions, articles and papers. And I was able to take up more invitations to travel abroad, often accompanied by Mark.

Since the beginning of our relationship we had travelled extensively in Europe, the USA and Mexico, and Australia, often combining holidays with research and lecturing trips. The tempo increased after my notional retirement. By the turn of the millennium those of us working on gender and sexuality had become part of a torrent of international links with growing research networks, international organisations, conferences and lecture tours. Sex research in general and LGBT research in particular had gone global, sustained by the internet revolution, cheap airplane travel and social media. I spoke widely on my own work, both to academic and community-based audiences, and invariably had lively and informed feedback – from Scandinavia to Mexico, Estonia to Costa Rica, and Cuba to Australia. But this was more than a Western scholar jetting in to impart wisdom. It was one aspect of a growing dialogue across different histories and experiences where we learnt from each other.

Global and transnational histories were becoming increasingly important in the academy, and this reflected a growing sense of the importance of understanding the ways in which sexuality and gender norms had been shaped by global flows, visibly accelerating since the sixteenth century through the heyday of imperialism in the nineteenth century to the globalised world of today. This had never been one-way traffic, west to east, north to south. The languages and ideologies around sexuality and gender now have an international currency. They underpin international organisations for human sexual rights and transnational campaigns. They are also the source of acute disagreements – about the meaning and role of human rights discourses especially, as well as the legacy of Empire – and outright opposition. Widespread discussion about the social and historical making of gender, for example, which was a key aspect of the work I was most closely associated with and spoke widely about, has become the focus of a sustained backlash. 'Gender ideology' has become the target of conservative forces in Latin America, post-communist regimes in Eastern Europe, and the Vatican, which as I write has issued a reaffirmation of the natural differences between men and women, and their centrality to family life. The global rise of a trans movement and consciousness of the fluidity of gender definitions has fanned a backlash, even among some feminists. Reactionary nationalisms are blowing on the flames.

Latin America has been the fulcrum of many of these tensions, between a rapid modernisation of sexual and gender norms, especially among the urban middle class, and a super-heated neo-traditionalism, usually backed by the Catholic Church, together with a rapidly growing Christian evangelicalism, regularly funded by conservative movements in the USA. In this context the local and international work of often embattled reformers and activists is vital, and from the early 1990s I was able to establish links with some of them. There was considerable interest in my work in Latin America, with several of my books and articles translated into Spanish or Portuguese, and this gave me an excuse to visit and get to know Central America better. In early 1995 Mark and I had visited Mexico, at the invitation of the dynamic sex educationalist and reformer Esther Corona, who has remained a warm friend of both of us ever since. I gave a number of lectures in Mexico City, and met many of the leading participants in the sex reform movement, from journalists in the gay press to academics, well-established political activists to leading psychologists and educationalists. I was present at early discussions to set up a new federation of sex education societies. Two decades later we were guests at the twentieth anniversary conference of what had become FEMESS – Federación Mexicana de Educación Sexual y Sexología, a thriving hub of clinicians, educationalists, researchers and activists that helped shape policy and programmes in Mexico and beyond.

It was through Esther that I developed some links with Cuba, which in many ways exemplifies the tensions and contradictions in this increasingly globalised discourse on sexuality and gender. Like many of my generation I had keenly followed the Cuban Revolution in the late 1950s and early

1960s, but had been quickly disillusioned by its treatment of homosexuals, and moved by the stories of those who had escaped. From my immersion in gay liberation from 1970 I passionately believed that treatment of same-sex love was an essential yardstick for judging radical intent and revolutionary integrity. Cuba fell far below such standards and I was highly sceptical of its claims. I remember being sharply attacked when I expressed this view at a conference as late as the early 2010s: this was, a participant said, a Western, imperialist stance that ignored the significance of the struggles of the Global South. I was familiar with these arguments, which have a long history: essentially, if necessary, LGBT rights must wait until the revolution is secured.

Cuba, however, was more interesting than such stereotypes. In 1994 I was speaking at a conference at Mexico City, and through Esther met a young Cuban woman who expressed interest in what I had said in my lectures, and what she had read of my work, and invited me to come to Cuba to teach at a summer school. It was Mariela Castro, niece of Fidel and daughter of Fidel's brother Raúl and his wife Vilma Espin. She was Cuban royalty but also charged with the leadership of Cuba's official sex education programme. I couldn't make the dates she suggested for a visit and long regretted afterwards that I had missed the opportunity to see what was going on in Cuba. Nearly twenty years later I met Mariela again, at a conference in Glasgow. She reminded me of my promise to visit, and this time I committed myself firmly to going.

By now the sex education organisation she led, Centro Nacional de Educación Sexual, or CENESEX, had become the motor for major changes in attitudes towards sexual health, homosexuality and trans people, and was in effect a government department promoting change. Her father was now president. Mark and I agreed to visit for the annual IDAHOBIT event on 17

May 2013, and I gave various lectures and attended a conference on global sexualities and social justice. This visit turned out to be a wonderful experience. We were warmly welcomed as Mariela's guests for the week, and at the IDAHOBIT event itself I paraded alongside Mariela as she led the newly invented tradition of a conga through central parts of Havana to the festival party in the park. In the evening we were guests at a huge rally at the Karl Marx Theatre, where Mariela was the guest of honour, and appeared on stage to a huge ovation. Subsequently the Communist Party's daily newspaper, *Granma*, had a favourable report on my visit, which greatly impressed the three Argentinian women we later travelled with on a tour of the island, who drew the newspaper piece to our attention.

We fell in love with the country. It was a nation still in dire poverty in large parts, and the two currencies in circulation, the local one for the population as a whole, and the dollar-related one for tourists, designed to bring in foreign currency, underlined deep inequalities in the socialist island. We were acutely aware that the tips we gave to tourist guides were worth ten times the local rate, so our tips could be worth as much as a doctor or teacher earned in a month. Despite some economic liberalisation, especially again related to tourism – battered classic cars of the 1950s as taxis, small home-based restaurants, bed and breakfast accommodation – the country was still very much under rigid Communist Party control, with revolutionary committees still closely observing behaviour in every local community. But it was not difficult to find a lively queer culture in most cities across the island, and a thriving cruising scene in Havana itself. Everyone we spoke to was full of praise for Mariela's work, especially given her direct line to the president (her father) and the upper echelons of the Communist Party. The story was that even Fidel, now in retirement, had regretted his earlier anti-gay policies and supported liberalisation of attitudes. The British Embassy asked me what they could do to support Mariela in promoting further reform.

The situation was not, however, straightforward. While a number of LGBT-identified people had survived the years of revolution as committed communists, and even in a few cases as protected members of the elite, it was obvious that open expression of same-sex attractions or gender nonconformity were still difficult for many people. The revolutionary enthusiasm of the early years to build the new socialist man and woman in many ways confirmed deeply ingrained and highly gendered family structures, and racialised divides. Oral history interviews conducted in the 2010s portrayed a picture of continuing shame and guilt about homosexuality, especially among fervent party members. It was difficult not to worry about how deeply embedded the changes were.[140]

Mariela herself has continued to lead the campaign for further advances and as a member of the National Assembly has recently been a strong advocate of same-sex marriage and of amending the constitution to embody that. She has become an international icon of LGBT and human sexual rights. But there was also growing opposition in the party and assembly to further change, fuelled by the rising Evangelical Christian movement (funded from the USA). The American opening-up to Cuba instigated by President Obama was rapidly closed by President Trump, who banned foreign travel by the Castro family. The prolonged collapse of the Venezuelan regime, which provided Cuba with cheap oil, and a tightening embargo, produced another major economic crisis. In the midst of this, the IDAHOBIT was cancelled in May 2019 by the government, citing the economic and international situation. Mariela and CENESEX reluctantly backed this, and an unofficial protest conga by activists was quickly halted by the authorities. At the moment it is unclear what the implications of this are. Inevitably, however, one can only wonder if LGBT advance is again to be sacrificed to the needs of 'the revolution'.

FAREWELL

My mother reached her ninetieth birthday in August 2011. We had a surprise party for her, just across the road in the local rugby club. She was expecting a small gathering. Instead there were a hundred friends and family. She loved the atmosphere and as usual took to her feet and danced as much as she could. In the following week she went to two or three more parties, energised by the excitement. But a few weeks after, she began to ail. For the last few years before her she was increasingly confined to the ground floor of the house she had lived in for nearly ninety years, moving around with sticks and a walking frame. She was never short of visitors, and most of her family still lived nearby. My brothers and their families were always at hand to provide support. Robert's wife Paula was a constant presence, shopping, doing the laundry, looking after Mam's finances, while Dennis' daughters visited every Saturday and tidied up the house – otherwise my mother would have tried to do it herself. She was resolutely independent, resisting any move to anywhere else. She still insisted on cooking for herself, and when she tried Meals on Wheels for a few days she quickly rejected them as too tasteless. Very reluctantly she agreed to regular visits by carers, in the morning and evening, ostensibly to prepare her for getting up and going to bed. In practice she always got up, washed and breakfasted before the morning visit, and had dinner before the evening one. She enjoyed the visits as company. The carers bandaged

Mam's swollen legs and gossiped to her. She knew all about their lives and families. When she died they came to the service.

The end came soon after her ninety-third birthday, in September 2014. She fell in the kitchen early in the morning, after washing but while going to make a cup of tea. When the carer arrived and found her on the floor she was still conscious. My brother Dennis arrived soon after and she said to him, 'I've had enough'. As she weakened over the next week she took charge of her dying as best she could. She said farewell to each of us in turn, and told Mark to look after me. The house was full of family most of the day, and Dennis, Robert, Mark and I had a rota to be with her through the nights. But when she finally gave up the struggle only Robert and Paula were present with her. Mark and I had popped out to get something to eat, expecting a long night by her bedside. It was not to be.

Everybody's mother is special to them. She led an ordinary life, in extraordinary times, and survived. She lived through the acute social strife of the 1920s, her father's premature death, the poverty and struggles of her teenage years, the challenges of the war years, the ups and downs of marriage and bringing up children, my father's depression and death, and her long years of widowhood and eventual ill health. Nothing bent or broke her generally cheerful disposition. She had a way of always expecting the worst but hoping for the best, which saw her through many crises. And she was acutely emotionally intelligent, watching, empathising, judging when to intervene or say nothing.

Mam's family was everything to her, her pride and joy, and we in turn were proud of her. She would do anything for her three boys and their partners, and we would have done anything for her. She loved to talk about our achievements, whether passing exams, successes in our careers, becoming a local councillor, running marathons, being loving parents of their own children. My citation when I was awarded an OBE was hung in pride of place in her living room. In our different ways we have all striven to live her ideal of a good life: close family ties, mutual toleration (despite occasional angry flare-ups), loyalty, neighbourliness and respect, for ourselves and others. The funeral was my mother's farewell. It was also a family embrace. At the invitation of my brothers and nephews Mark was one of her bearers. A circle had been closed.

MEMORY, MEMORIES

When I retired from full-time university life in 2008 my successor as dean, Mike Molan (another Welshman), said with his usual cheerful cynicism that I need not worry too much about seeking a legacy: 'The waters will soon close over your head'. I couldn't resist quoting the words back to him in my speech at his retirement ten years later. But of course he was broadly right. Several reorganisations after I left the university, the old new faculty I painfully built up has long gone, as have the research centre my successor named after me and many of the staff I appointed. The ethos is quite different (though quite a lot of reinventing the wheel). Ken Plummer also reminds me that the life cycle of a set of ideas is about fifteen years, so some of my own early theories and arguments as described in my books have now lived through nearly three generations. Several of my books have been continuously in print for over forty years, but their life-support systems have depended on regular updates. The waters pass easily through the fingers and blow in the wind.

Yet writing this memoir has reminded me forcefully that to forget the past is to lose the future. I am not talking here of the ephemera of a career necessarily reliant on constant change as successive generations of students come forward with new needs, hopes, aspirations and ideals. A good teacher, a committed researcher and writer about the present as much as the past has to respond to these or die. Nor am I thinking of the frailties of scholarship and the battle of ideas. If the scholarship is good, works will survive, even if they have to be rediscovered a hundred years hence in a dusty cupboard or more likely now in an obscure part of the internet. My real point is about the importance of memory, and how memory sustains and enables. In my early days as a gay man, I had no way of linking to a living past, a possible present or a hopeful future because I had no ease of access to memories of people like me. I had to find and make those connections for myself.

Now there is a wealth of memories embodied in a rich archive of feeling and experience encapsulated in books, libraries and museums, artefacts like the AIDS memorial quilt, oral and video records, television and radio programmes, billions of records online, and the constant telling and retelling of stories that bring the dead alive and give the living a sense of connectedness with past lives. The LGBT archives that now exist provide a resource, a collection of stories, a set of representations, a memorial, a time capsule, a field of inquiry and construction, all embodying and solidifying new structures of feeling, and contributing to a counter-public, an alternative public sphere. One of our battles, wrote Joan Nestle, reflecting on the establishment of the Lesbian Herstory Archives in New York, 'was to change secrecy into disclosure, shame into memory', for memory was an 'alchemy' that transformed mockery, hatred and fear into community.[141]

Reading the memoirs of people I knew has a special resonance, offering a community of belonging across distance. I think of the pleasure of reading Alan Wakeman's memoir, and tingling again with the excitement of early gay liberation, which created new horizons for him and for so many of us: the excitement of personal empowerment and collective belonging as we reinvented ourselves. I ache with remembrance as I read in my old friend Emmanuel's memoir, *Making Emmanuel Cooper*, an account of Sunday tea in his parents' house: the tinned fruit, the Carnation milk, the homemade trifle, and the plate of bread and butter that accompanied every meal. Emmanuel came from a mining village in Derbyshire, a hundred miles or more from my mining village in South Wales, but over the distance of space and time (Emmanuel was a crucial six years older than me) the lineaments of a common working-class material culture emerge. Yet this reminds me in turn that despite a common working-class identity forged by struggle and politics in the twentieth century, the Rhondda was distinctive.

Another memoir that takes me back to my roots, Dai Smith's dithyrambic *In the Frame: Memory in Society, Wales 1910 to 2010*, wonderfully recreates this difference, and there is one particular reference that brings this home to me. We were exact contemporaries in the Rhondda, he born just a few months before me. He attended the same school for a while, Porth County, though he had left before I arrived. We overlapped at various points in our careers. But what particularly echoes in the memory is Dai mentioning in passing that we called T-shirts 'Sloppy Joes' in the 1950s. I recently checked online the origins of this usage. It obviously suggests American influences, but it is striking how limited its usage was in Britain. Perhaps another Welsh peculiarity, like calling plimsolls 'daps' or spring onions 'jibbons'. But this is not the oddness of isolation but perhaps of South Wales' long global links. We were different in so many ways but we were connected to a larger world, and that world has come home to us.

Those 'continuing tensions' between different worlds that I quoted from Raymond Williams earlier in this chapter animate the memoirs and memories I mention here, and they echo very precisely the key worlds that I have sought to dance between: the world of my birth and continuing loyalties, and the cosmopolitan and metropolitan gay world that has become my life. What seemed an isolated struggle to live the contradictions can now be witnessed through memory as a collective history, a product of complex social and cultural as well as personal transitions. And these transitions are unfinished, partial, contested, especially but not only in the heartlands of non-metropolitan Britain that people like myself and Emmanuel came from. The conflicts over Brexit were in part fuelled by the contradictions working their way through a deeply divided society in a globalising world. It is difficult not to feel a darkening of the skies, and the impossibility of finding a way through in the wake of the disastrous electoral defeat of the Labour Party in 2019. That was certainly the end of something.

Yet it is difficult too not to listen to the memories of the people, peoples, I identify with, often across difference, who have made me, without a stirring of hope. Writing this memoir has allowed me to piece together a mosaic of struggles, endurance, aspirations, care, friendship and love that convinces me the waters do not, cannot, entirely cover our heads: not drowning, still waving. It remains possible, indeed necessary, to straddle different worlds and find a viable sense of belonging, all the way home.

REFERENCES

PREFACE

1   Mike Parker and Paul Whitfield, *The Rough Guide to Wales*, London: Rough Guides, May 2003, p. xxi.

2   T.A. Davies, 'Impressions of Life in the Rhondda Valley', in K. S. Hopkins (ed.), *Rhondda Past and Present*, Ferndale: Rhondda Borough Council, 1980, p. 11. I draw here on an earlier discussion of my life in the Rhondda in Jeffrey Weeks, *The World We Have Won: The Remaking of Erotic and Intimate Life*, Abingdon: Routledge, 2007, pp. 23–33.

3   Daryl Leeworthy, *Labour Country: Political Radicalism and Social Democracy in South Wales 1831–1985*, Cardigan: Parthian, 2018.

CHAPTER 1   A QUEER BOY FROM THE VALLEYS

4   E. D. Lewis, 'Population Changes and Social Life 1960–1914', in K. S. Hopkins (ed.), *Rhondda Past and Present*, Ferndale:

Rhondda Borough Council, 1980, pp. 110–18; Dai Smith, *In the Frame: Memory in Society, Wales 1910 to 2010*, Cardigan: Parthian, 2013, p. 392.

5   E. D. Lewis, op. cit., p. 110.

6   Vividly portrayed in Sue Bruley, *The Women and Men of 1926: The General Strike and Miners' Lockout in South Wales*, Cardiff: University of Wales Press, 2010.

7   Hopkins, *Rhondda Past and Present*, p. xi.

8   Simon Szreter, 'Falling Fertilities and Changing Sexualities in Europe since c.1850. A Comparative Study of Different Demographic Patterns', in F. X. Eder, L. A. Hall and G. Hekma (eds.), *Sexuality in Europe: Themes in Sexuality*, Manchester: Manchester University Press, 1999, p. 163.

9   P. O'Leary, 'Masculine Histories: Gender and the Social History of Modern Wales', *Welsh History Review* 22 (2), 2004, p. 265.

10   N. Dennis, F. Henriques and C. Slaughter, *Coal Is Our Life: An Analysis of a Yorkshire Mining Community*, London: Tavistock, 1969 (first published 1956).

11   Philip Dodd, 'Grimethorpe', in A. Buonfino and G. Mulgan (eds.), *Porcupines in Winter: The Pleasures and Pains of Living Together in Modern Britain*, London: The Young Foundation, 2006, p. 36.

12   Nickie Charles, 'The Refuge Movement and Domestic Violence', in J. Aaron, T. Rees, S. Betts and M. Vincentelli, (eds.), *Our Sisters' Land: The Changing Identities of Women in Wales*, Cardiff: Cardiff University Press, 1994, p. 48.

13   Dai Smith, 'Leaders and Led', in Hopkins, op. cit., p. 40.

14   Leo Abse, *Private Member*, London: Macdonald, 1973, p. 155.

15   Ken Plummer, *Narrative Power: The Struggle for Human Value*, Cambridge: Polity Press, 2019, p. ix.

16   Jeffrey Weeks and Kevin Porter, *Between the Acts: Lives*

of Homosexual Men 1885–1967, London: Rivers Oram Press, 1998 (first published 1991), pp. 15–27.

17   Ibid. pp. 70–90.

18   Rhys Davies, *Print of a Hare's Foot: An Autobiographical Beginning*, London: Heinemann, 1969; Meic Stephens, *Rhys Davies: Decoding the Hare: Critical Essays to Mark the Centenary of the Writer's Birth*, Cardiff: University of Wales Press, 2001; Meic Stephens, *Rhys Davies: A Writer's Life*, Cardigan: Parthian, 2013; Huw Osborne, *Rhys Davies*, Cardiff: University of Wales Press, 2009.

19   See particularly Norena Shopland, *Forbidden Lives: LGBT Histories from Wales*, Bridgend: Seren, 2017; Daryl Leeworthy, 'Hidden from View? Male Homosexuality in Twentieth-Century Wales', *Llafur*, 2015, pp. 97–119; Daryl Leeworthy, *A Little Gay History of Wales*, Cardiff: University of Wales Press, 2019.

20   Hopkins, *Rhondda Past and Present*, p. xiii.

21   Ibid.

CHAPTER 2   LONDON CALLING

22   See Mary McIntosh, 'The Homosexual Role', *Social Problems*, 16 (2), 1968, pp. 182–92.

23   Carl Wittman, *A Gay Manifesto*, New York: A Red Butterfly Publication, 1970, at https://www.historyisaweapon.com/defcon1/wittmanmanifesto.html, accessed 19 August 2019.

24   Randolph Trumbach, 'London's Sodomites: Homosexual Behavior and Western Culture in the 18th Century', *Journal of Social History*, 11 (1), Fall, 1977, pp. 1–33; Randolph Trumbach, *Sex and the Gender Revolution, Vol. 1, Heterosexuality and the Third Gender in Enlightenment London*, Chicago: Chicago

University Press, 1998; Alan Bray, *Homosexuality in Renaissance England*, London: Gay Men's Press, 1983.

25 Jeffrey Weeks, *What is Sexual History?*, Cambridge: Polity Press, 2016, pp. 46–7. For sources see Matt Cook, *London and the Culture of Homosexuality 1885–1914*, Cambridge: Cambridge University Press, 2003; Matt Houlbrook, *Queer London: Perils and Pleasures in the Sexual Metropolis, 1918–1957*, Chicago: Chicago University Press, 2005.

26 Chris Waters, 'The Homosexual as a Social Being in Britain, 1945–1968', *Journal of British Studies,* 51 (3), July, 2012, pp. 685–710.

27 Bryan Magee, *One in Twenty: A Study of Homosexuality in Men and Women*, London: Corgi, 1969 (first published 1966), p. 13.

28 James Baldwin, *Giovanni's Room*, London: Corgi, 1963. This is the edition I bought in Oxford in late 1963. I would have been 18 at the time.

29 James Baldwin, *Another Country*, London: Corgi, 1965.

30 Jeffrey Weeks, *Coming Out: Homosexual Politics in Britain from the Nineteenth Century to the Present*, London: Quartet, 1977, p. 176.

31 D. J. West, *Homosexuality*, Harmondsworth: Pelican, 2nd revised edition, 1969 (first published 1955), p. 261.

32 Donald West, *Gay Life, Straight Work*, London: Paradise Press, 2012, pp. 59–60.

33 A. E. G. Wright (Antony Grey), *Personal Tapestry*, London: The One Roof Press, 2008.

34 Leeworthy, *Labour Country*.

35 Raymond Williams, *Culture and Society 1780–1950*, Harmondsworth: Penguin, 1966 (first published 1958).

36 Raymond Williams (ed.), *May Day Manifesto 1968*, Harmondsworth: Penguin Books, 1968.

37 Raymond Williams, *The Long Revolution*, Harmondsworth: Penguin, 1965.

38 Dai Smith, 'Foreword', in Raymond Williams, *Border Country*, Library of Wales, Cardigan: Parthian, 2006 (first published 1960), p. ix.

39 Williams, *Border Country*, p. 436.

40 Dai Smith reminds me that there is a same-sex moment in an unpublished novel by Williams. Personal communication; Dai Smith, *Raymond Williams: A Warrior's Tale*, Cardigan: Parthian, 2008.

CHAPTER 3 DREAMS OF LİBERATİON

41 Edmund White, *The Beautiful Room is Empty*, London: Picador, 1988, p. 184.

42 Peter Scott-Presland, *Amiable Warriors: A History of the Campaign for Homosexual Equality and Its Times, Vol. 1, A Space to Breathe 1954–1973*, London: Paradise Press, 2015, Chapter 5, pp. 335–432.

43 Alan Wakeman, *Fragments of Joy and Sorrow: Memoir of a Reluctant Revolutionary*, London: Gemini Press, 2015, p. 35.

44 *NLR* was a product of the British New Left, which grew in the late 1950s following splits in the CPGB and the emergence of new mass movements, notably the Campaign for Nuclear Disarmament. The journal itself was established in 1960 on the amalgamation of two earlier magazines, *The New Reasoner* and *Universities and Left Review*, with Stuart Hall as first editor. Following an internal coup in 1962, *NLR* under the editorship of Perry Anderson soon became the vehicle for high intellectual Marxism, heavily influenced by European theories, where it has broadly remained.

45   Ken Plummer, *Telling Sexual Stories: Power, Change and Social Worlds*, London: Routledge, 1995.

46   Dennis Altman, *Homosexual: Oppression and Liberation*, 40th Anniversary Edition, St Lucia: University of Queensland Press, 2012 (first published 1971), p. 20.

47   Wakeman, *Fragments*, p. 109.

48   The most detailed account of the London GLF experience is still Lisa Power, *No Bath but Plenty of Bubbles: An Oral History of the Gay Liberation Front 1970–73.* London: Cassell, 1995.

49   Originally a talk in 1969, then an essay, Jo Freeman's 'The Tyranny of Structurelessness' was published in various versions and collections, and subsequently online. See the versions published in the *Berkeley Journal of Sociology*, Vol. 17, 1972–73, pp. 151–165, and *Ms.* magazine, July 1973, pp. 76–78, 86–89; and the discussion at https://www.jofreeman.com/joreen/tyranny.htm, accessed 4 September 2019.

50   Power, *No Bath*, p. 299.

51   Alberto Melucci, *Nomads of the Present: Social Movements and Individual Needs in Contemporary Society*, London: Radius, 1989.

52   *Manifesto*, London: Gay Liberation Manifesto Group, 1971. Peter Tatchell's views can be found at www.petertatchell.net/lgbt_rights/london-gay-liberation-front-manifesto-1971/, accessed 4 September 2019. For a comparison between the 1971 and 1978 versions see https://brian618.whyayh.com/reference/GLFmanifesto.diff.html, accessed 4 September 2019.

53   Stuart Feather was a leading light in this tendency. See his account: *Blowing the Lid: Gay Liberation, Sexual Revolution and Radical Queens*, Winchester: Zero Books, 2015.

54   Jeffrey Weeks, 'Ideas of Gay Liberation', *Gay News* 6, September, 1972, p. 6.

55   Power, *No Bath*, p. 89.

56 See my discussion of the Freudo-Marxists in Jeffrey Weeks, *Sexuality and Its Discontents: Meanings, Myths and Modern Sexualities*, London: Routledge and Kegan Paul, 1985.

57 Michel Foucault, 'Friendship as a Way of Life', interview by R. de Ceccaty, J. Danet, and J. Le Bitoux for the French magazine *Gai Pied*, April 1981.

CHAPTER 4 WRITING THE REVOLUTION

58 *Psychiatry and the Homosexual: A Brief Analysis of Oppression*, London: Pomegranate Press, n.d (1972). The quotations are from pp. 1–2.

59 *With Downcast Gays: Aspects of Homosexual Self-Oppression*, London: Pomegranate Press, n.d (1973), p. 18.

60 Andrew Hodges, *Alan Turing: The Enigma*, London: Burnett Books, 1983.

61 On sexual generations see Ken Plummer, 'Generational Sexualities: Subterranean Traditions and the Hauntings of the Sexual World. Some Preliminary Research', *Social Interactions*, 33 (2), 2010, pp. 163–91; Jeffrey Weeks, *What is Sexual History?*, Cambridge: Polity Press, 2016, pp. 19–20.

62 See Dennis Altman, *Homosexual: Oppression and Liberation*, 40th Anniversary Edition, St Lucia: University of Queensland Press, 2012 (first published 1971), Chapter 7, pp. 237–48.

63 Kwame Anthony Appiah, *The Lies that Bind: Rethinking Identity. Creed, Country, Colour, Class, Culture*, London: Profile Books, 2018.

64 James Baldwin, 'The Devil Finds Work', in James Baldwin, *The Price of the Ticket: Collected Nonfiction 1948–1985*, New York City: St Martin's Press, 1985.

65 The (in)famous conference at Barnard College, New

York, in April 1982, ignited a fierce and continuing debate about the relationship of sexuality to feminism, and Gayle Rubin's key article, 'Thinking Sex' played a central role. Major contributions to the pro-sex debates can be found in an important volume edited by the main organiser of the conference: Carol S. Vance (ed.), *Pleasure and Danger: Exploring Female Sexuality*, London: Routledge and Kegan Paul, 1984, which contains Gayle Rubin's article. In both the USA and UK, pornography was the fulcrum of controversy. See Lynne Segal and Mary McIntosh (eds.), *Sex Exposed: Sexuality and the Pornography Debates*, London: Virago, 1992.

66　Janice Raymond, *The Transsexual Empire*, Boston: Beacon, 1979.

67　Tom O'Carroll, *Paedophilia: The Radical Case*, London: Peter Owen, 1980.

68　Jeffrey Weeks, 'Where Engels Feared to Tread', *Gay Left: A Socialist Journal Produced by Gay Men*, 1, Autumn, 1975, pp. 3–5. Copies of all ten issues of *Gay Left* can be found online at http://gayleft1970s.org/.

69　Emmanuel Cooper, contribution to 'Personal Politics: Ten Years On', *Gay Left*, 8, Summer, 1979, p. 6.

70　'Collective Statement', *Gay Left*, 1, Autumn, 1975, p. 1.

71　Bob Cant, 'A Grim Tale: The IS Gay Group 1972–75', *Gay Left*, 3, Autumn, 1976, pp. 7–10.

72　'Communists Comment', *Gay Left*, 4, Summer, 1977, pp. 9–13.

73　Angus Suttie, 'From Latent to Blatant', *Gay Left*, 2, Spring, 1976, pp. 3–5.

74　Sue Bruley, 'Women in Gay Left', *Gay Left*, 3, Autumn, 1976, pp. 5–6.

75　'Love, Sex and Maleness', *Gay Left*, 4, Summer, 1977, pp. 2–6.

76　Bob Cant, 'Gays and Fascism', *Gay Left*, 5, Winter, 1977, pp. 26–9; Errol Francis, 'Political Pertinence', *Gay Left*, 10, Spring, 1980, pp. 45–6.

77   'Richard Dyer, 'Gays in Film', *Gay Left*, 2, Spring, 1976, pp. 8–11.

78   Emmanuel Cooper, 'Gay Art', *Gay Left*, 7, Winter, 1978/79, pp. 6–8. See David Horbury (ed.), *Making Emmanuel Cooper: Life and Work from his Memoirs, Letters, Diaries and Interviews*, London: Unicorn, 2019, Chapter 13, pp. 215–32.

79   Gay Left Collective (ed.), *Homosexuality: Power and Politics*, London: Allison and Busby, 1980. The book was republished by Verso in 2018.

CHAPTER 5   MAKİNG HİSTORY PERSONAL

80   Lord Beaverbrook, *Politicians and the War 1914–1916*, London: Oldbourne, 1960; Lord Beaverbrook, *Men and Power 1917–1918*, London: Oldbourne, 1959.

81   Richard J. Evans, *Eric Hobsbawm: A Life in History*, London: Little Brown, 2019, p. 429. There is a nice account here of the various travails Hobsbawm encountered in obtaining a senior job, despite his acknowledged brilliance. His Marxism at the height of the Cold War was enough to invalidate his claims.

82   See my entry on Mary in the *Oxford Dictionary of National Biography*: Jeffrey Weeks 'McIntosh, Mary Susan (1936–2013)', https://doi.org/10.1093/ref:odnb/106148.

83   See Mary's account of this in 'Postscript: Jeffrey Weeks and Kenneth Plummer interview Mary McIntosh', Kenneth Plummer (ed.), *The Making of the Modern Homosexual*, London: Hutchinson, 1981, pp. 44–9. 'The Homosexual Role' essay itself is reprinted on pp. 30–44.

84   Michel Foucault, *The History of Sexuality, Volume 1, An Introduction*, London: Allen Lane, 1978.

85   E. P. Thompson, *The Making of the English Working Class*, Harmondsworth: Penguin, 1967. This was the first copy of the book I purchased. The original publication was in 1963 from Victor Gollancz.

86   Jeffrey Weeks, 'Sins and Diseases: Some Notes on Male Homosexuality in Nineteenth Century England', *History Workshop Journal*, 1, Spring, 1976, pp. 211–19.

87   Jeffrey Weeks, 'Foucault for Historians', *History Workshop Journal*, 14, Autumn, 1982, pp. 106–19; 'Invented Moralities', *History Workshop Journal*, 32, Autumn, 1992, pp. 151–66; 'Making the Human Gesture: History, Sexuality and Social Justice', *History Workshop Journal*, 70, Autumn, 2010, pp. 5–20.

88   I was personally closest to the women historians, especially Anna Davin and Sally Alexander, who strongly supported my gay history work, Barbara Taylor, whom I worked especially closely with on the book reviews, Jane Caplan, Anne Summers and Carolyn Steedman. Although my personal relations were a little warier, I was influenced intellectually as well by Gareth Stedman Jones, probably Raphael's closest friend on the collective, and by Michael Ignatieff, who much later, in an unlikely career trajectory, was to become a telegenic star of late-night intellectual TV, and later still leader of the Canadian Liberal Party. When he was elected to the leadership several of us were approached by journalists seeking gossip or dirt on a former member of a socialist collective. Sadly for them, there was none that we were prepared to give.

89   Raphael's wife gives an unforgettable portrait: Alison Light, *A Radical Romance: A Memoir of Love, Grief and Consolation*, London: Penguin/Fig Tree, 2019.

90   Raphael Samuel, *Theatres of Memory: Past and Present in Contemporary Culture*, revised edition, London: Verso, 2012 (first published 1994).

91 Jonathan Ned Katz, *Gay American History: Lesbians and Gay Men in the USA*, New York: Thomas Crowell, 1976, pp. 1–2.

92 Ken Plummer, *Telling Sexual Stories: Power, Change and Social Worlds*, London: Routledge, 1995.

93 I was impressed by other gay historical work appearing in the USA, especially on the early twentieth-century German movement around Magnus Hirschfeld from Jim Steakley. Closer to home, regular essays on gay history by Rictor Norton were appearing in *Gay News*, and we socialised a little, but our differences in emphases soon became canyon-like, and I became the main target for critique in his later books.

94 The book, finally published in 1981, was self-consciously creating a genealogy of the approach we were collectively developing, which by now we were beginning to call social constructionist (for full references see note 4 above). Mary's 'The Homosexual Role' and the interview with Mary reflecting on the origins and influence of the article was the starting point, and was followed by accounts by Ken of the new sociology of homosexuality, and by me of the new theoretical discourses on homosexual history. Various aspects of these overarching themes were explored in the other essays, from transvestism and transsexuality to the uneven impact of medicalisation and the machoisation of the contemporary gay male scene. Annabel Faraday's essay on lesbian perspectives offered an early and prescient critique of the male assumptions embodied in gay history so far.

The Open University connection had a more directly personal impact on my life. My future partner, Mark McNestry, saw me in another Open University programme when he was an adolescent. I was one of the first out gay men he saw on TV. Years later, when we met, he still vividly remembered it.

95 For an account of the arguments see the contributions

to Edward Stein (ed.), *Forms of Desire: Sexual Orientation and the Social Constructionist Controversy*, London: Routledge, 1992.

96 Republished in Stein, *Forms of Desire*, 1992.

97 Eve Kosofsky Sedgwick, *Epistemology of the Closet*, Berkeley: University of California Press, 1990.

98 Alan Bray, *Homosexuality in Renaissance England*, London: Gay Men's Press, 1983.

99 This new generation of queer historians include Matt Cook, Matt Houlbrook, Alison Oram and Laura Doan. See Brian Lewis (ed.), *British Queer History: New Approaches and Perspectives*, Manchester: Manchester University Press, 2013. Another crucial figure, closer to my own generation and from a cultural studies background, was Frank Mort, who was close to people in and around *Gay Left*. His work wasn't explicitly in any sense 'queer history', but it offered valuable insights into the shifting moral economy and the evolution of disease models that clearly responded to the new context of gay liberation and especially the challenge of AIDS. See Frank Mort, *Dangerous Sexualities: Medico-Moral Politics in England since 1830*, London: Routledge and Kegan Paul, 1987.

100 Gert Hekma at the University of Amsterdam was the polymathic convenor of much of the Dutch activities, but Theo van der Meer at the Free University and Judith Schuyff at the University of Utrecht developed important historical work. As my own work appeared I made good friendships with lesbian and gay colleagues in Germany and Scandinavia, especially the social policy expert Benny Henriksson in Sweden and the sociologist Henning Bech and historian Karin Lützen in Denmark. My main contact in France was the Brazilian anthropologist Rommel Mendès-Leite, who also became a close friend.

101 Other people I met on these early trips included John D'Emilio, Alan Bérubé and George Chauncey, three of the most

important gay historians of their generation, and central to the development of gay scholarship in the 1980s and 1990s. John's work paralleled my own: beginning with an exploration of the movement itself, he then went on (with Estelle Freedman) to write a pioneering history of American sexuality, *Intimate Matters*. Alan had been inspired by Jonathan Ned Katz's *Gay American History*, and for him gay history was central to the struggle. As a college dropout, his practice of a community-oriented history defined his life for many years. George, then a student at Yale, had written to me after my review of John Boswell's book, criticising my lack of generosity and querying my critique of Boswell's panorama of gay men throughout history, but we met very amicably at the Metropolitan Museum on my first visit to New York, and established a good friendship. He was at this point still working on his PhD dissertation, but he already had a prodigious knowledge of gay scholarship, including my own.

102   Jonathan Ned Katz, *The Invention of Heterosexuality*, New York: NAL/Dutton, 1995.

CHAPTER 6   LOVE AND LOSS

103   Gayle Rubin's paper 'Thinking Sex: Notes for a Radical Theory of the Politics of Sexuality' was first published in Carol S. Vance's edited collection of papers from the conference, *Pleasure and Danger: Exploring Female Sexuality*, London: Routledge and Kegan Paul, 1984, and in various other places since. Carol Vance was academic coordinator of the conference. See 'Diary of a conference on sexuality', *GLQ: A Journal of Lesbian and Gay Studies*, 17, 1, pp. 49–78, at https://doi.org/10.1215/10642684-2010-016.

104   See Amber Hollibaugh and Cherríe Moraga, 'What we're rollin around in bed with: sexual silences in feminism',

in Ann Snitow, Christine Stansell, Sharon Thompson (eds.), *Powers of Desire: The Politics of Sexuality*, New York: Monthly Review Press, 1983, pp. 394–405.

105   Other colleagues and friends included Janet Sayers, later a well-known historian of feminist psychoanalysis, Kate McLuskie, a leading Shakespearean expert, and Jan Montefiori, a poet and expert on Rudyard Kipling, all of whom were to become luminaries in their fields.

106   Alan Hollinghurst, *The Swimming-Pool Library*, London: Chatto and Windus, 1988, p. 3.

107   Matt Cook, '"Archives of Feeling": AIDS in the UK 1987', *History Workshop Journal*, 83, 1, Spring 2017, pp. 51–78.

108   The standard history remains Virginia Berridge, *AIDS in the UK: The Making of Policy, 1981–1994*, Oxford: Oxford University Press, 1996. See also Simon Garfield, *The End of Innocence: Britain in the Time of AIDS*, London: Faber and Faber, 1995. The best chronicler of the crisis as it unfolded is Simon Watney: *Policing Desire: Pornography, AIDS and the Media*, London: Commedia/Methuen, 1984; *Practices of Freedom: Selected Writings on HIV/AIDS*, London: Rivers Oram Press, 1994; *Imagine Hope: AIDS and Gay Identity*, London: Routledge, 2000.

109   *Pride*, film directed by Matthew Warchus, BBC Films, 2014. See Tim Tate, *Pride: The Unlikely Story of the True Heroes of the Miners' Strike*, London: John Blake, 2017. See also Diarmaid Kelliher, 'Solidarity and Sexuality: Lesbians and Gays Support the Miners 1984–5', *History Workshop Journal*, 77, 1, Spring, 2014, pp. 240–62. For an account of the strike in Wales see Daryl Leeworthy, *A Little Gay History of Wales*, Cardiff: University of Wales Press, 2019; Daryl Leeworthy, *Labour Country: Political Radicalism and Social Democracy in South Wales 1831–1985*, Cardigan: Parthian, 2018, pp. 472–88.

110   Eric Hobsbawm, 'The Forward March of Labour Halted?', *Marxism Today*, September, 1978, pp. 279–86.

111   Stuart Hall, Chas Critcher, Tony Jefferson, John Clarke and Brian Roberts, *Policing the Crisis: Mugging, the State, and Law and Order*, 1st edition 1978, 2nd edition, with two additional chapters on the impact of the work, London: Red Globe Press, 2013.

112   Jeffrey Weeks, 'Love in a Cold Climate', *Marxism Today*, January, 1987, p. 12.

113   Elizabeth Wilson, *Prisons of Glass*, London: Methuen, 1986, pp. 192–204.

114   Martin Jacques, 'Introduction', complete run of *Marxism Today*, at http://banmarchive.org.uk/collections/mt/index_frame.htm, accessed 11 October 2019.

115   For Percival's comments see *The Guardian*, 22 November 1986; for Anderton's *The Independent*, 12 December 1986. For the general climate and reference to the Gay's the Word action see Jeffrey Weeks, *Coming Out: The Emergence of LGBT Identities in Britain from the 19th Century to the Present*, 40th Anniversary Edition, London: Quartet, 2016, pp. 245–8.

116   Weeks, *Coming Out*, p. 241.

117   Quoted at https://lgbtplushistorymonth.co.uk/wp-content/uploads/2020/02/1384014531S28Background.pdf, accessed 1 July 2019.

118   'Clause and Effect: A Roundtable Discussion', *Marxism Today*, June, 1988, pp. 22–8.

119   This section draws on my account of the exhibition in Jeffrey Weeks, *Invented Moralities: Sexual Values in an Age of Uncertainty*, Cambridge: Polity Press, 1995, pp. 155–7.

CHAPTER 7 İNTİMACY MATTERS

120   The project was with my colleague David Dunkerley.

121   Dennis Altman, 'Legitimation through Disaster: AIDS

and the Gay Movement', in Elizabeth Fee and Daniel M. Fox (eds.), *AIDS: The Burdens of History*, Berkeley: University of California Press, 1988, pp. 302–14. For the 'war-time emergency' metaphor see Virginia Berridge, *AIDS in the UK: The Making of Policy, 1981–1994*, Oxford: Oxford University Press, 1996.

122   See Mark McNestry and Mike Hartley, *Developing a Local Response: Gay and Bisexual Men's Needs in relation to HIV and AIDS*, London: Bexley and Greenwich Health Promotion, 1995; Metro, *Our History 1983–2020. From the Greenwich Lesbian and Gay Centre to Metro Charity*, London: Metro Charity, 2020.

123   Jeffrey Weeks, *Invented Moralities: Sexual Values in an Age of Uncertainty*, Cambridge: Polity Press, 1995.

124   Cited in Steve Connor, 'The "gay gene" is back on the scene', *The Independent*, London, 1 November 1995.

125   Brian had been my PhD student at Bristol, exploring the experience of people with HIV confronting illness and death. Catherine's research had been about self-insemination among lesbians, so with my own research experience we covered some of the key issues behind the new relational ethics of the lesbian, bi and gay worlds. Brian later became Professor of Sociology at the University of Manchester, and Catherine Professor of Sociology at the University of Durham.

126   Jeffrey Weeks, Brian Heaphy and Catherine Donovan, *Same Sex Intimacies: Families of Choice and Other Life Experiments*, London: Routledge, 2001.

127   Anthony Giddens, *The Transformation of Intimacy: Sexuality, Love and Eroticism in Modern Societies*, Cambridge: Polity Press, 1992.

128   Janet Finch, *Family Obligations and Social Change*, Cambridge: Polity Press, 1989; Janet Finch and Jennifer Mason, *Negotiating Family Responsibilities*, London: Routledge, 1993.

129   A fine comparison of the late nineteenth and late

twentieth centuries is Elaine Showalter, *Sexual Anarchy: Gender and Culture at the Fin de Siècle*, London:Virago, 1992.

130   See my discussion of these critiques in Jeffrey Weeks, *What is Sexual History?*, Cambridge: Polity Press, 2016, Chapters 3 and 6. See Jasbir K. Puar, *Terrorist Assemblages: Homonationalism in Queer Times*, Durham, NC: Duke University Press, 2007; Sarah Schulman, *Israel/Palestine and the Queer International*, Durham, NC: Duke University Press, 2012. See also Dennis Altman and Jonathan Symons, *Queer Wars*, Cambridge: Polity Press, 2016.

131   For a variety of reactions see Nicola Barker and Daniel Monk (eds.), *From Civil Partnership to Same-Sex Marriage: Interdisciplinary Reflections*, London: Routledge, 2015. For the growing embeddedness of same-sex unions in the ordinary discourse of the queer world see Brian Heaphy, Carol Smart and Anna Einarsdottir, *Same-Sex Marriages: New Relationships, New Experiences*, Basingstoke: Palgrave Macmillan, 2013.

CHAPTER 8   ALL THE WAY HOME

132   Dai Smith, *In the Frame*, p. 326. I found an unexpected echo in another memoir, from another country. In his *Returning to Rheims* (London: Allen Lane, 2018) the French cultural critic Didier Eribon recounts his journey from working-class, communist roots; self-imposed exile in Paris as he negotiates his gayness; and his later return to the city he grew up with and a partial reconciliation with his mother, by which time his family had moved to the far right. *Border Country* is again a point of reference. The particular experience described by Williams becomes a universal signifier.

133   Peter Laslett, *The World We Have Lost*, London: Methuen, 1965.

134   The phenomenon is powerfully dissected in Paul

Gilroy, *After Empire: Melancholia or Convivial Culture*, Abingdon: Routledge, 2004.

135   Gertrude Himmelfarb, *The De-Moralization of Society: From Victorian Values to Modern Values*, London: Institute of Economic Affairs, 1995, pp. 217–18.

136   Dan Healey, *Russian Homophobia from Stalin to Sochi*, London: Bloomsbury, 2017; Ken Plummer, *Cosmopolitan Sexualities: Hope and the Humanist Imagination*. Cambridge: Polity Press, 2015.

137   See Rachel Trezise, *In and Out of the Goldfish Bowl*, Cardigan: Parthian, 2000; *Fresh Apples*, Cardigan: Parthian, 2005.

138   Raymond Williams, 'Community', in *Keywords*, London: Flamingo, 1984, p. 76; James Baldwin, *Evidence of Something Not Seen*, London: Michael Joseph, 1986. See Jeffrey Weeks, 'The Idea of a Sexual Community', in *Making Sexual History*, Cambridge: Polity Press, 2000, pp. 181–93, which I draw on for this section.

139   *The Guardian*, 15 June 2019, p. 1.

140   See Ian Lumsden, *Machos, Maricones and Gays: Cuba and Homosexuality*, Philadelphia: Temple University Press, 1995; Carrie Hamilton, *Sexual Revolution in Cuba: Passion, Politics and Memory*, Chapel Hill: University of North Carolina Press, 2012; Noelle M. Stout, *After Love: Queer Intimacy and Erotic Economies in Post-Soviet Cuba*, Durham, NC: Duke University Press, 2014.

141   Joan Nestle, 'The Will to Remember: The Lesbian Herstory Archives of New York', *Journal of Homosexuality*, 34 (3/4), 1998, p. 229.

PARTHIAN MODERN WALES

Who the Welsh are today and who we may wish to become tomorrow is inextricably tied to the origins and outcomes of modern Wales: and that is the rupture with the past which occurred with such rapid force and with all its multifarious consequences from the late eighteenth century. The dynamic of Wales for two hundred years would be industrial and urban. Our culture and society, our economy and politics, our towns and cities and the intertwined countryside, our languages of expression and our creative arts, our sense of ourselves as a people whether in good times or bad, all derives from that passage into modernity which we were amongst the very first in the world to take.

This exciting new series, in lively and accessible volumes, presents and examines this crucial process and its whole aftermath by dispelling the fog of myth which has too often descended to blanket us. Instead, we offer the insight of analysis and the witness of the informed. Our approach will continue to be diverse as we range across non-fictional genres to uncover the complexity of our singular historical condition.

Dai Smith, Series Editor

The Modern Wales Series is published with the support of the Rhys Davies Trust

the RHYS DAVIES TRUST

WALES: ENGLAND'S COLONY?

Martin Johnes

From the very beginnings of Wales, its people have defined themselves against their large neighbour. This book tells the fascinating story of an uneasy and unequal relationship between two nations living side-by-side.

PB / £8.99
978-1-912681-41-9

RHYS DAVIES: A WRITER'S LIFE

Meic Stephens

Rhys Davies (1901-78) was among the most dedicated, prolific and accomplished of Welsh prose writers. This is his first full biography.

'This is a delightful book, which is itself a social history in its own right, and funny.'
– The Spectator

PB / £11.99
978-1-912109-96-8

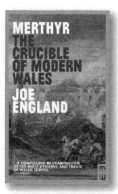

MERTHYR, THE CRUCIBLE OF MODERN WALES

Joe England

Merthyr Tydfil was the town where the future of a country was forged: a thriving, struggling surge of people, industry, democracy and ideas. This book assesses an epic history of Merthyr from 1760 to 1912 through the focus of a fresh and thoroughly convincing perspective.

PB / £18.99
978-1-913640-05-7